CHE

Elizabeth I

Elizabeth I was Queen of England for almost forty-five years. The daughter of Henry VIII and Ann Boleyn, she was declared illegitimate after her mother's execution and led a sometimes scandalous existence until her accession to the throne at the age of twenty-five. Elizabeth oversaw a vibrant age of exploration and literature and established herself as a national icon, "the Virgin Queen", whose legend endures to this day. But Elizabeth was England's second female monarch, and was greatly influenced by the experiences of the reign of her half-sister Mary before her. As religious wars raged in Europe, Elizabeth had to work hard to balance the management of an inherited Catholic realm against the demands of her more zealous fellow Protestants.

This engaging new biography casts fresh light on some of the most familiar features of Elizabeth's reign: Mary Queen of Scots and her continuing efforts to take the throne; the Spanish Armada; and the origins of English overseas colonial expansion. It examines Elizabeth's early life, influences and religious beliefs and offers new insights into her reign, her politics and her problematic reluctance to marry. Taking an objective and rounded view of Elizabeth's whole life, Judith M. Richards has written the perfect introduction for anyone with an interest in this most fascinating of historical figures.

Judith M. Richards was previously senior Lecturer at La Trobe University, Australia, and is now a history research associate there. Her earlier publications include an acclaimed biography of Mary Tudor.

Routledge Historical Biographies
Series Editor: Robert Pearce

Routledge Historical Biographies provide engaging, readable and academically credible biographies written from an explicitly historical perspective. These concise and accessible accounts will bring important historical figures to life for students and general readers alike.

In the same series:

Bismarck by Edgar Feuchtwanger
Calvin by Michael Mullett
Oliver Cromwell by Martyn Bennett
Edward IV by Hannes Kleineke
Gladstone by Michael Partridge
Henry VII by Sean Cunningham
Henry VIII by Lucy Wooding
Lenin by Christopher Read
Louis XIV by Richard Wilkinson
Mao by Michael Lynch
Martin Luther King Jr. by Peter J. Ling
Martin Luther by Michael Mullet
Marx by Vincent Barnett
Mary Queen of Scots by Retha M. Warnicke
Mao by Michael Lynch
Mussolini by Peter Neville
Nehru by Ben Zachariah
Neville Chamberlain by Nick Smart
Emmeline Pankhurst by Paula Bartley
Richard III by David Hipshon
Trotsky by Ian Thatcher
Mary Tudor by Judith Richards

Forthcoming:

Churchill by Robert Pearce
Franco by Antonio Cazorla-Sanchez
John Maynard Keynes by Vincent Barnett

Elizabeth I

Judith M. Richards

Routledge
Taylor & Francis Group

LONDON AND NEW YORK

First published 2012
by Routledge
2 Park Square, Milton Park, Abingdon, Oxon OX14 4RN

Simultaneously published in the USA and Canada
by Routledge
711 Third Avenue, New York, NY 10017

Routledge is an imprint of the Taylor & Francis Group, an informa business

British Library Cataloguing in Publication Data
A catalogue record for this book is available from the British Library

Library of Congress Cataloging in Publication Data
Richards, Judith M., 1938-
  Elizabeth I / Judith M. Richards.
  p. cm. -- (Routledge historical biographies)
  Includes bibliographical references and index.
  1. Elizabeth I, Queen of England, 1533-1603. 2. Great Britain--History--Elizabeth,
  1558-1603. 3. Queens--Great Britain--Biography. I. Title.
  DA355.R526 2012
  942.05'5092--dc23
  [B]
  2011020376

ISBN: 978-0-415-48158-8 (hbk)
ISBN: 978-0-415-48157-1 (pbk)
ISBN: 978-0-203-18090-7 (ebk)

Typeset in 11/12 Garamond 3
by Saxon Graphics Ltd, Derby DE21 4SZ

MIX
Paper from
responsible sources
FSC
www.fsc.org
FSC® C004839

Printed and bound in Great Britain by the MPG Books Group

FOR ANDREW AND JENNIFER

Contents

List of Plates

Between pages 148 and 149

Image Captions and Credits

1 The Family of Henry VIII, c.1545 (oil on canvas), English School, (16th century)/The Royal Collection ©2011 Her Majesty Queen Elizabeth II/The Bridgeman Art Library

2 Elizabeth I when Princess, c.1546 (oil on panel), Scrots, Guillaume (fl.1537–53) (attr. to)/The Royal Collection ©2011 Her Majesty Queen Elizabeth II/The Bridgeman Art Library

3 Queen Elizabeth I by Nicholas Hilliard ©National Portrait Gallery, London

4 Locket ring belonging to Queen Elizabeth I, c.1575 (gold with enamel, rubies, diamonds & mother-of-pearl), English School, (16th century)/By kind permission of the Chequers Trust/Mark Fiennes/The Bridgeman Art Library

5 Portrait of Queen Elizabeth I. Zuccaro, Federico (1542–1609). c.1557–1609 ©The Trustees of the British Museum

6 Robert Dudley, 1st Earl of Leicester by unknown artist ©National Portrait Gallery, London

7 Portrait of Queen Elizabeth I (1533–1603) in Ceremonial Costume (oil on canvas), Zuccari, or Zuccaro, Federico (1540–1609)/Pinacoteca Nazionale, Siena, Italy/Alinari/The Bridgeman Art Library

Acknowledgements

I owe debts to many friends and colleagues in and beyond Australia for their support and encouragement while writing this study. Above all, Susan Doran has very generous in sharing her extensive knowledge of Elizabeth and of her reign. The conclusions I have drawn from her generous help are, however, entirely my own responsibility. I must also acknowledge once more my friend and colleague, Lotte Mulligan, for her friendship, support and encouragement, as I have had occasion to do over many years. The unstinting support of the staff of the La Trobe University Library and their extraordinary capacity to track down even the most arcane material has been invaluable, and is much appreciated.

This is my second biography for the Routledge Historical Biographies series, and I owe much to Robert Pearce. His astuteness in editing the drafts and his commentary on the progress of each work has done much to help me through to the final format. For that I thank him, as I do the many others who have supported me while these works were in progress.

Introduction

As ancient wisdom has it, 'Of making many books there is no end' (Ecclesiastes 12.12). Among the many demonstrations of that truth is the number of books written about Elizabeth I, who ruled England from 1558 to 1603. There are many reasons her reign has been found so fascinating. In part it was because she was a female king, unusual but not unprecedented, but also in part because she reigned so long. Above all, she was unique amongst English monarchs for at least 500 years in that she did not marry. That she ruled for more than 40 years as a single woman was even more intriguing. One effect of her unmarried status has been that she has also been a focus for much romantic imaginings and speculation, more so than any other monarch, except perhaps for her remarkable father, Henry VIII, who married so unusually often.

In all that, the persistent image of Elizabeth is that of a female, unmarried monarch who necessarily forged her own path through all the difficulties of being a woman on the throne in turbulent times. There is certainly some truth in that view, but she also had more precedents for how to rule – and also even greater problems to manage – than many studies have recognised. Indeed, part of the rationale for this particular biography of her is that, having recently completed a biography of Elizabeth's elder sister Mary Tudor, as Elizabeth's biographer I come to the study of the younger sister from an unusual perspective. Perhaps Elizabeth's most enduring challenge was that, contrary to popular tradition, the realm she inherited was still predominantly Catholic, despite the religious changes of Henry VIII and Edward VI. Indeed, in Mary's reign the Catholic Church had been so reinvigorated that Elizabeth, rather than sweeping to the throne on a wave of Protestant enthusiasm in 1558, had to tread a very careful path when putting in place – and sustaining – her religious changes.

One reason historians were slow to recognise perhaps her greatest challenge, the religious transformation of England to a country with a Protestant majority, was that the years immediately following her accession saw the production of much Protestant material directed to establishing the legitimacy of Elizabeth's rule. Such a propaganda campaign was necessary for two major reasons. The first is familiar, but until recently was seldom recognised for the problem it was at the time. In the eyes of most of her subjects, Elizabeth began her rule as Henry VIII's illegitimate daughter, of dubious origins and doubtful reputation. By way of contrast, her elder sister Mary (Mary I, 1553–8) had in her youth enjoyed many years as the popular princess of England and was the daughter of the even more popular Katharine of Aragon. Elizabeth, however, was bastardised before she was three, the daughter of the widely loathed Anne Boleyn, and a symbol of Henry's repudiation of his popular first wife and of his break with Rome. During the reign of her brother Edward VI (1547–53) the adolescent Elizabeth had also been the subject of a scandalous and much discussed enquiry into the details of her relationship with the ambitious Thomas Seymour. Moreover, as was also widely known, though less discussed since, Elizabeth had been implicated in at least one significant plot against her sister's throne, and widely suspected of knowledge of others.

For such reasons, the resources of the relatively new art of printing and the skills of many writers were required from the beginning of Elizabeth's reign to establish her moral, religious and personal suitability to rule. In that propaganda there was little place for Elizabeth's elder sister, Mary I, except when cast as the cruel and 'Spanish' Catholic, during whose regime many Protestants were burned as heretics. Although Elizabeth had frequently attended mass in Mary's reign, in the eyes of the Catholic Church, she was almost certainly a heretic. Perhaps also because in papal eyes Elizabeth was certainly a bastard, and because she shared the views of her father Henry VIII and brother Edward VI about the proper supremacy of the crown over the papacy, as over all other powers, there was never a serious possibility that she would maintain her sister's acceptance of papal authority. On the other hand, Mary's restoration of more church music and ritual helped Elizabeth in turn to establish a modified version of the Edwardian church. Moreover, the first Tudor queen regnant had established the ritual and ceremonial adaptations and legal clarifications necessary for the establishment of female monarchy; these Elizabeth accepted, but without acknowledging her sister's innovations.

The realm Elizabeth inherited was marked by deep religious divisions which fed into both political tensions and several assassination plots against her. Beyond her realm were powerful international opponents with religious, political, diplomatic and, increasingly, economic grounds for seeking her downfall. Despite that, and despite the growing demographic, economic and social problems within England, she maintained her rule for 45 years. She reigned at a time when the term 'personal monarchy' was a meaningful description of royal authority, so her biography must also take full account of the fact that she was a woman, as her advisers sometimes remarked to each other in exasperation; she was, after all, effectively only the second English queen regnant to exercise full royal authority.

Elizabeth's role as ruler of England placed her at the apex of the social, religious and political structure, carrying with that enormous responsibilities. Like any monarch, Elizabeth was expected to listen to her advisers, but like any monarch of the times she was also, as one authority put it, 'the life, the head and the authority of all things that be done in England'. That she was a single woman overseeing all those more usually masculine fields of activity raised again those gender problems (and more) which had confronted her sister Mary I. Her decision to remain single meant that, although Elizabeth owed something to Mary for the precedents her sister had set, once she was on the throne there were other problems which Elizabeth faced without a husband and, at times, because of the absence of one. Her refusal to marry and provide an heir gave rise to much scurrilous gossip at the time; since then there has been and continues to be much speculation about the reasons why she remained single. If, however, the reason for her remaining unmarried is still an interesting question, so are many other questions about this queen, including what part she actually played in the much celebrated 1588 destruction of the Spanish Armada, in determining policy through the decades of her reign, and in the determining the careers of the leading men in England whose rise at her court was the crucial, indeed definitive, component in their wider success.

In brief, then, the Elizabeth of this study experienced in her first decades disgrace, humiliation and infamy quite as much as the formally royal esteem her portrait from that time represents (Plate 2). She came to the throne with little preparation to rule, and succeeded to a realm which was dependent on her Catholic and Spanish brother-in-law for support against France and against the claims of Mary Stuart, Queen of Scotland, to the English throne. She inherited a realm in which most of the population were Catholic; a determined minority were strongly Protestant, but without agreed views about the proper Protestant forms and rituals to be introduced. She survived those problematic early years to remain on the throne so long that few of her subjects could remember a time when she was not there, and during her reign England emerged as an increasingly important sea power; moreover while she was on the throne literature, and especially drama, flourished as never before. One further – and major – problem in writing a biography of Elizabeth is twofold: the one of distinguishing the queen herself from the flattery and propaganda which surrounded her from her accession, and the other of knowing which of the many utterances published in her name actually represented her own beliefs.

A fascinating queen in fascinating times, her biography has properly been the subject of many and varied tellings. This is offered as one more account.

1 Elizabeth, briefly Princess of England

A divisive beginning

Elizabeth Tudor was born in the royal palace at Greenwich on 7 September 1533, the child of Henry VIII and his second wife, Anne Boleyn. The birth went well for mother and child, and the infant was healthy. Still, Elizabeth's arrival was something of a disappointment since both parents, encouraged in their hopes by royal doctors, midwives and, above all, astrologers, were confidently expecting a son. King Henry VIII already had a healthy daughter, Mary – her mother was his first wife, Katharine of Aragon – and an illegitimate son, Henry Fitzroy, Duke of Richmond. To secure the Tudor dynasty, of which he was only the second ruler, what the king most needed was a legitimate, healthy son. When he decided to end his first marriage, to Katharine of Aragon, her failure to provide a healthy male heir was one of Henry's proofs that his first marriage had been against God's law: her failure to produce a healthy male heir demonstrated God's displeasure that Henry had married his elder brother's widow.

Anne Boleyn, his second wife, had supported, cajoled and scolded her prospective husband for several years before he achieved the annulment of his first marriage. When success finally seemed near enough in late 1532, she had agreed to sleep with the king. She carried the resultant pregnancy safely through her marriage to Henry VIII in late January 1533 and her coronation in May. After both Katharine and the pope failed to fall in with Henry's wishes to end his first marriage, he had finally declared himself a sufficient authority, under God, to replace the papacy by himself as head of the Church in England and now subject only to God. Although that process was not completed until after Elizabeth's birth in May 1533 his new Archbishop of Canterbury, Thomas Cranmer, was empowered to declare Katharine had never been rightfully wife to Henry. Under that dispensation, and bypassing papal sanction, Elizabeth was born the legitimate daughter, and Mary declared illegitimate.

The processes whereby the pope's authority had been superseded by that of the king had not been popular. That Queen Katharine's marriage was repudiated, and Queen Anne set in her place, divided court, clergy and the population at large; such divisions were based partly on religious grounds, but were also a consequence of the considerable popularity of Katharine and almost equal hostility to Anne, widely seen as responsible for the whole sequence of the king's religious and marital changes. The infant Elizabeth was from her birth a symbol of the political and religious divisions between traditional Catholics and adherents of the new and changing religious order, divisions that were to haunt the English realm throughout her reign. These divisive religious issues connected to Henry's marital adventures were to shape major aspects of the reigns of all three of his children, Edward VI, Mary I *and* Elizabeth I. Of the three, however, Elizabeth was the original and most obvious symbol of the profound and enduring divisions in church and state resulting from Henry's innovations. It may be helpful to explain what was involved in the king's first two marriages in more detail.

From Queen Katharine to Queen Anne

As previously indicated Elizabeth's first 25 years at least were shaped in many ways by the circumstances of her birth. When Henry VIII, then 17, came to the throne in 1509 one of his first acts was to marry Katharine of Aragon, the widowed wife of his elder brother Arthur. There was some unease at his decision because, if her first marriage had been consummated, then Henry's relationship to Katharine was within the forbidden degrees of affinity. Katharine always denied the consummation of that marriage, but as an additional precaution a papal dispensation for her second marriage had also been obtained.

Observers were generally agreed that the early years of her second marriage were successful in almost every way, except in the crucial matter of ensuring a (male) heir. After the brief – six week – life of their son, another Henry, in 1511 Katharine gave birth in 1516 to Mary Tudor, her only child to survive. By 1525, given Katharine's age (she was approaching 40), recent miscarriages and general health, Henry had little prospect of any more children with his wife. He was very fond of his daughter, who was treated as effectively Princess of Wales (male heirs to the throne were formally given the title of Prince of Wales). He was proud of her musical and other accomplishments and took pleasure in her company; but manifestly she was not a son – and no woman had ever reigned successfully in England.

Just when Henry first expressed his doubts about the legitimacy of his first marriage is not certain, but they were being widely discussed at court and beyond by 1527. His doubts about his marriage to Katharine were reinforced by his growing attraction to Anne Boleyn, at his court from 1522 as an attendant to Queen Katharine. The king had previously had several mistresses, of whom the historically more important were Elizabeth Blount, mother of Henry Fitzroy, Duke of Richmond, and Anne Boleyn's married elder sister, Mary Carey, whose subsequent children by her husband were to provide Elizabeth's immediate family. But Mary Carey's younger sister had no intention of following her sister's more submissive path to the king's bed as his mistress.

Anne Boleyn's leading biographer, E.A. Ives, has argued that Henry's own intentions were also quite different on this occasion. At first, Ives wrote, both Anne and Henry anticipated a quick end of his marriage to Katharine, and that their marriage would swiftly follow. They had no reason to expect significant opposition from the Papacy, the only authority in Catholic Christendom with power to approve royal divorces, for popes had often obliged monarchs by annulling their marriages. So Henry turned his mind readily enough to having his first marriage annulled. (Annulment of his marriages, it might be noted, was always Henry's preferred language, since throughout his life, and despite six marriages, he disapproved of divorce.)

His decision that his first marriage to Katharine of Aragon, his wife since 1509, had never been legitimate was based on the text of Leviticus 20 v. 21, which forbade a man's marrying his brother's widow. Other scriptural texts, including Deuteronomy 25 v. 5, actually instructed a brother to marry the widow of his deceased childless brother, but Henry preferred the earlier text.[1] His argument that his first marriage was against God's law (and therefore could not be justified by papal sanction) seemed all the stronger when he considered the death within weeks of his only son, perhaps a divine punishment.

But Henry faced unexpected problems as he began to move for an annulment of his marriage with Katharine. He had always expected that the most serious opposition to Henry's divorce would come from the Hapsburg Charles V, Holy Roman Emperor, the most powerful ruler in Europe, and protective nephew of Katharine. Charles was always careful of his family's reputation. On the other hand, Henry may well have expected that, because the pope was closely allied with France and therefore opposed to Hapsburg interests, Pope Clement VII would be indifferent to Hapsburg hostility to his divorce. By May 1527, however, there was open warfare between the pope and the Holy Roman Emperor, leading to the Emperor Charles V capturing Rome and taking Clement VII prisoner.

Thereafter Clement was in no position to defy the Emperor, and Henry's anticipated annulment of his marriage became much more problematic. As Henry turned to seeking a 'divorce' despite papal reluctance, his subjects were forced to decide between their traditional obedience to the pope and the powerful ideology that taught that resistance to the monarch was treason and against God's law. Nevertheless, some leading women, including Henry's favourite sister Mary, Dowager Queen of France, now married to his good friend Charles Brandon, Duke of Suffolk, found it hard to abandon Katharine, England's much-admired queen for more than 20 years. Some, but fewer, leading nobles had the same difficulty. Katharine also had considerable popular sympathy within England among the clergy and women. As it became ever more obvious that the king's future marriage plans were focused on Anne Boleyn, the protests widened within as well as beyond England. There were street riots in London, and at least once noble retinues brawled when their respective lords clashed in their support for the current or the prospective wife.

Henry VIII's marriage to Anne Boleyn in late January 1533 was so secret that not even Thomas Cranmer, an ally of the Boleyns since

1529, knew the precise date; the haste was necessary because by then the king knew that Anne was pregnant. The secrecy was essential because Henry's second marriage was being celebrated before his first marriage had been formally annulled. By mid-1533, however, Henry had undermined the power of papal dispensations so much that his new Archbishop of Canterbury, Thomas Cranmer, could feel free to confirm that Katharine's marriage to Henry had never been legitimate; a proclamation to that effect was issued on 5 July 1533. Katharine was henceforth to be known only as Princess Dowager, her status now redefined as that of Prince Arthur's widow. These moves did not put an end to public protests and intermittent public displays of support for the first queen, who was now moved away from the court to places ever more remote from London. To add to the complexities, the cause of the old queen was closely associated with the familiar papal religious authority, the cause of the new queen with the reformist agenda of men like Luther and, increasingly, those promoting even more advanced religious changes.

Contemporaries reported occasions in London when, after the clergy followed their new instructions to pray publicly for Queen Anne, congregations walked out of their churches. It was said that when Anne's coronation procession passed through the capital on 1 June 1533 there were very few cheers from the assembled onlookers. The printed account of that occasion – itself a significant innovation in the use of print to spread the carefully shaped 'good news' of the new queen widely across England – made many references to the sounds of musical instruments, none to the sounds of cheering, let alone any reference to the actual numbers assembled.

Despite the contradictory accounts of some observers, the message of the pamphlet, *The most noble, triumphant Coronation of Queen Anne, wife unto the most noble king Henry VIII*, was that all the ceremonies surrounding the coronation of Queen Anne had been most properly magnificent, and that the new queen had had shown 'a joyful, thankful countenance' throughout. The pamphlet also carried the promise that Anne would bring Henry the son he so desired. She was visibly pregnant at her procession through London. The messages adorning the pageants along her path through London streets praised her virtue and her chastity, promising Anne that 'when thou shalt bear a new son of the King's blood; there shall be a golden world unto thy people.'[2] Another message set out the diplomatic implication of this marriage: that her marriage confirmed a French – and therefore anti-Hapsburg – alliance.

The next day was Anne's coronation day, celebrated with all the usual ceremony and the customary church rites. Enough of the elite of the land had dutifully gathered to support her coronation ceremony and to endorse their king's new queen at a great feast. Although it was always evident to Henry – and everyone else – that there was widespread unease at the king's break with traditional papal authority, members of the nobility always had to weigh up the dangers to their status, their possessions, their lives and their families if they openly resisted their God-ordained king. Lesser subjects also had to weigh up their public interests – and lives – against their private convictions.

Some observers speculated that hostility to Henry's second marriage – and the subsequent declaration that Princess Mary was illegitimate – was so widespread that if only Katharine had supported any proposed insurrection there would have been armed risings across the realm. Henry himself expressed some anxiety about that possibility. Katharine, however, insisted on her duty of obedience to the man she still regarded as her lawful husband. Nevertheless, Henry's repudiation of papal supremacy and of his first wife continued to take its toll; a number of traditional Catholics were to die as traitors to their king, including both Sir Thomas More and Bishop John Fisher, executed in mid-1535 for refusing the oath declaring the legitimacy of Henry's second daughter, Elizabeth. For both, the sticking point was less the legitimacy of Elizabeth, much more the oath's preamble rejecting all papal authority. The two issues, however, were always inextricably linked.

In the following years, less scholarly but more aristocratic conservative families such as the Courtenays and Poles, both with strong Plantagenet descent lines and therefore some possibility of claims to the throne, were brought almost to extinction by Henry's anxiety about their religious conservatism and possible support for his elder daughter. All in all, it is plain to see why the aftermath of the religious transformations which accompanied Henry's divorce from Katharine and marriage to Anne Boleyn had significant consequences for Elizabeth throughout her whole life, and why English religious divisions (and their foreign supporters) were to be always a problem for her.

The Princess Elizabeth and the Lady Mary

As already noted, when Queen Anne Boleyn gave birth, the child was not the son so widely prophesied. It was said some astrologers had fled for fear of the consequences of their error, but publicly at least Henry had accepted his new daughter serenely enough, in the expectation that sons would follow. One person, however, for whom the arrival of Queen Anne Boleyn's daughter did augur badly was Katharine's daughter, Mary. As long as the infant was expected to be a boy, it was unlikely to have much impact on Mary's status, since a male child would always take precedence over her, but another daughter gave rise to more nuanced issues, which helped set the pattern for the recurrent difficult relations between the two sisters as long as Mary lived.

At Elizabeth's first great royal occasion, her christening four days after her birth, there were several reminders of divided loyalty towards the first or second queen, and of the political imperative for critics of the new order to conceal their misgivings. The christening was a splendid occasion, quite as magnificent as the ceremony for Henry's first daughter had been, although neither occasion had been marked by such celebrations as the jousting which had marked the birth of Henry's brief-lived son in 1511. The new princess's godparents were the obliging Thomas Cranmer, Archbishop of Canterbury, the duchess of Norfolk and the marchioness of Exeter. Significantly, both the suitably high-status godmothers were known supporters of Katharine and Mary, but neither could afford to offend the king by refusing to take part. The marchioness's equally conservative husband, the marquis, and John Lord Hussey, Mary's chamberlain, also played the parts allotted to them precisely to test their loyalty to the king's new domestic order.

After the main part of the ceremony, Elizabeth was proclaimed 'the high and mighty princess of England', explicitly displacing the 17-year-old Mary from that title. Perhaps at Anne Boleyn's instigation, but certainly with the king's active support, Mary was several times pressured to acknowledge the illegality of her mother's second marriage, her own illegitimacy and the precedence now due to her infant sister. She adamantly refused to accept any such propositions. When just two months old, Elizabeth was given her own household and established at Hatfield, sufficiently close to

London to make parental visits easy. The journey there was the infant's first major public appearance, and she was escorted through London by two dukes and an impressive number of lords and gentlemen to emphasise the high status of the new princess. Chapuys, the Hapsburg ambassador, had no doubts that Henry had arranged a longer route for the whole retinue – through the more populous parts – in order to impress on as many bystanders as possible the royal status of this new daughter.

In the following days, the remnants of Mary's household were removed from her and she was moved into her sister's household, where the older daughter was surrounded by women whose interests lay entirely with the Boleyn ascendancy, and all were overseen by Anne Boleyn's aunt, Lady Sheldon. It is, of course, impossible to know how much Elizabeth ever saw or understood of the recurrent tension and/or hostility in her infant household between Mary and the supporters of her mother in those early years, but it was not a promising start for any hope of good relations between the king's two daughters.

Elizabeth's life as princess

Lady Margaret Bryan supervised the household of the new royal infant as she had previously headed the nursery of the infant Mary – and was to do again for Prince Edward; clearly Henry had great confidence in her. If the regulations Henry had set out in Mary's infancy were followed again, as they most likely were, Elizabeth's early life was shaped by strict etiquette: every man approaching the infant princess was required to doff his cap, every woman to curtsey to her. None but the greater nobility were permitted to approach so close they could kneel and kiss her hand. Only her social equals – effectively members of her most immediate family – were permitted to kiss her on the cheek. Her formal dress reflected the same highest social standing, and the need to set her apart. Even Elizabeth's caps distinguished her; they included two purple ones – purple always being the colour of royalty – of taffeta and satin, and each with a net of damask gold to catch her hair.

It is unlikely that Elizabeth knew much of her mother or father, since the infant was most frequently lodged in the country and only occasionally visited by her parents. But one glimpse of the king's ultimate control of the household is a note, dated 9 October 1535, recording that the king, acting on advice from Lady Bryan and other members of the household, had decided that Elizabeth, now two, should be weaned. Although the princess's main place of residence was the old palace at Hatfield, she also spent time in other houses, above all at Eltham and Greenwich, places where she was more likely to be with her parents. (Like any great household, Elizabeth's moved frequently, to allow for the thorough cleaning of the drains and accumulated refuse from whichever house had been occupied, a process referred to as 'sweetening' the house.)

Little reliable information survives about the earliest year of Elizabeth; she was, after all, princess for less than three years. She visited and was visited by her parents, separately or together at intervals. On occasion, she was visited by other members of Henry's court, who dutifully reported on her unusual promise, even from the age of six months – as politically wise subjects did for each royal child. The household was supplied with all the necessary furnishings to establish the standing of the royal princess for any visitor. When questions were asked about the increased expenses of the household, however, some of it was attributed to the extra requirements and demands which Mary made – in part because of her insistence on eating apart from the main household, precisely to avoid any need to enact her submission to her sister's precedence.

Care was always taken that the royal infant was shown in a sufficiently rich setting, with sumptuous hangings around the chamber. As relations with the Hapsburg emperor deteriorated further over the treatment of both his aunt Katharine and his cousin Mary, the French pursued the time-honoured practice of seeking a marriage alliance to confirm a political one. The first diplomatic overtures to that end had taken place in early April 1534; just some six months old, Elizabeth was displayed naked to three French visitors. (It was common before any marriage negotiations to demonstrate that the royal infant had no hidden deformities.) An account surviving from May 1535, included £49 15s 'for certain liveries for the household of the king's daughter', which may have signalled further French negotiations, a proposal which resurfaced intermittently for several more months.

If there was any substance in the rumour that Francis I wanted Mary for his elder son the Dauphin and Elizabeth for a younger son,[3] that may be another reflection of Elizabeth's more problematic origins. Otherwise, Elizabeth's dubious status in the eyes of the European Catholic monarchs meant that, whatever the complexities of their international rivalries, few were so desperate as to contemplate seriously marriage between Henry's 'bastard' and their family members. Beyond England she was very seldom referred to as the princess that Henry VIII insisted that she was. The kindest of the more usual terms for referring to her was 'the little one'; for most Europeans 'Princess' was the term still applied to Mary. Quite often foreign ambassadors referred to Elizabeth simply as 'the little bastard'.

When Katharine of Aragon died on 7 January 1536, Henry had good reason to be relieved. One response was to declare that he was finally free of 'fear of war' with the Emperor, for he had been quite as well aware as the various ambassadors of recurrent talk of possible rebellion and/or foreign invasion on behalf of his first – and Catholic – wife and daughter. On 21 January Chapuys reported to Charles that, hearing of Katharine's death, some of Anne's associates declared all that was now needed was for Mary also to die. He added that Henry, to celebrate his first wife's death, had gone to mass the next day:

> clad all over in yellow, from top to toe, except the white feather he had in his bonnet, and the Little Bastard was conducted to mass with trumpets and other great triumphs. After dinner the King entered the room in which the ladies danced, and there did several things like one transported with joy. At last he sent for his Little Bastard, and carrying her in his arms he showed her first to one and then to another.[4]

The death of Queen Anne Boleyn, and Henry's second illegitimate daughter

It is just possible that Elizabeth might have remembered those spectacular – and very noisy – triumphs, although she could hardly have understood the reason. But in the same month that Katharine died, Anne miscarried, for the second time, of what was said to have been a male foetus. Chapuys – never a reliable source of court gossip (his information was, at the very best, second hand and was certainly more indirect on this occasion) – reported that after that miscarriage Henry had declared that God obviously disapproved of his second as much as his first marriage, since He had ensured that neither of Henry's wives gave him male heirs. Given the source, that might have been dismissed as unreliable, but subsequent events soon suggested otherwise.

What was quite as ominous for Anne were the reports circulating by January that Henry had a new love, the sister of a rising star at court, Edward Seymour. Little is known about Jane Seymour, except that she had been a lady in waiting first to Katharine of Aragon then to Anne Boleyn. There are some reports of Anne storming at Henry after finding Jane seated on Henry's knee as early as mid-1535; Jane soon accepted other favours, which suggest she may have been a willing enough participant in the scheme said to have been hatched by Cromwell, her relatives and some more conservative nobles to bring about the fall of Anne Boleyn.[5] The queen obviously understood that she was facing some urgent threat when she was seen on 30 April, with her daughter in her arms, pleading unsuccessfully to Henry through a window. That was the last time mother and daughter were together, for within two days Anne was in the Tower, and the first of the several men alleged to have committed adultery with her had 'confessed' to his offences.

Historians still debate what validity, if any, there was in the allegations of Anne's sexual promiscuity, although the dominant opinion is that she was innocent of the charges. The significance of the charges and the guilty verdict here is that they served as justification for the complete destruction of the queen's reputation. One indicator that more was afoot than simply disposing of an allegedly adulterous wife was that once Anne was in the Tower and facing her trial, Jane Seymour moved to Hampton Court, nearer the king. Two days before her execution Cranmer declared that Anne's marriage to Henry was null and void, on grounds which have always remained secret, but probably drew on the king's liaison with her sister Mary before he married Anne, since that consummated liaison made Henry and Anne effectively brother and sister in the eyes of the church.

Once Anne's marriage had been invalidated, Elizabeth joined Mary as another illegitimate – but always acknowledged – daughter of the king. But for many years the grounds for Anne's execution and the invalidation of her marriage were to provide material for those hostile to Elizabeth to speculate about her having inherited her mother's morality, since it was a common belief that immorality could pass from one generation to the next. There were also many rumours about who, actually, was her father. (After Anne's death, Chapuys took it as self-evident that Elizabeth was the daughter of Norris, one of the men executed on the charge of adultery with Anne. Mary, when she was queen and finding Elizabeth a most unpromising heir, several times asserted that Elizabeth was the daughter of Anne's musician, Mark Smeaton, the only one of the accused to confess – after torture – his 'guilt'.) Elizabeth was to be subject to such innuendo from her critics for many years. For her, however, perhaps the most enduring consequence of the public explanations for Anne Boleyn's execution was that she could never move for her own mother's public rehabilitation, since if Anne was innocent of the charges against her, then the king her father was either profoundly gullible or criminally complicit in the judicial murder of his second wife.

Even without Henry's increasingly close relationship with Jane Seymour during the last days of Anne Boleyn, the evidence points to the second of those possibilities. On the day of Anne's execution, 19 May 1536, Cranmer formally granted a dispensation of affinity between Henry and Jane Seymour for marriage, since both could trace their lineage back to Edward III (d. 1377). The following day Henry and his new love were betrothed, an occasion conventionally marked by a feast which must have been in preparation for some days. The pair married privately at Whitehall ten days later, and Queen Jane was soon introduced to Henry's court. The Succession Act of July 1536 completed Henry's preferred new order, confirming as it did Elizabeth's new status; now she, like her elder sister was illegitimate and excluded from the line of succession to the throne. Mary, with some help from Queen Jane's influence, was soon restored to her father's favour, after a sufficiently abject submission, and rapidly regained precedence over her infant sister, in relative size of household and other ways.

The new succession legislation cleared the way for whatever children Jane Seymour might bear, a prospect made even more pressing when Henry's other possible (illegitimate but male) heir,

Henry Fitzroy, died suddenly in late July. (Remarkably, some reports attributed his death to Anne Boleyn, who was, by then, a Tudor propaganda embodiment of evil.) No statutory reaffirmation of her illegitimacy, however, had an immediate impact on Elizabeth, since her father always acknowledged her as his daughter. Her household continued with much the same personnel as before, although with rather less ceremonial and expense. The people closest to the little girl remained with her, under the continuing supervision of Lady Margaret Bryan.

There were, however, new problems for the household, which Bryan set out in a letter sent to Cromwell probably in late July, although such problems were not ones likely to concern a child not yet three. Her governess declared herself confused as to Elizabeth's precise status now that she was no longer the king's acknowledged heir; the child was in need of new garments, having outgrown her previous ones, and there was no material in the house to meet her needs. Sir John Shelton, married to Anne Boleyn's aunt and recently made controller of the combined household for the king's two daughters, was asserting his new authority in ways she believed threatened Elizabeth's daily routine and welfare. Nevertheless, and despite the 'great pain' Elizabeth was suffering from her teeth, Lady Bryan concluded, 'she is as toward a child and as gentle of condition as ever I knew in my life.'[6]

Elizabeth remained in the country for most of the time in the following years. Despite nominally sharing a household with her younger sister, Mary spent much more time at the royal court after Henry had taken his third wife. Whatever resentment she still felt towards Elizabeth's mother, Mary, when writing to her father within weeks of their reconciliation, reported that Elizabeth was 'such a child … as I doubt not but your Highness shall have cause to rejoice of in time coming'.[7] As Mary resumed a prominent position at court, Henry appears to have restored her precedence in every way, while still providing affection and support for her little sister. One observer reported in late October that 'Madame Marie [Mary] is now the first after the Queen, and sits at table opposite her, a little lower down …. Madame Ysabeau [Elizabeth] is not at that table, though the King is very affectionate to her. It is said he loves her much.'

The age difference between the two sisters always meant that they were treated differently, with Mary more commonly in the King's immediate party. As one example, when Henry decided in late 1537 that he, Queen Jane and 'my lady Mary' would travel to Greenwich for Christmas one way, 'my lady Elizabeth' and the rest of the household not appointed to wait on the king were to go in another party.[8] Another consequence of the age difference was that in effect Elizabeth had her own household while Mary was at her father's court. Lady Bryan remained with her until she was called upon to undertake care of the infant Edward, born to Jane Seymour in October 1537. Before then, in mid-1536 Katharine Champernowne, better known as Kat Astley as she became after her marriage in 1545, joined Elizabeth's household as a lady in waiting. She was to become Elizabeth's governess in 1547, and remained unusually close to Elizabeth until her death in 1565. She may well have been Elizabeth's closest confidante for some 20 years. Despite various reports about the kindnesses of Henry's wives to his little daughter, Elizabeth was more often away from rather than at court in her early years. Once she became simply Henry's second daughter she was of little political interest, and therefore seldom appears in any official records.

She did, however, still make occasional public appearances as part of Henry's family. The birth of Edward, hailed as 'the most dearest son of King Henry the VIIIth', provided one such occasion. Henry had decreed a uniquely magnificent christening service for his long-desired male heir. Mary, with Archbishop Cranmer and the Duke of Norfolk, stood godparent to the infant. Although just four, Elizabeth also attended: she carried the baptismal chrisom (a white robe put on the infant after baptism), and was herself carried by Edward Seymour, brother to Queen Jane.

Otherwise, there are only fragments from her life in those years. Her early education, like that of her royal siblings, concentrated on classical learning and religious instruction. She exchanged gifts with family members at the appropriate times (the surviving accounts of Mary's Privy Purse expenses indicate that she was among those who were generous to her little sister in those early years), and was at court for such significant occasions as the celebration of Henry's brief marriage to Anne of Cleves. She did not see much of his next queen, her cousin Katherine Howard, but at the age of eight may have understood something of the reasons for her execution in early 1542. There is no evidence on which to speculate about whether she understood any similarities between the death of her Howard stepmother and that of her own mother, but she is unlikely to have seen enough of Katherine to grieve for her. Nevertheless, one story survives (but was first recorded decades later) that it was about this time Elizabeth commented to her young companion Robert Dudley that she would never marry. That tradition, however, is the less plausible since there is no surviving evidence that the two met during that period.

As Elizabeth grew older, she was several times one more bargaining chip in Henry's recurrent and complex schemes for diplomatic intermarriage between his and other great families. Her part in such proposals was made more problematic by reminders of her scandalous mother and her own illegitimate status. But she was prestigious enough to be the subject of prolonged diplomatic manoeuvres between the English and Scottish courts in 1543. Elizabeth, then 10, was described by her father as 'endowed with virtues and qualities agreeable with her estate' as he proposed her betrothal to the son of the then Earl of Arran.[9] Her estate, as a king's acknowledged illegitimate daughter, was still high, if not of the first order, and was deployed as part of Henry's complex negotiations for a marriage between his son and the infant Queen Mary of Scotland.

The final years as Henry's daughter

When Henry married his sixth and final wife, Katharine Parr, on 12 July 1543, there was no secrecy about it. Rather, their marriage at Hampton Court was witnessed by a group which included both the king's daughters. A year later, however, a letter from Elizabeth, dated 31 July 1544 when she was 11, laments that she and Katharine had been separated, apparently for that whole year. The reason for what Elizabeth described as her 'exile' is not known, but she asked her stepmother to intercede for her with her father, since she still dared not write to him on her own behalf. Soon after, while Henry was off waging war in France and Katharine was regent, Elizabeth did return to court. She was apparently also restored to her father's favour by September that year, when Henry sent affectionate greetings to all three of his children from France. A version of the happy royal family almost all together was painted in 1545, but the striking feature is that a portrait of the long-dead Queen Jane, mother of Henry's male heir, was substituted for the childless Katharine in the centre (Plate 1). As mother to Henry's legitimate son, the dead Jane took precedence over any living wife.

More generally, Elizabeth, like her two royal siblings found Katharine an attentive and supportive stepmother, and she responded warmly to such interest. Several letters from Elizabeth to her have survived, as have some she wrote on her stepmother's behalf. Nevertheless, the child still spent much of her time away from the royal couple, and was usually the focus of much less attention than her long-desired brother or even her elder sister, now seen as one of the ornaments of Henry's court and a constant companion of Queen Katharine. So it was that although she now enjoyed more affection and attention than she could remember, Elizabeth was still ranked third in her father's order of interest.

While Katharine oversaw several aspects of Elizabeth's upbringing, including her musical education, the child sent her several gifts of her own making, including a translation of Marguerite of Navarre's *Mirror of the Sinful Soul.* This moderately reformist work was much in tune with Katharine's own religious inclinations, and the next year Elizabeth presented her father with a translation of Katharine's own *Prayers or Meditations* in French, Italian and Latin. As was always the case with gifts from young royal children, it is impossible to know just what role a tutor played in such gifts, but at the very least it suggests Elizabeth already shared something of the scholarly accomplishments Henry's other children developed.

Since Katharine Parr had a long-standing interest in portraiture, it may well have been her influence which led to the first formal portrait of Elizabeth, painted in about 1546, which provides an almost unique indication of Elizabeth's personal appearance, before the stylised works of the later years took over (Plate 2). Perhaps its most interesting feature is how little information it conveys about the apparently demure and composed king's daughter. After several reworkings of his preferred line of succession, reflecting his marital changes, and several proposed alternatives which never made it as far as taking form in legislation, Henry's final Act of Succession (35 Henry VIII c. 1) restored both daughters to the line of succession, albeit with Elizabeth in third place; this portrait may reflect the extent to which Elizabeth enjoyed what was to be a unique period of relative family tranquillity, which lasted until Henry's death on 27 January 1547.

None of Henry's family, let alone his current wife, had been allowed near him for the last month of his life, and his death was kept secret for three days, before Edward, now nine years old, was proclaimed king. There had been some uncertainty whether the boy would have a regent – the names of both Katharine Parr and his sister Mary were put forward by observers for such a position – but from those days of secret negotiations it was Edward's uncle Edward Seymour who emerged as Duke of Somerset and Lord Protector. His younger brother Thomas revealed *his* ambition by asking his brother's approval to woo Mary, who, he was assured, would never accept him. He also considered both Anne of Cleves and Elizabeth as prospective brides before he settled for secretly marrying the widowed Queen Katharine Parr; she had previously been wooed and almost won by him before Henry had chosen her as his next wife, and the marriage improved his access to the royal family, an access of which he was to take full advantage.

The king's disreputable daughter?

Contrary to the usual conventions about mourning periods for widows, Katharine Parr married Thomas Seymour within four months of Henry's death, giving rise to widespread and adverse comment. Amongst those profoundly shocked by the news of Katharine's speedy remarriage was Mary, who wrote to Elizabeth as soon as the secret marriage was known, suggesting there should be some united display of disapproval from them. In reply, Elizabeth agreed that 'the king, our father' had been 'shamefully dishonoured by the queen, our step-mother', but argued that neither of them was in a good position to display her disapproval of the hasty remarriage, 'without running heavy risk of making our own lot much worse than it is', and therefore recommended 'dissimulation'. Nevertheless, Elizabeth reassured her sister, in future she would 'always pay much deference to [Mary's] instructions and commands'.[10] That may have been Mary's introduction to Elizabeth's undoubted capacity for the dissimulation she was to practise in the following years, for Elizabeth was soon a member of Katharine's household, now shared by Thomas Seymour.

In that Parr/Seymour household, Elizabeth became the subject of a major public scandal which was to leave a serious scar on her reputation, a reputation already vulnerable because of her mother's shameful death. Later, in her answers to close questioning about the relationship between the king's daughter and the queen consort's husband, Kat Astley, still Elizabeth's governess, suggested that Seymour's conduct towards the king's daughter had become unusually familiar in later 1547, and only intensified in the months that followed. The apparently mutual flirtation came to some sort of crisis in the spring of 1548, when the pregnant Katharine reportedly saw her husband embracing Elizabeth. By May, the king's daughter, perhaps banished from Katharine's household by the queen, had moved to that of the Dennys. Sir Anthony had stood high in Henry VIII's favour and his wife was sister to Kat Astley, so the choice was hardly surprising.

On 30 August Katharine gave birth to a daughter, only to die herself within the week. Soon there were reports that Katharine's widower was aiming even higher for his next marriage; reports had it that he planned to marry Elizabeth and, always jealous of his brother's pre-eminence, seize the young king, whose favour he had worked steadily to win. His purpose, it was said, was to supplant his brother Edward as Lord Protector to their nephew, now Edward VI. Kat Astley, who had previously supported Seymour's interests, agreed that she had indeed raised the question of Elizabeth marrying him, but insisted that the king's daughter had given very proper – and evasive – answers to her hints. It seems likely, from Seymour's strong interest in the details of Elizabeth's income and resources, that he did indeed contemplate marriage with her, but the rest is more speculative. In the end, it was Thomas Seymour's wild scheming and some remarkably loose talk which drew more adverse attention to himself; he was arrested in January 1549.

Then, as well as the more recent charges which ended with his conviction for high treason, the older scandal of his behaviour towards Elizabeth was resurrected. That was carefully investigated by the Privy Council in early 1549. Details of the interrogations spread beyond the initial enquiries to become the matter of public gossip within England and internationally. Despite vehement denials from Elizabeth of any improper behaviour whatsoever, there were widespread rumours even that Elizabeth was pregnant, forcing her to request some public denial of the rumour. No such official denial was forthcoming, but although the speculation gradually died down, the whole episode 'brought both her chastity and her judgment into question'.[11] Seymour refused to defend himself from many of the charges put to him, and was executed in March; despite many romantic tales to the contrary, there is very little evidence that Elizabeth ever mourned for him.

Rather, as the scandal began to die down, Elizabeth reportedly set about repairing her reputation, in part by transforming herself into a model Protestant maiden and integrating herself into the new Protestant order emerging during Edward's reign. Roger Ascham, her tutor from early 1548 until 1550, accompanied her to the Denny home at Cheshunt, and her scholarship prospered under his supervision. According to his account, in both his letters and his book *The Scolemaster*, she received an excellent education in languages both ancient and modern, and in classical studies. (As will be discussed in the final chapter, scholars now believe that Ascham – and others – overstated her scholarly accomplishments.) His own religious position in the religiously troubled times of Edward's reign was moderately reformist, as was that of Kat Astley; if Elizabeth knew much of her mother's own religious positions it would have been an added incentive to accept the religious changes progressively introduced from early in Edward's reign, and accept them she ostensibly did.

John Aylmer, one-time tutor to Lady Jane Grey, reported indeed, significantly in 1559, that Elizabeth had become such a model Protestant maiden that only once in the seven years after her father's death did she willingly dress herself in the rich gowns and jewellery that she inherited, but there is little contemporary evidence to support that particular retrospective claim. It would surely have been remarked more widely if Elizabeth had really foregone the rich dress of her royal status in life, at a time when dress was strictly regulated to ensure it accurately reflected the social status of the wearer. A recurrent theme in this study will be the considerable amount of Protestant myth-making by those about Elizabeth from the time of her accession.

Elizabeth as Edward's preferred sister?

Although Elizabeth was more often at Edward's court than was Mary, that was partly because Mary several times refused invitations to court for fear of further religious confrontation between herself and her royal brother.[12] (Mary refused to accept the legality of the successive reformist religious changes until her brother the King, now formally God's vice-regent in England, was of an age to make an informed judgment on the changes being prosecuted in his name.) Elizabeth was, however, also more usually in the country, at Hatfield, Ashridge or Enfield in Buckinghamshire, than at court. By her father's will, and a significant reinterpretation of it by the early Edwardian council, those were the main houses to go to her, though she could not take legal title to them until she had reached her age of majority, 16, and even then there was a further struggle as she resisted the wish of Northumberland in 1550 to take Hatfield for himself. (By late 1549, the power of Edward Seymour as Lord Protector had been broken and John Dudley, soon to become Duke of Northumberland, emerged as the king's pre-eminent councillor.) Thereafter Elizabeth was the legal owner of extensive property, although still not as much as Mary. As one scholar recently concluded, whereas Mary had 'obtained large, capacious residences and their surrounding estates, Elizabeth had to make do with lesser houses and small, dispersed parcels, which ranged from Northamptonshire to Lincolnshire and Dorset'. Elizabeth's subordinate status vis-à-vis her elder sister was still being expressed in every visible way.[13]

In February 1553 Edward VI, aged 15 and until then a relatively healthy person, fell ill of a complaint which he could never entirely shake off. There were marked fluctuations in his condition, but by May concern about his health was widespread. Neither of his sisters had been permitted to visit him, and by June it was clear he would not recover. Nevertheless he was lucid enough to insist on gathering his judges at his bedside to alter the line of succession. He would not accept his father's will – and the statute enacting it – since it specified that in the absence of his own heir Mary would succeed him or, failing her, Elizabeth. His publicly stated reason for disinheriting them was that both were illegitimate. Moreover, he argued, either sister, being still unmarried, might marry a foreigner, thereby bringing into England foreign customs and perhaps foreign (Catholic) religion, destroying the Protestant order progressively introduced in his reign. Instead, the young king insisted, he would have their cousin Jane Grey (granddaughter of Mary Tudor, who was the younger sister to Henry VIII and Dowager queen of France) as his heir.

The accounts of the teenage age king forcing his will upon his judges and his councillors is impressive for what it suggests about the force of his personality, although he was not yet 16. Even though he never acted alone – he was particularly supported by Northumberland, whose son Guilford had recently married Lady Jane Grey – there is now little doubt that Edward had taken some time in the previous months to work out an alternative line of succession. There is no sign in his deliberations that he ever considered Elizabeth as a possible heir, any more than he had Mary. And when he was dead, and his preferred line of succession announced, there was nothing that Elizabeth could do but wait upon the outcome of Mary's mustering of forces to support her own claim to the throne. Mary still stood high in popular esteem, and had the resources to rally her supporters – two attributes Elizabeth lacked. Once again, Henry's younger daughter was reminded, as she had so often been in the first 20 years of her life, that being the king's second daughter was no certain guarantee of either high status or political success.

2 From suspect 'second person' to Queen of England

Elizabeth and the triumph of Mary Tudor

As outlined in the previous chapter, after Edward VI died on 6 July 1553 his councillors issued an unexpected and unusually detailed proclamation announcing that the new monarch was Lady Jane Grey. That proclamation set out Edward's reasons for believing Lady Jane was the best candidate, and reminding the people that both Henry's daughters were illegitimate (as indeed, formally they still were) and therefore, his argument went, both disqualified from inheriting the throne. Furthermore, since neither of Henry's daughters was married, either might marry some foreign prince and thereby reintroduce foreign (that is, Catholic) religion. This unexpected announcement, however, ignored the widely publicised statute of Henry VIII that had written into law the old king's preferred line of succession.

Nothing is known of Elizabeth's immediate reactions, although her consistent hostility to the surviving Grey sisters during her own reign may offer a clue. Indeed, one problem in writing about Elizabeth's life during Mary's reign is that so little of her own writing has survived from those years. An even greater problem is that later versions of her life in these years were written only after Mary was dead and after Elizabeth was on the throne. The best-known and most enduring 16th-century polemic of them all was a vehemently Protestant work first published in 1563 and commonly known as John Foxe's *Book of Martyrs*.[1] Just one example of his selectivity is found when he wrote of the events of July 1553; Foxe repeated the reasons for Mary's exclusion from the throne, but made no mention of Elizabeth being excluded on exactly the same grounds, with the implication that only Mary was said to be of illegitimate birth.

Elizabeth never wanted 'Queen Jane' on the English throne any more than did Mary, but the younger sister had little choice but to wait upon the outcome of her elder sister's challenge to the new regime. She took no part on either side of the struggle but pleaded illness and took to her bed. (One trait the two Tudor sisters shared was a marked tendency to plead illness and take to their beds when some disagreeable event or choice threatened.) Elizabeth's caution was prudent, but it proved to be unnecessary, for the story of Mary's accession to the throne was one of unexpected success. That was the more surprising since the supporters of Jane Grey had control of all English military and naval resources, of London, and of the armoury and treasure in the Tower. How Mary triumphed and claimed the throne has been variously explained by her popularity, by her legal status as next heir after Edward, by popular support for her religion and by pure chance. Whatever the reasons, the reign of Queen Jane was over in nine days; the most part of the Edwardian Privy Council declared it had always preferred Mary, and dutifully proclaimed her queen of England on 19 July. 'Queen Jane' remained in the Tower, but with a different quality of accommodation from that of the royal apartments.

Elizabeth had played no part in Mary's success. But as soon as her sister had triumphed, she wrote to Mary with congratulations for her successful accession and asked the new queen's advice: when she joined Mary's entourage for the royal entry into London, should she dress in mourning for Edward or in celebration of Mary's accession? The answer is not known, but Elizabeth prudently chose the latter. Accordingly, ten days after Mary's official proclamation as queen, Elizabeth rode into London at the head of a large number of horsemen (onlooker estimates of the number in her train ranged from 1,000 to 2,000) all dressed in Tudor colours of green and white; another Tudor daughter had entered the capital to join the triumphant Mary Tudor's official entry into London on 3 August. And in that procession, Elizabeth was given a prominent position, entirely appropriate for the now 'second person' to the throne. That was her first public appearance as acknowledged 'next heir'.

In the months immediately following, Elizabeth was treated publicly with all the respect due to her new status. Her place of high honour in Mary's first royal entry into London was hers again when Mary undertook the traditional monarch's progress through the capital the day before her coronation. Although the eyewitness accounts were confusing, even contradictory, the official records make it clear that Mary went that day as queens consort had always done, dressed in white cloth of gold and riding in a litter with her hair loose. Elizabeth, travelling in another litter with Anne of Cleves, was placed in the most honourable position, immediately after the queen herself. Anne of Cleves, it might be remembered was briefly Henry VIII's fourth wife, and granted the status of Henry VIII's 'sister' after the annulment of their marriage. She was always a favourite with his children.

Since the reigns of neither the 12th-century Matilda nor of Lady Jane Grey had been marked by such an event, the following day saw the first coronation of an English queen regnant, and Elizabeth was again in close attendance. She therefore saw Mary crowned as kings had been crowned, and anointed as kings had been anointed. One concession to her sex was that at the relevant point in the ceremony the queen touched the coronation spurs rather than having them put on her. Throughout the days of coronation rituals, Mary set precedents which Elizabeth watched and was to follow as second queen regnant. Mary always insisted that her office as queen took precedence over her identity as female. For her it followed, therefore, that she, crowned as all English and French kings had been crowned for centuries, also shared their special power to exercise the royal healing touch for her subjects afflicted with what was called the 'king's evil', but is now better known as scrofula. Elizabeth observed and in due time followed Mary's practice, to considerable polemical effect.

Nevertheless, those early public displays of proximity and respect between Henry's two daughters were not long (indeed, if ever) an accurate indicator of their personal relationships. Mary's first parliament had confirmed her legitimacy by reiterating the legality of her mother's marriage to King Henry. What followed was the implication that Elizabeth's illegitimacy was necessarily confirmed, since if Henry's marriage to Katharine of Aragon was valid, his marriage to Anne Boleyn had always been invalid. The Venetian ambassador for one believed that was at the point at which relations between the sisters worsened. And there was also the delicate matter of religious practice. Mary could never forget that during Edward's reign Elizabeth had been willing to accept his increasingly Protestant religious order. While she was queen, Mary's doubts about the reality of Elizabeth's apparent acceptance of the Catholic religion were never entirely set to rest.

Although tension emerged most obviously over questions of religious practice, there were further problems. Mary sometimes gave precedence to Lady Margaret Douglas, the legitimate and Catholic daughter of Henry VIII's elder sister, Margaret, by her second marriage. Margaret Douglas, a companion of Mary for many years, and in Mary's household for much of that time, had been at Henry's court since she was 15. And as her suspicions of her younger sister strengthened, the queen even suggested that perhaps her 'sister' was not the daughter of Henry, but fathered by Anne Boleyn's musician. He was the one man to plead guilty to the charge of sexual relations with her. If that were the case, Mary hinted, Elizabeth had no claim to the throne even if her royal 'father' had always acknowledged her as his daughter. (It might be noted that many, if not all, modern historians believe Smeaton's confessions were spurious, forced from him by torture.)

On matters of religion, as on many other issues, the practice of dissimulation or half-truths was a skill anyone wanting to survive at successive Tudor courts needed. Queen Mary, no amateur at that art herself during previous reigns, may have remembered Elizabeth's comment that dissimulation was her preferred course of action. She wrote that to Mary when they were discussing possible responses to Katherine Parr's shamefully rapid remarriage after their father's death. When Mary questioned Elizabeth about her erratic attendance at mass, Elizabeth claimed that she had never been brought up in the ancient faith, a rather weak return to half-truths. After all, until Henry's death his household had been required to attend mass according to the traditional rites – and his family had all done so. It is the case that she had never lived under papal authority, but Elizabeth's attendance at mass was the issue under discussion. Her response did not improve Mary's attitude to her half-sister.

We know very little of Elizabeth's life in the years that Mary reigned, but a Venetian ambassador wrote a detailed description of her at 21. He reported:

her figure and face are very handsome, and such an air of dignified majesty pervades all her actions that no one can fail to suppose she is a queen. She is a good Latin and Greek scholar, and besides her native tongue she speaks Latin, French, Spanish and Italian very well, and her manners are very modest and affable.[2]

But graceful manners and linguistic fluency, it transpired, were not enough to maintain Elizabeth's reputation in the eyes of either her queen or the queen's advisers.

Elizabeth and early opposition to Mary

As well as facing suspicions about her true religious preferences, Elizabeth had other reasons for feeling uncomfortable at Mary's court. As reports first circulated that Mary planned to marry Philip of Spain, rumours of plots to thwart her foreign marriage began to spread. The motives of the conspirators were mixed; some plotters were members of the Edwardian establishment who had lost status with the accession of the new monarch, some had marked religious reformist tendencies and feared more Catholic influence. Why, however, the Duke of Suffolk, father of Lady Jane Grey, joined in any conspiracy is harder to explain, since nobody seems to have suggested restoring 'Queen Jane'. Most conspirators denied they meant any harm to Mary, a claim which seems improbable given the widespread report that the plotters planned to marry Elizabeth to Mary's rejected English suitor Edward Courtenay, Earl of Devon. The most plausible Plantagenet heir, from the royal dynasty displaced in 1485 by Henry VII, Courtenay was one of the earliest conspirators in the plot.

In modern times, the name most often connected with the uprisings is that of Sir Thomas Wyatt; a generation before, his father had hoped to marry Anne Boleyn before Henry VIII claimed her. How much that history drove Wyatt to promote the interests of Anne Boleyn's daughter has never been clear, and other motives he might have had are also still a matter for speculation. Elizabeth chose to retire from the court to her own place when rumours about the plots were already rife, but there is no indication of just how much she knew. Her departure did not obviously signify any public disgrace, and Mary's parting present to her was a sumptuous sable hood, sable being then still an exotic and expensive fur, more commonly used for trimmings rather than complete garments. To that generous gift Mary added pearls, Elizabeth's favourite jewel.

As she was leaving, Elizabeth begged Mary to believe nothing bad of her before she had had a chance to answer any hostile reports. Elizabeth may well have had good reasons for making such a request, for just before her departure she had received a visit from two of Mary's most prominent advisers, Paget and the Earl of Arundel, explicitly warning her against any contacts with either English heretics or French interests. As another move to reassure Mary, on her way to her house at Ashridge, formally a priory in Buckinghamshire, Elizabeth sent a message back to Mary asking for the robes and furnishings necessary for the celebration of mass in her chapel, surely a curious afterthought in her preparations for the move. Moreover, she made no effort to carry out another promise to Mary, that she would remove from her household anyone suspected of Protestant tendencies.

Much more dangerously, once settled at Ashridge Elizabeth received at least two messages from the 'Wyatt' conspirators hinting at the proposed uprising against her sister; she was advised that for her safety she should move further from London and to a more easily defended castle. She also sent at least one message to Wyatt, apparently couched in terms of general good will. What was to count so heavily against her in what followed was her failure to pass on to Mary any of the warning signs she had received of an imminent uprising. She also remained silent about the activities her household undertook as precautions against the planned uprising which, as would be demonstrated, were unfortunately for her well known to the authorities.

By mid-January 1554, the many rumours circulating about the proposed four-pronged uprising against Mary frequently mentioned Elizabeth's name. One conspirator thought that although 'we ought not have a woman bear the sword ... if a woman bear a sword, Lady Elizabeth ought to bear it first.'[3] Mary's advisers were quick to learn the general outline of the plot since the one-time conspirator Courtenay, nominated as Elizabeth's future husband, had already confessed everything to his long-time friend and mentor, Bishop Stephen Gardiner, Mary's Lord Chancellor. For now, Gardiner shielded his protégé but gradually made clear how well informed he was about the plots. Some conspirators faded away, to France where possible, but the Duke of Suffolk was ignominiously captured in flight from his home. Wyatt and his Kentish companions, however, fought their way north and launched an attack on London which was only defeated after some strenuous street fighting within the city. It was after the suppression of that rebellion that Suffolk, his daughter Lady Jane Grey and her husband were among those executed to make the regime safer.

Throughout those dangerous days, Elizabeth remained silently at Ashridge. One ironic result of Wyatt's attack was that Queen Mary gained a significant propaganda victory. She not only displayed considerable courage in refusing to flee to Windsor, as much of her court had, but also delivered a much-acclaimed speech at Guildhall by which she rallied the citizens of London to her support; it was indeed a speech worthy of emulation in following years by the next queen. Thomas Wyatt was captured and resolutely denied, under interrogation and on the scaffold, that Elizabeth had been in any way implicated in the plot.

But the authorities did not need his testimony, for they had other evidence against the queen's sister. On 26 January 1554, the day after Wyatt raised his rebellion, a copy of a letter written in Elizabeth's own hand (an unusually private act) to the queen was found in a packet of letters to the French king. Both her contemporaries and subsequent historians have found it hard to see how her personal letter to the queen could have been copied without Elizabeth's knowledge. That apparent contact with the French was very close to, if not actual, treason. The French ambassador had backed Jane Grey as queen, and had encouraged the Wyatt plot from the early stages. By both her actions and her failures to act, Elizabeth was at least keeping open her options, as she had done while Mary fought for the throne, when she had committed herself to neither side although publicly reiterating her loyalty to Mary. At 20, as in her earlier years, her place in the royal line of succession was insecure; her own best interests lay in protecting that place in whatever way she could.

Mary, however, could hardly condone Elizabeth's actions since they suggested, on even the most generous reading, ambivalent loyalty from her heir apparent. The queen had 'invited' (i.e. ordered) her sister to court 'for her own safety' as soon as details of Wyatt's plots were known, but Elizabeth's household officers sent word she was too ill to move. The 'invitation' was renewed in much more imperious terms as soon as the rising was suppressed, and Mary's own doctors were sent to assess Elizabeth's condition. She was indeed ill, they reported, but she could travel, if slowly, in the royal litter which Mary had sent to her. Elizabeth then had no choice but to set out for London, but in carefully planned short stages.

It was not until 22 February, ten days after leaving Ashridge, that Elizabeth passed through the streets of London; as she did so, she had the curtains of her litter drawn back so all could see her wan and pallid appearance. Even the Spanish ambassador, usually her most unsympathetic critic, remarked on how ill she seemed, although he still commented sourly on her 'proud' demeanour. Her entourage was much less splendid than on previous occasions, but she still travelled through the streets of London, as a bystander recorded, with a hundred 'velvet coats' riding before her 'chariot open on both sides' and another hundred behind her in coats of scarlet trimmed with velvet, 'her grace being sick'.[4]

Her apparent illness did not win Elizabeth any sympathy where she most needed it. When she reached the palace at Whitehall, Mary refused to see her; rather, the heir to the throne and her attendants were confined to one set of rooms, with a guard set before the doors. As virtual prisoners, Elizabeth and her little household were kept in isolation for almost a month. She almost certainly knew by then that the intensive questioning of those conspirators still in England was designed to explore all possible contacts between Elizabeth, her household and the plotters. She was closely questioned about how much she knew of her household's plans to muster her forces at Donnington, a castle just north of Newbury, more distant from London, and well situated and fortified for defence. Although all such allegations were outlined, and doubts and suspicions were explored, nothing conclusive about Elizabeth's complicity with the Wyatt plot was discovered; in part this was because of the capacity for linguistic evasions, not to say dissimulation, which Elizabeth again displayed in answer to her questioners.

Wyatt's trial ended with his conviction on 15 March; the next day some 20 of Mary's advisers, led by Lord Chancellor Gardiner, visited Elizabeth, still confined to her part of the palace. They remained suspicious about her knowledge of the Wyatt uprising, and advised her of the Queen's decision that she should be sent to the Tower while the network of conspiracies was further investigated. Before being removed, Elizabeth was given permission to write to her sister. In her letter, dated 16 March 1554, she reminded Mary of their previous parting and of her then 'last demand: that I be not condemned without answer and due proof'. Instead of that, she wrote, although unheard, she had indeed been found guilty since the Tower was 'a place more wonted for a false traitor than a true subject'. She insisted that she was indeed the queen's true subject, and added that 'as for the copy of my letter sent to the French king, I pray God confound me eternally if ever I sent him word, message, token, or letter.' She signed herself 'Your highness' most faithful subject, that hath been from the beginning and will be to my end'.[5] And then she was taken by river to the Tower of London.

Elizabeth in the Tower – and after

One prisoner already in the Tower wrote down what he heard of Elizabeth's arrival there, including her insistence on her innocence and her complete loyalty to her sister, her anxiety because so many soldiers were present, and the distress of some of those with her at the treatment of the queen's sister.[6] That material was later much elaborated by John Foxe in his 1563 *Book of Martyrs* to become the most quoted description of Elizabeth's arrival at the Tower. Although, as David Starkey notes, Elizabeth was housed in the royal apartments in the Tower, had her usual attendants with her, and her own household attended to all her needs,[7] Foxe reported that after Elizabeth was 'clapped in the Tower', she was later 'tossed from thence, from prison to prison'. Even on the more accurate account, however, it is not surprising if Elizabeth was very distressed when despatched to the Tower. However comfortable her accommodation, two things in particular must have given her considerable anxiety: that she had incurred her monarch's deep mistrust, and that she was now held where her own mother had been beheaded. She must have felt she had good reason to be fearful.

At the time Foxe wrote his account of her time at the Tower, Elizabeth was queen, and he added to it many details designed to demonstrate her sufferings and humiliations at the hands of Mary. Foxe's extraordinarily influential and enduring work was meant primarily as an exposition of the sufferings of true Christians at the hands of false Christians; the deaths of true believers martyred as heretics in Mary's reign were demonstrations of the cruelty of the false church. But he had problems with celebrating Elizabeth, now queen, since she had frequently attended mass during Mary's reign, and never explicitly suffered for her religion. In 1563 Foxe's concern was to do what he could to show Mary had indeed treated Elizabeth harshly. In later editions, as he became increasingly dismayed by what he saw as Elizabeth's religious conservatism, Foxe specifically contrasted the behaviour of some in her household who did challenge the mass with Elizabeth's repeated attendance at it. But all that lay in the future in 1554.

Despite Elizabeth's repeated protestations of her total innocence and of her unqualified loyalty to Queen Mary, modern commentators often look at the composition of Elizabeth's household during the years of Mary's reign and assess her differently. Like many others in those years, Elizabeth had adopted the reformed Edwardian religion and then in Mary's reign conformed enough to Catholic practice, and attended mass sufficiently, to meet the legal requirements. But, as Mary and her Council frequently complained, she also retained many people of dubious religious tendencies in her household, and several with likely connections to the Wyatt uprising. Nevertheless, by late May 1554 nothing definite had been established against Elizabeth, and she was removed from the Tower. She travelled by barge from there to Richmond, then from Windsor to Woodstock, a royal residence since Anglo-Saxon times and extensively refurbished in the reign of Elizabeth's grandfather, Henry VII.

The man given the unenviable task of guarding Elizabeth, both controlling all access to her *and* at the same time treating her with all the respect due to the queen's sister, was Sir Henry Bedingfield. It is difficult not to feel sorry for him as one reads his reports of his guardianship, or even Foxe's very different narratives of that time, during which, he wrote, she was finally released only to become 'prisoner in her own house, and guarded with a sort of cutthroats'.[8] Foxe focused on emphasising the difficulties and dangers Elizabeth faced under harsh supervision; Bedingfield, on the other hand, stressed his attention to, and problems in following, the orders of the queen and council. One point which emerges through both sources is both how charming and how extraordinarily difficult Elizabeth could be in her dealings with her keeper, often first tormenting and then seeking to beguile Bedingfield.

Queen Mary married Philip II of Spain on 21 July 1554, an event marked by a range of sumptuous celebrations and feasting which the greater nobility were all expected to attend. The most prominent absentee was Elizabeth, still exiled from the court although the conditions under which she lived were more relaxed. Bedingfield remained with her at Mary's command until the following April, and he still reported frequently on Elizabeth's activities, and complained of her household. She attended mass as required, he noted, but her household included some who occasionally disrupted the Catholic rites, or were found to have seditious (Protestant) literature in their possession. But, although there was always the anxiety that English malcontents, frequently with French support, would use her name for their conspiracies, Elizabeth did enjoy an increasing degree of freedom.

Elizabeth's release from 'durance vile'

Elizabeth was finally released from her seclusion at Woodstock, and summoned to court in May 1555. By then Mary believed that she was pregnant, and shortly to be delivered of an heir to the throne. Despite many suggestions there is still no definitive explanation for Mary's putative pregnancy, but what is clear is that her doctors and some midwives continued to encourage her in the expectation of a child well after her original delivery date. In the event, Mary was not delivered of a child, and thereafter Elizabeth's position, both at court and politically, improved markedly. Philip for one saw her as the most acceptable next heir. His view was not surprising since the most likely alternative candidate for the throne was Mary Stuart, Queen of Scots, granddaughter of Henry VIII's elder sister Margaret. Born in 1542 Mary Stuart, nominal Scottish queen since her infancy, had been at the French court since 1548 and by 1554 was betrothed to the heir to the French throne. Hapsburg interests would have been seriously damaged if she had succeeded to the English throne as well. The surviving sisters of Lady Jane Grey seem not to have ranked as serious candidates and were without significant support.

When it was accepted that there would be no royal infant, Elizabeth returned to Hatfield, and was as much at liberty as she had ever been. Her household was again headed by her familiar companions Kat Astley and Sir Thomas Parry, the latter having first joined her household about 1548. But the likelihood of Elizabeth becoming queen in due course was again threatened by the emergence of yet another plot against Mary, once again making free use of Elizabeth's name and promoting her as an alternative queen, possibly with her tacit approval. This time the leading conspirator was Sir Henry Dudley, related to the late Duke of Northumberland and with long-standing connections to the French court. The most alarming aspect of the conspiracy was the number of higher-ranking officials of Mary's government also found to be implicated, and the extent of French support promised for 'munitions, arms and money'. Elizabeth's household was again suspected of supporting Henry Dudley, although Elizabeth herself was never questioned; some say that decision was at the command of Philip himself.

Nevertheless, the surviving state papers include a range of reports that apparently associated Elizabeth with the conspiracy. As one conspirator put it, once their rebellion had prevailed 'Elizabeth is a goodly liberal dame, nothing so unthankful as her sister. ... Then shall men of good service and gentlemen be esteemed.'[9] There were suggestions of a purpose to 'banish the Spaniards and popery', but the central aims of the conspiracy are still disputed. Its main result for the increasingly confident heir apparent was that at least two of her household were imprisoned when they were implicated in the plot. As a search of Kat Astley's possessions uncovered her extensive collection of anti-Catholic books and pamphlets, she was also despatched (again) to the Tower. Under interrogation in May 1556, Astley, long Elizabeth's closest confidante, agreed she had deserved Mary's displeasure 'another way'. To that vague allusion to her religious unorthodoxy, Astley added that, had she ever done or said anything against the queen, 'of whose virtues I have had long experience', then indeed it was right that Elizabeth should never see her again.

That Elizabeth was not questioned after this plot was in part because her brother-in-law Philip II was then seeking to marry her to his cousin, good friend and most important ally, Emmanuel, Prince of Piedmont. Nevertheless, because of her suspected involvement in the Dudley conspiracy, Elizabeth was once again placed under the supervision of a person chosen by Mary. This time the man chosen, Sir Thomas Pope, proved a much more congenial companion for her than ever Bedingfield had done. It helped that he was not required to fulfil that role for long. Edward Courtenay, Earl of Devon, who had regularly been proposed by conspirators as a husband for Elizabeth, died abroad in his semi-permanent exile in September 1556; the following month Pope's supervision of Elizabeth ended. Indeed, soon afterwards Elizabeth was once again invited to attend the royal court, presumably since there would be no more attempts to replace Mary by Elizabeth and Courtenay together, and the prospects of persuading her to marry a candidate whom the reigning couple preferred seemed brighter.

The last two years of Mary's reign were relatively tranquil for Elizabeth, apart from repeated, and always unwelcome, suggestions of whom she might marry. She spent much of her time at Hatfield, one of her favourite houses, but she was without her favourite companion. Although Astley had been released from the Tower within months of her incarceration, she was forbidden to rejoin Elizabeth's household and, indeed, did not do so until her mistress's accession to the throne. Nevertheless, relations between the Tudor sisters improved enough for Elizabeth to be given permission to visit London once more; she arrived there on 27 November, expecting to spend Christmas with the court, but left London again on 3 December. The abrupt end to her visit was most likely because she had rejected yet another suggestion from Mary that she should marry Philip's good friend, Emmanuel of Piedmont.

Other candidates for Elizabeth's hand also presented themselves. Being a relatively neutral candidate, the future Erik XIV of Sweden was an unusually eligible prospect when he proposed marriage with Elizabeth, but in April 1558, to Mary's complete satisfaction, Elizabeth responded that:

> In the king my brother's time there was offered to me a very honourable proposal or two ... [but she asked her brother] for leave to remain in that state I was, which best pleased me. I am

at present of the same mind, and intend so to continue, with her majesty's favour. There is no life comparable to it. ...

What I shall do hereafter I know not, but am not at this time otherwise minded than I have declared, though I were offered the greatest prince in Europe.[10]

In that preference at least, Elizabeth was to show consistency.

Elizabeth's life continued with relative tranquillity for the rest of her sister's reign. Mary fell ill in October 1558, and by mid-November it was obvious that she was dying. Philip, still involved in the wars with France, during which England had lost Calais (its last European foothold), sent his confidant the Count of Feria to visit Mary and then Elizabeth. Feria reported that Mary knew he was there, but was too weak to read the letter Philip had sent her. After visiting her, he travelled to Hatfield to visit the heir apparent. There he received a rather frosty welcome, for Elizabeth rejected his suggestion that she had any obligation to Philip. Rather, he reported that she placed:

great store by the people and is very confident they are all on her side – which is certainly true. She declares it was the people who put her in her present position and that she will not acknowledge that your majesty or the nobility of the realm had any part in it.[11]

There were, in fact, no obvious alternatives to Elizabeth as next heir, unless one looked to the Catholic Mary Queen of Scots, now married to the Dauphin of France. Her claim to the English realm had very little support, even among Catholics, on the grounds that she was born a foreigner *and* married to the French heir. Such a complete reversal in England's international relations was unthinkable, for it was not only the Hapsburgs who feared the implications for England when France and Scotland were so closely allied.

Given the scheming which had followed the deaths of the two previous monarchs, it is hardly surprising that as her accession approached Elizabeth was not content to depend solely on statute law, let alone on those she called 'the people', despite her brave words to Feria. Her household had made contingency plans for raising an armed defence of her claim, and planning seems to have included military contacts across much of England. She had also been in contact with members of Mary's court; such contact was usual on both sides since courtiers and politicians, like potential monarchs, usually wished to protect their future careers. As it transpired, the outcome of all that, and of Mary's deathbed nomination of Elizabeth as her heir, meant an unusually smooth transition from one English monarch to the next.

Elizabeth had faced many challenges in Mary's reign, often of her own making. More significantly, it is apparent that by the time Mary's final illness set in, Elizabeth had learned many strategies for political survival. In the words of one eminent Elizabethan scholar:

> the beacon which guided her actions was not one of religious or political principle but, first of all, survival and, beyond that, the pursuit of power. ...
>
>   In this self-taught course of instruction, the princess learned many of the skills of the practical politician, mostly those of a darker kind – dissimulation, outright deceit, evasion, the careful concealment of one's own aims.[12]

While still in detention at Woodstock, Elizabeth had made very much the same point more simply. Then, as tradition has it, she used a diamond to write on a window

> Much suspected [of] me,
> Nothing proved can be.
> Quoth Elizabeth the prisoner.

And she had survived; it was now her turn to reign and thereafter to manage the attempted subversions of her reign by other ambitious malcontents.

'Elizabeth by the grace of God Queen of England, France and Ireland'

Those words announced the death of Elizabeth's 'dearest sister of noble memory, Mary, late Queen of England'. Mary I died in the morning of 17 November 1558. Archbishop Heath, Mary's Lord Chancellor, immediately advised parliament of her death and

Elizabeth was proclaimed queen before noon the same day. That evening Cardinal Pole, Mary's Archbishop of Canterbury, also died, from the devastating sickness at that time endemic in England. When she confirmed Elizabeth as her successor, Mary made two requests to the new monarch: that the official religion should be maintained in the new reign, and that the dying queen should be buried with her mother in a new grave. If the first request is best described as wildly optimistic, the second request was even less likely to be granted, since it would inevitably have reopened all the complexities of Henry's marital history, and the issue of which of his two daughters was *really* illegitimate – unless, of course, as he had sometimes argued, they both were.

The much-repeated account of Elizabeth falling on her knees at the news that she was indeed now queen and declaring 'It is the Lord's doing; it is marvellous in our eyes' appeared first some 70 years after her accession, in a hagiographic account of the late queen written by her godson John Harington. The official proclamation had, equally improbably, declared the new queen's 'great grief' at Mary's death. Elizabeth explained to the first Marian councillors visiting her that as an individual she of course grieved for her late sister, but accepted that she was now become 'a body politic to govern'. This assertion that, though a woman, she was indeed qualified to rule was by then a familiar one, having been frequently invoked by Mary I, but there were always some who raised concerns about the propriety of female rule.

The most notable case is that of Protestant reformer John Knox, who notoriously wrote his *First Blast of the Trumpet against the Monstrous Regimen of Women* against three Catholic queens, and particularly Mary I of England, only to find that by the time it was published the English throne was occupied by Elizabeth. He never successfully mollified Elizabeth's resulting aversion to him. Elizabeth's hostility may have been the stronger because he was only one of a number of Protestants who attacked female (Catholic) rule just in time to be confronted with another, but Protestant, queen regnant. In each case it is difficult to distinguish between 'female' and 'Catholic' in the argument, but the authors insisted (without notable success) to Elizabeth that there was never any intention to attack a godly princess like herself.

The celebrations for Elizabeth's accession followed the traditional pattern; across the country the bonfires and feasting for the new reign were supervised, as was customary, by relevant officials to ensure that the occasion was properly joyful. Machyn reported that *Te Deums* were sung 'in every church in London', but some churches delayed doing so for two days, perhaps reflecting uncertainty about the new queen's religious preferences. Elsewhere, beyond London, the delay was frequently longer.

Elizabeth herself was preoccupied with the demands of establishing a new regime; by the time she left Hatfield her council was taking shape. William Cecil, who was to be her pre-eminent councillor for the rest of his life, had first been employed by Elizabeth in 1550. Long in her confidence, and now emerging as her closest adviser, he had drafted the oath for her new councillors the same day Mary died. Elizabeth included six Marian councillors, of whom three were from the older nobility, in her new Council; they all served Elizabeth until their deaths. It might indicate her resistance to more radical Protestantism that her first council included only one explicitly Protestant Marian exile, the Earl of Bedford. Another position went to Nicholas Bacon, brother-in-law and friend to Cecil. Before her first parliament met he was named Lord Keeper, making it his responsibility, among other duties, to address parliament on the queen's behalf.

A week after Mary's death, Elizabeth moved from Hatfield. On 23 November she was escorted, it was said, by a company of 'a thousand and more of lords, knights and gentlemen, ladies and gentlewomen' as she travelled to Barnet, then still well outside London. There she was met by the sheriffs of London and moved to the Charterhouse, on the very outskirts of London. When the new queen made her first entry into her capital city on 28 November, the diarist Machyn abandoned all attempts to estimate the numbers in her train, noting instead that Elizabeth wore purple velvet, and recording the names of some of those who now held important positions. He also recorded her welcoming reception to the 'joy and comfort of all true English men and women, and to all people'.[13] The following weeks were occupied with marking the end of the previous regime, above all by the funerals of Mary I and of Reginald Pole, whose death significantly eased the path to religious change for the new regime.

The Count of Feria, now the representative of Philip II in

England and consistently suspicious of Elizabeth, sent his king mixed messages about the new queen. On 14 December 1558 he wrote that she was 'a young lass, who, although sharp, is without prudence. ... She seems to me incomparably more feared than her sister and gives her orders and has her way as absolutely as her father did.' Two weeks later he reported that soon after her accession Elizabeth had made a speech to the women in her service commanding them never to speak to her on business, but given the considerable influence exercised, for example, by Kat Astley, that seems an unreliable account of Elizabeth's statement.

Crowning England's second queen regnant

Traditionally, coronation rituals and celebrations for a new monarch were spread over four days. The first saw the royal journey by water to the Tower of London with the Lord Mayor and leading Londoners on attendance. The second day of activities included the creation of new knights of the Bath and associated ceremonies; the third was taken up with a stately and elaborate procession through the city of London, and on the last day the coronation itself took place. Curiously, the most comprehensive account of the rich displays and complex rituals of those four days when Elizabeth was crowned came not from English sources, but from Il Schifanoya, the then Venetian ambassador. His report was informed by the traditional belief that the richness of royal magnificence displayed on such occasions reflected the power and legitimacy of the monarchy; the local focus necessarily addressed other issues, for Elizabeth was the daughter of Henry's most disgraced queen, with a dubious past in terms of both sexual behaviour and loyalty to her sister and monarch, and known to favour an unpopular religion.

On her progress through London, Elizabeth's coronation ceremonial retained the adaptations which Mary had established for a queen regnant in dress and procedures, but the details of her cloth-of-gold dress and her rich entourage were all recorded in detail only by the Venetian ambassador. He was also among the few who detailed some of her attendant nobility; no one seems to have paid much attention to Robert Dudley, already very close to the queen as her newly confirmed Master of the Horse. But whereas there had been several reports on the numbers – some said, unprecedented numbers – at Mary's coronation, no one reported on the size of the crowds for Elizabeth's procession. In brief, as at least one historian has concluded, the initial reception of the Protestant queen was 'lukewarm'.[14] Surviving records, apart from the pamphlet discussed in what follows, confirm that lukewarm response, and even the pamphlet makes no reference to numbers in the crowd, although that was a familiar means of measuring popular responses.

Given that she was widely known for her Protestant preferences in a country that was then predominantly Catholic, there was a compelling need to represent Elizabeth as a potentially ideal queen. This task was undertaken in a lengthy account of her progress written by Richard Mulcaster, who had also been involved in designing the pageants for that day, As an account of the coronation procession, the pamphlet offered little information about either the traditional magnificence and display or the more prominent personnel in leading roles. But because it is a uniquely detailed description, albeit focused almost entirely on the interaction between the queen and her subjects, the pamphlet, *The passage of our most dread sovereign Lady Queen Elizabeth through the City of London to Westminster the Day before her Coronation* has long been regarded as the definitive account to the events of that day.

It is easy enough to see why. The only other printed account of a pre-coronation progress through London was that published for Queen Anne Boleyn, and a comparison of the two demonstrates immediately how much more sophisticated and complex was that written for Elizabeth, with a degree of coherence and polemical force never previously seen for such an occasion. Mulcaster's account also focused on the monarch herself, with an almost complete exclusion of the higher nobility and clergy that many understood were integral to any regime. The emphasis was on the behaviour of Elizabeth herself, on her detailed responses to the didactic pageants erected by the City of London, on the 'loving' response of her subjects to a 'loving' queen, and her warm reactions to subjects from the lower echelons of society who caught her eye. (The idealised relations between 'loving' subject and 'loving' monarch by then were familiar terms for defining monarch–subject relations.)[15] It offered reassurance that Elizabeth would be a responsive and caring monarch, and, more cautiously, a good Protestant. It also described in careful detail the several pageants along the route, elucidating their purposes and ensuring the messages were properly understood. The publication was, indeed, a brilliantly conceived exercise, portraying the new monarch in the most admirable light and foreshadowing her religious agenda.

Rather than accepting that account literally, however, it is better read as a statement of what the author wanted Elizabeth's subjects to believe about the new queen. It was necessary, after all, to counter years, if not decades, of negative reports about the daughter of Anne Boleyn, the girl who had succumbed to the charms of Thomas Seymour, the young woman who permitted and perhaps encouraged her household's involvement in plots against the previous queen, her sister. Although the accounts of no other observers, English or foreign, reported anything like Elizabeth's responses described there, the descriptions of the pageants themselves are much more dependable, being also described by other observers, though never in such didactic detail.

The customary genealogical pageant was noteworthy for the first public recognition of Anne Boleyn as Henry VIII's wife since she had been beheaded more than 20 years before. The pageant, which centred on Elizabeth's joyful reception of the Bible in English, was reassuring about her Protestant inclinations, and remarkable for her appropriation of Mary's most familiar motto, 'Truth, the daughter of Time'. The printed account was also an exercise in reminding the audience of Elizabeth's detention in the Tower, although the reasons for her being detained, including her complicity in treason against her sister, were nowhere mentioned. The prayer she reportedly uttered before she left the Tower was one in which she likened her state then to Daniel, saved from the 'greedy and raging [Marian] Lions', yet another reminder that only divine intervention had brought Elizabeth out of the Tower and to the throne.

The final day of celebration, when the actual coronation took place, posed some problems. It occurred on Sunday 15 January 1559, a date chosen after astrological advice from the eminent scholar John Dee. A great religious occasion, it was usual to have the Archbishop of Canterbury officiating but, since Pole's death, that position was vacant. Of the surviving Marian bishops, almost all were disqualified from that office, either by being unacceptable to the queen for their religious past or by their own reluctance to take part.

How important the occasion was for Elizabeth is suggested by her own significant contribution to the cost; but only Owen Oglethorpe, Bishop of Carlisle, was prepared to perform the necessary anointing of the new monarch with holy oils and the crowning itself. This choice itself suggests the extent of Elizabeth's problem in finding a qualified cleric: she had previously walked out of a Christmas celebration when, against her instructions, Oglethorpe had elevated the Host during the Eucharist. Nor did Oglethorpe's coronation service save him from house arrest for the last months of his life after he opposed Elizabeth's religious programme in the House of Lords.

The Venetian ambassador, who reported the almost orthodox Catholic nature of the coronation ceremonies, commented austerely that Elizabeth had returned from the ceremony 'very cheerfully, with a most smiling countenance ... so that in my opinion she exceeded the bounds of gravity and decorum'.[16] It is hard to imagine what he might have written had he observed the behaviour described in the pamphlet detailing her progress through London and her warm responses to observers' comments.

Elizabeth, however, of dubious royal descent, of suspect loyalty to the previous monarch and of uncertain religious affiliation, had every reason to rejoice that she had survived to see that day. Like Mary before her, Elizabeth had resisted any suggestion that parliament should meet before her coronation; like her sister she was monarch by inheritance, statute law and divine providence, and therefore in no need of any parliamentary confirmation. The new government's policies, however, including the new monarch's preferred religious practice, had to be endorsed by the first Elizabethan parliament, and that was to meet within days. So what would then be established would define the nature of her government over a realm in an unusually divided and troubled condition. The precise nature and extent of the problems in establishing her regime were about to become quite clear.

3   Establishing the new reign

Elizabeth's subjects in 1558

Elizabeth's usual residences in or near London were a first port of call for any well-connected foreigners visiting England; their reports of the magnificence and ceremonial displayed reflected the general belief that court splendour represented the wealth of the whole realm. More generally, Elizabeth has often been similarly viewed as the focal point for all her subjects. In many ways, however, the England Elizabeth inherited was less a single identity, more a collection of greater and lesser communities, all structured by a traditional and very hierarchical system. And all except the very greatest in the land conventionally identified themselves first by their parish and then by the county where they lived; very few indeed of the queen's subjects would have first thought of themselves as English. It is not surprising, then, that for the majority of her subjects there were many more pressing matters than the identity, let alone the personality, of their monarch. It is hard to know now how much most of her subjects ever knew of Queen Elizabeth, but a telling anecdote describes one female onlooker – a London resident at that – who on first seeing her, cried: 'O Lord! The queen is a woman.' Since Elizabeth was, in fact, the *second* queen regnant, immediately following her sister Mary, that astonished exclamation indicates how little might be known about any ruler, even in the capital city. Elizabeth's England was much more a series of greater and smaller communities than a coherent realm.

The many familiar portraits and abundance of printed praise for Elizabeth that shape much of our modern understandings of her were originally directed at the literate few, confined to the upper levels of the social hierarchy. Where most of her subjects learned something of Elizabeth's existence, and increasingly of her religious preferences, was through their parish churches. They had long been a community focal point, and were often the channel by which monarchs communicated their commands to their subjects through such means as proclamations. During Elizabeth's reign, as in Mary's, attendance at the local church was a legal requirement – and a test of loyalty to the ruler. And by the end of her reign almost every church attendee could gaze on Elizabeth's coat of arms, which became for many subjects probably the most familiar image of her rule.

By then her subjects should also have been well versed in the importance of their monarch. In 1559 a Book of Homilies was published, with instructions that each of the homilies should be read out across the year. The homily 'On Obedience' reiterated the natural hierarchy of creation as then understood, that all people have 'appointed to them their duty and order. Some are in high degree, some in low, some kings and princes, some inferiors and subjects.' The congregation was warned: 'Take away kings, princes, rulers, magistrates judges ... no man shall ride or go by the highway unrobbed. ... No man shall sleep in his own house or bed unkilled, no man shall keep his wife, children and possessions in quietness.' Such statements serve rather less as an account of the monarch's actual power than as compelling reminders of the violence endemic in all levels of 16th-century society, and the perceived need for a monarch to maintain some degree of social order.

For the upper levels of that very stratified society, the place of the monarch was much more important than for the more lowly majority of her subjects. The royal court was a focus for men – and women – who aspired to further their wealth, power and influence. Political skills, military prowess and, in the case of Elizabeth's court, elegant appearance could attract the queen's attention and open up prospects of advancement. (According to a long-standing tradition, the rise of Sir Christopher Hatton was one example of the benefits of being a skilful dancer – having thereby first attracted the queen's attention, he subsequently became an important administrator.) For courtiers as for councillors, favoured males prospered in any Tudor court, although they could as easily fall into disgrace. The rise of Robert Dudley, the man whom Elizabeth may well have wanted to marry in the early years of her reign, is one spectacular example of a man made wealthy by the queen's favour.

That favour was expressed by extensive grants of land and in other ways, but there were many others who benefited in similar ways. Positions at court could be almost as rewarding for women as for men. Katherine Astley, from 1547 in charge of Elizabeth's household and increasingly her confidante before and following her accession, had an unusual degree of influence with Elizabeth and frequently controlled access to her, but many others found it worthwhile to place their daughters in such an advantageous environment.

The queen's first advisers

Like both her siblings, Elizabeth had received a humanist education, and throughout her reign she continued to study and drew upon classical sources as expressions of her own ideals, both publicly and privately. Unlike either of her siblings, however, Elizabeth came to the throne without any explicit preparation to be a ruler. The closest she came to exercising such authority was in the management of an unusually large household throughout her sister's reign, and there she established excellent relations with several men who were to serve her well when she was queen. Foremost among them was William Cecil. A junior member of the Edwardian Council, and in Elizabeth's service during Mary's reign, Cecil was appointed as her Secretary of State the day that Mary died (17 November 1558). As she confirmed his appointment, Elizabeth declared her confidence that he would always offer his best advice, even when he knew it clashed with her preferences. He usually did offer such advice, but was often to find it hard, if not impossible, to persuade her to heed his view.

Immediately following his appointment, Cecil took charge of many affairs, from writing the oath her councillors took to matters of international significance. Elevated to the peerage in 1571 as Lord Burghley, he then served his queen as Lord Treasurer until his death in 1598. Cecil often found his service to the queen frustrating, but despite his intermittent threats to resign he was to prove her longest-serving and most important councillor. He may have been instrumental in Elizabeth's early appointment of his brother-in-law Nicholas Bacon to the duties of Lord Chancellor. Since Bacon's father was only a Suffolk yeoman, however, Elizabeth, while entrusting him all the responsibilities of the Chancellor's office, gave him only the lesser title of Lord Keeper.

Another who rapidly came to prominence after Elizabeth's accession was Robert Dudley, who did so without any help from Cecil. Although the tales of their shared childhood in the days of King Edward VI have been doubted by modern scholars, it seems that Dudley was on good terms with the new queen some time before her accession; his appointment as her Master of the Horse came only one day after it. That position meant he was often in her company, and the more so, as Cecil complained, since he soon encouraged her passion for hunting. That royal pastime had the advantage, for him, of requiring Dudley's ever more frequent attendance on her. In Cecil's view, however, the sport was both dangerous for the queen and a distraction from attending to the serious business of her government.

Cecil, Bacon and Dudley were all firmly Protestant (although favouring different degrees of doctrinal reformation) but the wider membership of Elizabeth's first Privy Council, her most formal source of advice, also demonstrated the queen's consciousness of the need to include a wide range of the current religious and political views. Ten of her original members had previously served on Mary's council – indeed the Marquis of Winchester had been Lord Treasurer to both Edward and Mary before he served in the same capacity for Elizabeth. Even Mary's Archbishop of York was initially included, although within months he was removed for resisting Elizabeth's proposed headship of the church and her other religious changes. Two members of the wider Boleyn family were also included, foreshadowing Elizabeth's increased reliance on her mother's relatives in her later years.

One piece of advice Elizabeth received at her accession was from Nicholas Throckmorton, a man she had known since her time in the household of Katharine Parr; he suggested that: 'neither the old or new councillors ... should wholly understand what you mean, but [you should] ... use them as instruments to serve yourself with.'[1] Apparently she took that advice to heart, for her councillors complained frequently of her resistance to their advice throughout her reign and the difficulty of anticipating – or even persuading her to make – her own decisions. Even more disconcertingly – but in accordance with the practice of her predecessors – she discussed her issues of the moment with many others: familiar close companions like Kat Astley, her female courtiers and a wide range of men other than those designated official councillors. She was often particularly resistant to advice which was offered by her parliaments. Above all, her resistance to unpalatable advice was obvious from the start in two matters, widely seen as related and of the utmost urgency. In most minds, one pressing issue was whom she would marry, and the other was what religion she, with her prospective husband, would establish in her realm.

Redefining England's official religion

In the event, it was a still unmarried Elizabeth who oversaw the religious changes. Her personal piety has seldom been doubted, nor that her doctrinal preferences were at least mildly reformist. During her reign, several volumes of prayers were published in her name, with images of her at prayers in her own chapel. Even, it has been noted, some of those prayers 'were of her own composition and survive in her hand'.[2] The religious settlement she established, however, might usefully be seen as rather more an exercise in religious accommodation than of doctrinal rigour. It was always clear that she would repudiate papal authority, which had been restored during Mary's reign, but beyond that there was considerable uncertainty.

This uncertainty was fed by Elizabeth's own past religious practice. During her father's lifetime she had attended the traditional Catholic mass, which Henry VIII always retained. After conforming to the successive Protestant changes during the reign of her brother, in Queen Mary's time Elizabeth had attended the restored Catholic mass, although she also sometimes complained of illness when she attended. Perhaps by her actions Elizabeth was enacting her own belief that each monarch, through the Henrician doctrine of royal supremacy, had the right to define the public religion, or perhaps she was again evading making a firm commitment for as long as she could.

In 1558 the majority of her subjects still observed Catholic forms of worship. Furthermore, there were some hints from Rome that her parents' marriage might, after all, be accepted as legitimate by the Papacy should she retain orthodox Catholicism in her realm;

that would have removed the doubt about her legitimacy which Catholics had long entertained. But, quite apart from her personal beliefs, one powerful argument against such blandishments was that Elizabeth's greatest security lay in the fact that she was the only claimant to the throne acceptable to English Protestants. (The alternative plausible and indisputably legitimate Catholic claimant to the throne just across the English Channel will be discussed in the next section.) In the early weeks of her reign Elizabeth was, however, evasive about her religious intentions, not least because she needed the Catholic Philip II's support if she was to have any hope of regaining Calais from the French. But by the end of December the (Catholic) Venetian ambassador reported that, having believed Elizabeth's early promises that the official religion would remain as it was, he now lost faith in that, since those around Elizabeth were returning to their former religious 'bad habits'.[3]

Elizabeth was well aware that the entire ecclesiastical hierarchy she inherited was Catholic, and that Catholics dominated both universities. From Elizabeth's perspective, the death of Cardinal Pole, Archbishop of Canterbury on the same day Queen Mary died had been one rare stroke of good fortune in matters ecclesiastical. The surviving Catholic bishops, however, and a number of their aristocratic co-worshippers, were still sufficiently numerous and committed to the old religion to make the House of Lords a difficult place to win approval for her changes. That mattered because, since Henry VIII's first religious changes had been made through parliament, parliamentary authority was thereafter required for all ecclesiastical changes. Moreover, as well as the apparent strength of the Catholic established hierarchy, Elizabeth faced problems in winning approval from reformed theologians. When those Protestants who had gone into exile in Mary's reign returned to England from late 1558, they brought widely differing views of their preferred religious order, their views reflecting the particular European cities where they had settled. Those who had remained in England had different views again, less influenced by the vigorous theological debates on the continent. To accommodate the considerable diversity of reformed views would be a significant challenge indeed.

A form of Protestant religion, however, there was to be. Changes had been signalled even before Elizabeth's first parliament met on 25 January 1559. During the Christmas celebrations, she had ordered Bishop Oglethorpe not to elevate the sacramental host, a specifically Catholic form of honouring it, and had stalked out of the service after he disobeyed. Before the opening of parliament there was the customary service at Westminster Abbey, and she brusquely ordered away the lighted tapers with which the monks of that Abbey had greeted her. (The monks themselves soon followed.) The preacher she had approved for that occasion, Richard Cox, fully supported Cranmer's Edwardian reforms; for 90 minutes he preached to the (standing) parliamentarians of the need for religious reformation in England. After the Abbey service, and Cox's sermon, Elizabeth processed to the old Palace at Westminster, where she heard her Lord Keeper deliver on her behalf the opening oration to the new parliament. In that speech Bacon defined true religion as the proper medium between 'Idolatry and Superstition' (listeners should have understood 'Catholicism') and 'contempt or irreverent behaviour towards God and Godly things' (that is 'advanced' Protestantism, stripped of ceremonial).

The first bill for the Elizabethan religious settlement was introduced in parliament on 16 February; there was considerable resistance to the proposed changes, particularly in the House of Lords. The conservative resistance there should not have been a surprise but, on the other hand, many Protestant critics had hoped for a more radical reformed religion. They too had finally to accept the queen's preferred changes; after several weeks of dispute and manoeuvring the outcome desired by Elizabeth (and Cecil) was achieved. Papal authority in England was finally rejected, and the authority of the monarch as supreme head of the Church of England was restored, but with Elizabeth now described as 'supreme Governor' rather than 'supreme Head'.

That was a gesture to the Pauline prescription that women should not lead the church, but the change in title proved a distinction without any practical significance. Elizabeth exercised her authority to make the final judgement about the doctrine and practice of her church, frequently despite protests from her own clergy. Nor did Elizabeth give ground on her personal religious practice. She continued the use of a crucifix and candles in her private chapel, and her hostility to priests' marriage was more conservative than the views of most of her Protestant subjects. More advanced Protestants also disapproved of her decision to retain many of the musical traditions restored by her sister after the Edwardian reformations.

Finally, the new religious settlement saw Cranmer's Second Book of Common Prayer of 1552 restored, but modified by some changes drawn from his less radical 1549 version. In the Elizabethan version, the 1552 words 'take and eat this in remembrance that Christ died for thee' were preceded by the 1549 'The body of our Lord Jesus Christ, which was given for thee, preserve thy body and soul unto everlasting life'. That addition, acknowledging some form of real presence, accommodated much of the contemporary range of Protestant beliefs on that widely debated question. It even, perhaps, nodded in the direction of the Catholic doctrine of the Eucharist. When, however, a proclamation was issued declaring that communion in both kinds would be offered to all communicants, few could doubt that significant and distinctively Catholic doctrines were under attack. Elizabeth was, in that at least, moving beyond the Henrician settlement in which she had been raised.

It was all too predictable that in future years Elizabeth would face problems with discontented Catholics. Aware of the strength of resistance to the religious changes in England, she followed a more cautious policy in the strongly Catholic Ireland, establishing a church which has been described as 'doctrinally protestant but liturgically catholic'.[4] Although the religious settlement there was even more cautious than in England however, Elizabeth still insisted on her supremacy in religious matters. But in England she was also to face considerable dissent from those Protestants she regarded as too radical. On one occasion, in 1565, she twice interrupted a particularly well-attended sermon to insist that the preacher stop abusing the use of religious images. Elizabeth's church was intended to be as inclusive as possible, so she was always strongly hostile to those who demanded more sharply defined doctrinal reforms in either direction. It was, for her, ultimately *her* responsibility to define and maintain the form of public divine worship. The Church of England established in her reign continues to be the official church in England to this day, albeit accommodating a range of religious traditions and practices, rather than the uniformity Elizabeth demanded but did not get.

Mary Queen of Scots, Scotland and the disputed succession

Although when Mary I died she had acknowledged Elizabeth as her heir, there was an impeccably Catholic and impeccably legitimate claimant to the English throne. Mary Stuart, better known now as Mary Queen of Scots, was born in December 1542, the daughter of James V of Scotland and the French Mary of Guise. James V was the son of Henry VIII's elder sister Margaret, who had been married to the Scottish James IV. Because her father's death followed only days after Mary's birth, the infant had been nominally queen of Scotland since she was a week old. In Henry VIII's final years there was a determined – and violent – English attempt to betroth her to his son Edward, thereby uniting the two realms, but it failed and those Scots who supported their traditional alliance with France (and therefore traditional hostility to England) won the day.

By the time she was six, Mary had been despatched to the French court where she was educated, and later married to Francis, Dauphin of France. After Mary Tudor's death, and urged on by her father-in-law the French king Henry II, Mary Stuart had included in her coat of arms the arms of England, thereby making public her claim to the Tudor throne. Henry II died in July 1559, but Francis II proved equally interested in pursuing his wife's claim to England. Appeals went from France to the pope to declare Elizabeth a heretic and Mary Stuart the legitimate English queen. Perhaps ironically, it was the Catholic Philip II of Spain who intervened to protect Elizabeth from any such papal injunction; as happened so often, political interest had taken precedence over religious commitment. Philip's intervention had the unintended effect of giving Elizabeth more time to establish both her rule and her preferred religion. When Francis II died in 1560 and the widowed Mary returned to Scotland, her presence just across the border was a constant reminder that until Elizabeth married and produced an heir, her obvious heir was the Catholic and Scottish queen. That fear of Mary's succession was one reason, but only one of several, why Elizabeth came under pressure from many subjects so early and so often to marry and produce her own Protestant heir.

With the help of mainly French advisers, Mary of Guise, the mother of Mary Queen of Scots, had governed Scotland on her daughter's behalf since 1554, but by 1558 political and religious tensions had led to a group of Scottish Protestants seizing the political initiative. From 1559, as part of a strategy designed by William Cecil, the reformist Scots had secret English support as part of a wider attack on French interests. Cecil's intervention was part of his own dream, echoing that of Henry VIII, of a British Isles united in a reformed religion and free of foreign intervention. But for some time his main obstacle in pursuing that dream was his queen, who had several objections to his Scottish project. One was her hostility to any cause strongly supported by the Scottish reformer John Knox, already barred from travelling through England for his radical Protestantism, and especially for his notorious attack on female monarchy in his 1558 *First Blast of the Trumpet against the Monstrous Regimen of Women*. Although he was to claim later that his attack was directed only at Catholic female rulers, there was nothing in the text to support this claim. Indeed, the opening sentence of his work could easily be seen to contradict that: 'To promote a woman to bear rule, superiority, dominion, or empire above any realm, nation or city, is repugnant to nature, contumelie [disobedient] to God, a thing most contrary to his revealed will and approved ordinance, and finally it is the subversion of good order, of all equity and justice.' Elizabeth was *not* amused, let alone persuaded. Another, more general reason for Elizabeth's reluctance to intervene in Scotland was her much reiterated opposition to supporting rebels against any legitimate ruler.

Nevertheless, in 1560 while Mary Stuart was still queen consort of France, Elizabeth was persuaded to sign a treaty with the Lords of the Congregation, the Scottish Protestant leaders. She was also, even more reluctantly, persuaded to give some support to a military attack on Leith, then a French stronghold in Scotland; the initial failure, in part the result of Elizabeth's rather grudging support, was offset by the death of Mary of Guise and the failure of French reinforcements to arrive in time. After that victory, a new Scottish parliament was called (without any royal authority, and therefore strictly illegally) to establish Protestant doctrines as the official religion in Scotland. By late 1560, French support for efforts to maintain their hold in Scotland had collapsed, not least because they were also facing the prospects of religious wars within their own realm. Elizabeth was persuaded to sign a treaty with the Lords of the Congregation. As Wallace MacCaffrey has pointed out, the formal declaration that Scotland was a Protestant nation gave a new significance to Elizabeth's inherited title of Defender of the Faith: 'However unwillingly, she had assumed the role of protectress of a foreign Protestant community.'[5] That was often to be a complicating factor in her reign, as other Protestant communities sought her support against the Catholic rulers she regarded as their legitimate monarchs, and therefore as having the God-given right to define the public religion of their subjects.

After her husband died, and having failed in her efforts to make another brilliant European marriage, Mary Stuart had little choice but to return to her officially Protestant Scottish kingdom, which she had last seen in 1548. Once there, she made it clear that she would not oppose the de facto Protestant settlement but would continue to practise her own Catholic religion. And, for a while, it seemed that the two queens on the one island might co-exist with relatively good relations, despite Elizabeth's refusal to recognise the Scottish queen as her heir apparent, a recognition which Mary earnestly and repeatedly sought. In that refusal at least, Elizabeth was entirely consistent, always refusing to name her successor. William Cecil's successful support for Protestantism in Scotland, and the ousting of the French, greatly enhanced his standing, and he was now firmly emerging as Elizabeth's most effective man of business.

Fiasco in France?

The second foray into foreign affairs that Elizabeth approved turned out very differently. Calais, a fortified town overlooking the straits of Dover, had been the last remnant of England's once extensive continental holdings in what was by the 16th century French territory. That toehold was finally lost to England in early 1558, after Mary I had joined her Spanish husband's war against France. Although Calais had both trading and strategic value for England, it was perhaps valued even more as a symbol of England's once glorious continental past. Mary was much blamed for its loss during the next reign; Elizabeth was determined to recover it, and the push to do so began in 1562. By then religious wars had broken out in France, and French Huguenot (Protestant) rebels offered to restore Calais to England in return for English aid against their Catholic monarch. Robert Dudley, always a strong Protestant supporter, used the prospect of regaining Calais as a means of overcoming Elizabeth's usual aversion to aiding rebels, let alone religious rebels, against their lawful monarch.

The final outcome, however, was a debacle for England as the Protestant allies fell out; one reason was again Elizabeth's reluctance to commit sufficient resources, both men and money, to the project. Her allies were never persuaded by her insistence that she did not have the necessary resources, and one result was that the disillusioned Huguenots joined with other French forces to drive their ineffectual allies out of their last stronghold, Newhaven (Le Havre). Elizabeth insisted her army should make a final stand there, although the plague was raging through the town and her soldiers were dying at the rate, it is said, of up to 500 a week. By 1564 Elizabeth had no option but to accept French terms to end the war; in so doing, she had finally to renounce any English claim to Calais. Curiously, although that French adventure proved disastrous for Elizabeth, Dudley, the driving force for that entire project, continued to be the object of the queen's particular favour and affection.

Nevertheless Elizabeth, like many of her subjects felt the final loss of Calais deeply. It is much easier for later historians than for Elizabethan contemporaries to make a most reasonable argument that the loss of Calais was neither a financial nor a strategic disaster. With all the benefits of hindsight, it can be seen that with the loss of Calais Elizabethans finally turned away from trying to revive past continental glories, and turned instead to fresh opportunities opening up in the New World, opportunities which will be discussed in more detail later. But that was not an obvious alternative in the early years of Elizabeth's reign; the strength of the lingering nostalgia was reflected in the fact that Elizabeth and all successive English monarchs continued to include France in their royal titles until 1802.

Retreat from warfare, and turning to marriage diplomacy

Many in Elizabeth's Council had always been reluctant to support the more warlike policy in either France or in Scotland. The more conservative members had found such interventions against Catholic rulers profoundly distasteful, and Elizabeth herself had been ambivalent in both enterprises, reluctant to commit the men and financial requirements for policies that were, after all, aimed at subverting legitimate monarchs. Historians and biographers have long debated the extent to which her unpredictable behaviour on such occasions was because of her knowledge of how scarce were her resources, or a sign of her clever manipulation of her disparate group of councillors and favourites. Either way, her anxiety that the proposed policies would leave her vulnerable to more powerful neighbours was understandable. Particularly in the early years of her reign, no definitive conclusion can be reached. Elizabeth did learn the hard way that foreign interventions were costly and hazardous when a country lacked the resources necessary to sustain them; she was to avoid such interventions as much as possible for the rest of her reign but, as will become apparent, she never managed to extricate herself from ever-worsening relations with Spain.

One matter on which all her advisers were agreed was that the queen should (indeed, must) marry. That, they argued, was surely self-evident. England was a dynastic realm, and for some 500 years every English monarch had married, as marriage was traditionally seen as by far the best way to ensure the safe transfer of the crown from generation to generation. (There was always the warning from the case of Edward the Confessor, whose failure to produce a direct heir opened the way for the Norman invasion in 1066.) In the case of Elizabeth, the matter was even more pressing since she was the last of the children of Henry VIII. In the absence of any direct heir, the Scottish queen was still the leading claimant for the English throne, a prospect anathema to English Protestants. Moreover, in the case of a female monarch, men were agreed, a husband was also desirable to provide support in explicitly masculine matters – particularly warfare. The reign of Mary Tudor had demonstrated that a queen regnant could remain 'sole queen' even after marriage, and there had been legislation to ensure that was the case. However deplorable Protestants subsequently found aspects of Mary's reign, the terms of Mary's marriage treaty were seen as a starting point for ensuring that Elizabeth also could remain an effective queen regnant of England even if she married a foreign monarch.

Elizabeth was following a common monarchical pattern when she used potential and actual courtships, and several suitors found themselves wooing the queen over a number of years, not least because of her diplomatic interests. Her failure to marry was, however, unique in English history, and ignored continuing pressure from her subjects that she should do so. Her first parliament had formally reminded Elizabeth that kingdoms might be immortal but monarchs were not. Some parliamentarians also, pragmatically but perhaps less tactfully, suggested that she should take a consort who would 'relieve her of those labours which are fit only for men'. Elizabeth's earliest response to the parliamentary proposal include the declaration that she would be satisfied if her tombstone declared that a queen 'having reigned such a time, lived and died a virgin'. Elsewhere, she repeated her sister's early response to a similar request, that she was already married to her kingdom. Few of her subjects believed those early answers would prove to be definitive.

There was, after all, no shortage of candidates for her hand both within and beyond the realm, and all proposals reflected the primacy of political and religious considerations. In February 1559 Feria had made a formal marriage proposal on behalf of Philip II. That proposal had two purposes: to ensure that the English/ Hapsburg alliance against the French continued and that England retained its Catholic identity, for the proposal was always conditional on Elizabeth retaining the Catholic religion. When, soon after, Philip was betrothed to a French princess instead, Feria reported Elizabeth's comment that the king 'could not have been so much in love with her as I had said, as you had not had patience to wait four months for her'.[6] Her tone may have been flirtatious, but her purpose was political, and her anxiety was that any Hapsburg alliance with France would leave England seriously isolated, entrenching the loss of Calais and probably posing new threats.

Other foreign suitors presented themselves. The Protestant Eric XIV of Sweden renewed a proposal he had made to her during her sister's reign; he made at least two attempts to reach England and woo her in person, but on each occasion he was forced to turn back by storms. But Elizabeth saw no particular strategic benefit in marrying Eric of Sweden despite his more acceptable religion. Others candidates included several eligible Catholic Hapsburgs: two archdukes and five dukes. Marriage to any of those Hapsburg candidates would have preserved the previous alliance against France, still the most obvious threat to Elizabeth. There was no sign Elizabeth seriously considered any of her early foreign suitors, but she enjoyed the rich gifts their envoys brought, and the associated ceremonial and banquets. One of the immediate advantages was that the splendid diplomatic processions through London as they came to woo her were public demonstrations that other monarchs, both Catholic and Protestant, endorsed the legitimacy of Elizabeth as ruler of England, however dubious some subjects might think her birth or her religious preferences.

In the early 1560s Elizabeth, born in 1533, was still well within her marriageable and childbearing years. She certainly enjoyed all the attention that her many foreign suitors brought, but despite the diplomatic advantages of a foreign marriage Elizabeth, like Mary I before her, came under considerable pressure to marry within England. For both queens a foreign marriage proposal led to heightened fears of foreign entanglements, on the premise that even a queen regnant was likely to be dominated by her husband; another anxiety about marrying a foreign prince was that any resulting heir might simply absorb England into other possessions inherited from the father. Of English suitors the only duke at the time, Thomas Howard, fourth Duke of Norfolk, was already betrothed at Elizabeth's accession, and there were no other plausible English subjects approximating to Elizabeth in status. Nevertheless, many thought that there were other potential candidates; Henry Fitzalan, twelfth Earl of Arundel, who during Mary's reign had proposed his son as Elizabeth's husband, now dreamed of marrying her himself. He spent lavishly on jewellery for her ladies and on hospitality for her, but in the queen's eyes he was always something of a joke, not least because of his lack of political skills. Other English names were bandied about, but most with increasingly less plausibility.

The reasons that Elizabeth never married have long been a favourite topic of speculation among historians, but without any generally agreed conclusion. There is no evidence to support – and some to refute – the theory that she had been psychologically scarred by her mother's disgraceful death; one more plausible explanation that has been offered is that her councillors could never agree to support any specific proposal which she contemplated accepting either within or beyond England. At least in the early years of her reign, such conciliar division may have been the more important since she was still concerned about her ambiguous status as Anne Boleyn's daughter, ruling over a still predominantly Catholic realm. And there was always one widely reported complication to any marriage proposal. From very early in the reign there were many rumours about Elizabeth's relations with Robert Dudley, whose court position meant that he was frequently in her company.

As early as April 1559 Spanish sources reported that Dudley's wife, Amy Robsart, had 'a malady in one of her breasts and the Queen is only waiting for her to die to marry Lord Robert'.[7] In September 1560, Dudley's wife was found lying dead at the bottom of a staircase; there were no witnesses to her fall. The coroner declared her death to be by misadventure, but the rumour mill – with, it must be said, some grist to work on – found her death deeply suspicious precisely because it removed the barrier to Dudley's marriage to Elizabeth. It was, however, just those uncertainties which meant Elizabeth could not now seriously contemplate marrying him if, indeed, she ever had. But what was beyond dispute was that she publicly showed considerable affection for him and he grew rapidly in importance at the court. Scandalous reports of children born to the couple, some destroyed at birth, some reportedly alive and flourishing, were to emerge for several decades and had a wide circulation within and beyond England, but there is no evidence to support any such claim.

Elizabeth's displays of affection for Dudley remained a matter of public comment for many years. Dudley was always one of her closest confidantes, to the extent that one historian has written of 'her almost total emotional dependence on him and her insistence on his constant presence at court'.[8] As a consort, however, he was simply not acceptable to men who mattered at court, for several reasons. The manner of Dudley's wife's death, the well-known fact that his father and his grandfather were both executed for treason, that in the early years he had more debts than property and that he had no experience of the world beyond England all helped make him a poor match indeed in the eyes of other English subjects, especially in the eyes of William Cecil. Throckmorton wrote from Paris to Cecil that if the marriage went ahead the country would be ruined, a prey to foreign forces. Others discussed the possibility of an aristocratic revolt in the event of such a mismatch.

As his prospects for a royal marriage waned, and perhaps with Elizabeth's knowledge, Dudley sent an unexpected offer to Philip of Spain that if the king supported that marriage, the English church could be reformed along lines then being discussed by another session of the Council of Trent. Philip's refusal may have been one factor in Elizabeth's acceptance that marriage to Dudley was impossible. But thereafter she still protected and advanced the interests of her favourite, and Dudley in turn became her 'eyes' at court, keeping her well informed about court machinations. He remarried only in 1578, and then did so only secretly. Despite that secrecy, Elizabeth soon learned of the marriage and took partial revenge by demanding early repayment of outstanding loans; she remained resentful of his wife for the rest of her life, although her close relationship with Dudley himself was later restored.

If one imperative for Elizabeth to marry was to provide an heir for her throne, her failure to do so was compounded by her hostility, which endured to her dying days, to ever allowing any discussion, however tentative, of possible heirs. But as long as she remained childless, anxiety and debate about possible successors was a recurrent issue. She shared the view expressed by Cecil in October 1560 when he told the Spanish ambassador of the old English saying that 'the English run after the heir to the Crown more than after the present wearer.' That may have been an exaggeration in both her own and the previous reign, but Elizabeth during the reign of Mary had first-hand experience of just how easily potential rebels could invoke the heir presumptive's name to legitimise their own plots. Nevertheless, although she continued to entertain suitors over the years, Elizabeth's consistent refusal either to commit to any marriage proposal or to name an heir was, it will become clear in later chapters, the source of considerable social and political tensions, and even external threats, as her reign proceeded.

The issue of her marriage was the more pressing because throughout Elizabeth's reign there were several possible (if not always probable) claimants to her throne. If the will of Henry VIII was followed, then Elizabeth's heir might well have been Katherine Grey, younger sister of Jane who had reigned so briefly in 1553. Her claim seemed even stronger when Katherine secretly married a nephew of Queen Jane Seymour and produced a male heir. But the claim to the throne of Queen Jane Grey, the nine-day queen, had originally rested on the charge that Elizabeth, like her sister, was illegitimate and therefore debarred from the throne. With some reason, Elizabeth always resisted the Grey pretensions to the throne and, as will be discussed in more detail later, she imprisoned both husband and wife for marrying without her permission. Such marriages without royal sanction by any aristocrat were always a serious offence against the monarch, and that one was particularly galling.

If not the Grey family, there also were also the descendants of Lady Margaret Douglas, daughter of Henry VIII's elder sister. Raised in England, Lady Margaret was at one time considered by Henry as his possible heir, after he had declared both his own daughters illegitimate. She now had a son, Henry Stuart Lord Darnley, born and raised in England, who will reappear in this history as the second husband of Mary Queen of Scots. (From 1575, there was also to be Margaret Douglas's granddaughter Arabella Stuart, born and bred in England.) If none of those candidates seemed acceptable, there were still those who referred to the Tudor 'usurpation' of 1485, when Henry Tudor (Henry VII) defeated Richard III at the Battle of Bosworth, and dreamed of the restoration of the Plantagenets

There were several possible aspirants who could trace themselves back to that dynasty. That Elizabeth remained deeply suspicious of that lineage was made particularly plain in the case of Henry Hastings, Earl of Huntingdon. His mother was Katherine Pole, granddaughter of Margaret Pole, Countess of Salisbury, niece of Edward IV and Richard III. His prominent Plantagenet descent had long made Huntingdon an object of Elizabeth's suspicion, which was heightened when more radical Protestants, whose religious views he shared, mentioned him as a plausible heir should she die. In October 1562, Elizabeth fell seriously ill with smallpox; for a few tense days her life was seriously in danger. One result of her illness was that, when she believed herself to be dying, she swore solemnly that she was indeed still a virgin – an oath very likely to be true, but one which had no discernible impact on the endemic gossip about her relations with Dudley for the rest of her reign.

A more serious consequence of her near-death condition was that it reopened, much more urgently, the succession question. Some suggested Katherine Grey was the obvious heir in terms of the will of Henry VIII, but more usually Huntingdon's name was raised as most likely successor, not least because he was Robert Dudley's brother-in-law and was believed to have his total support. Despite Huntingdon's own behaviour as a consistently loyal subject, it was several years before Elizabeth forgave him for his name being bandied about as heir apparent during her illness – and then she sent him for many years to a position in the north of the country, well away from the centres of political life.

The 1563 parliament made several attempts to persuade the queen to marry, or settle the succession question, or both; these issues had been made yet more urgent by her recent brush with death. There was even one bill, drafted with the support of Cecil but never actually tabled, proposing that in the event of the queen's death her Privy Council should exercise all her powers until a (Protestant) successor had been established. This suggested that Elizabeth's continuing refusal either to marry or to name a successor could well throw into doubt the very principle of hereditary succession. Indeed, the proposal looked very like at least an interim rule by an effectively republican body.

Elizabeth's England after her early rule

What had Elizabeth achieved in those early years? It may now seem extraordinary, but if Elizabeth had died of smallpox in 1562, or indeed for any reason in the immediately following years, her historical reputation would be almost as woeful as that of her immediate predecessor, and sister, has traditionally been. Like Mary, she had managed one apparent but precarious achievement, in the matter of religion, but in 1562 that was not necessarily any more permanent than Mary's restoration of Catholicism. The majority of her subjects were still Catholic, although there was no doubt by 1562 that the public, official religion was Protestant. Just what kind of Protestantism was practised remained a matter of considerable variation, particularly at the level of the local parish; at that fundamental level, doctrinal differences flourished, in part because, whatever control Elizabeth might exercise over the upper church hierarchy, most benefices for lower clergy were in the control of local property owners, who commonly appointed men of their own religious views. (Dudley was only one of many noted for his promotion of more radical Protestants, but most landowners were not of that persuasion.)

If it remained the case that a significant number of Protestants were still dissatisfied with the queen's preferred religious order, and more would become so, it was also the case that, particularly in the northern parts of England, Catholicism was still widely observed, and maintained by the clergy. Catholics were required by law to attend the parish church, and faced repeated fines and ultimately imprisonment if they did not. Some in the more southern regions did indeed attend their parish church in the early years where, it was said, many Catholics passed the time by reading their missals rather than attending to the service being conducted. They frequently felt as strong a claim as Protestant parishioners to the parish church, always the focal point for many communal activities and where almost everyone's forebears were buried. Moreover, for generations wealthier local families had contributed to the upkeep and adornment of the local church, and felt a strong commitment to the traditional ways of the parish. So Elizabeth's preferred religious practice had been legally enacted but was far from being accepted across her realms.

Nor had Elizabeth's foreign policy been marked with great success. The intervention in France had been a debacle which served mainly to confirm the permanent loss of Calais. With her support Scotland had become an officially Protestant country, but there a Catholic queen now ruled. Mary Stuart never disguised the fact that her highest ambition was now to be recognised as Elizabeth's heir apparent, a recognition to which, by any criterion, she had a very strong claim. The one thing for which Elizabeth could not be held accountable was that 1563 was also a very bad year for plague, although there were many who saw the hand of God in such visitations. Elizabeth's early years on the throne were not a promising omen for a stable reign in the years ahead. And for two decades her most immediate problems were to involve the young queen recently returned to Scotland and/or her deteriorating relationship with her one-time brother-in-law and still king of Spain, Philip II.

4 Mary Queen of Scots, the English succession and other problems, 1563–7

Two unmarried queens, two thrones, one island

In 1563, Elizabeth was 30 years old, unmarried, and still refusing to address the pressing questions of her marriage or naming a successor – or, preferably, both. Meanwhile, in Scotland the Catholic Mary Stuart, for many the most likely heir to the English throne, was apparently securely established as queen of Scotland, but still in search of her second husband. Her overriding ambition to be named Elizabeth's heir placed serious limits on her marriage choices. It was alarming enough for Elizabeth when Mary looked for a French marriage, since that reaffirmation of the long-standing Scottish/French 'Auld Alliance' always posed a potential threat to England. When, however, Elizabeth learned that the Archduke Charles of Austria, younger son of the Holy Roman Emperor and once a candidate to marry her, was under discussion as a likely candidate for Mary, the Scottish queen was warned that the English would view such a marriage as a hostile act. Since by this time relations with Spain were already worsening, any such alliance of Catholic, Hapsburg and Scottish interests could pose a serious threat to England. Mary's brief flirtation with the idea of marrying Don Carlos, the son of Philip II, was even briefer for the same reason.

As well as being warned against marrying any member of the Hapsburg family if she ever hoped for formal recognition as Elizabeth's heir, Mary was told her chances of inheriting the English throne would improve considerably if she married an Englishman who had Elizabeth's approval. Possible candidates included both

Darnley, the elder son of Henry VIII's niece Lady Margaret Douglas, and the Duke of Norfolk, then between wives. Then Elizabeth followed up with a quite explicit proposal, that Mary Stuart should marry Robert Dudley. He was, at that time, a man widely believed to be responsible for his first wife's death, quite as widely but implausibly believed to have been Elizabeth's lover and, even less plausibly, the father of her child or children (the rumours varied about the number); he was, however, indisputably her favourite. Privately outraged at the suggestion, Mary was slightly more cautious publicly, but matters between the two queens still became so strained that in May 1564, Mary sent one of her most accomplished courtiers, Sir James Melville, to ease the now fraught relations.

A Scottish account of the English queen

Melville's first visit to the English court resulted in an unusually detailed account of his conversation with Elizabeth. He already had considerable experience of the French court, and knew several prominent men around Elizabeth. Since it was another four decades before Melville wrote his memoirs, albeit from notes he made at the time, some of his observations should be treated with care. Nevertheless, his reports both of the English queen's behaviour and of the advice her courtiers offered for dealing with her were entirely plausible. Throckmorton, for example, suggested that one way to move Elizabeth to meet Mary's wishes was for Melville to become particularly friendly with the Spanish ambassador, a strategy based on Elizabeth's considerable anxieties about Spanish influence in the British Isles – an influence which, indeed, was soon to become a very real threat in Ireland.

   Melville was at Elizabeth's court for nine days, and in her company every day. Elizabeth stressed to him that, had she decided to marry, it would have been to Robert Dudley; but she now thought he would be an appropriate partner for the Scottish queen. What she did not add was that she trusted Dudley to defend English – and her – interests against any Scottish conspiracies, but she did add that such a union would 'much incline her' to name Mary her heir. Melville was an observer when Elizabeth created Dudley Earl of Leicester, apparently to make him a more eligible match for Mary. He recorded that amidst all the ceremony of that solemn occasion, while Dudley was still kneeling before her, Elizabeth 'could not refrain from putting her hand in his neck to tickle him smilingly, the French ambassador and I standing by'. Later, when he was in Elizabeth's bedroom with other members of her court, he saw a miniature of Dudley, labelled 'My Lord's picture'; since it was Elizabeth's only picture of him, she refused Melville's suggestion he should take it to Mary. In every way, it would seem she was determined to leave the Scottish ambassador with no room for doubt about her attitude to her favourite, but it is less clear whether in that she was hoping to promote or stall the negotiations for his marriage.

Aspects of Melville's report suggest a queen surprisingly insecure about her own attributes, for she asked him many personal questions about the Scottish queen's appearance and accomplishments. Faced with such questions as which queen had the better-coloured hair and which queen was the fairer, it was as well Melville was an accomplished courtier, skilled in evasive answers. Told that Mary was taller, Elizabeth responded that, as she was just the right height, Mary was too tall. Melville went on to speak perhaps too warmly of Mary's musical skills, for later that same day, a courtier led him to a gallery so he might 'accidentally' overhear Elizabeth playing the virginals; ignoring her coy disclaimer that she never played in the hearing of men, he assured her that she played 'excellently well', even better than his queen. Although anxious to leave, he was required to remain longer at the English court, it transpired so that he might admire the queen's dancing. His assessment was (perhaps ambiguously) that his 'queen danced not so high and disposedly [with lofty dignity?] as she did'.[1]

Despite her apparent preoccupation with the attractions and accomplishments of the Scottish queen, suggestive of her own anxiety about an unfavourable comparison, Elizabeth already knew that Mary had rejected the proposed marriage with Dudley. Presumably, however, Cecil was sadly disappointed, as were other like-minded councillors and advisers, including those hereditary nobles who had previously warned there would be a rebellion should Elizabeth marry a person of such dubious lineage as Dudley. For all those suspicious of Dudley, a major attraction of the Scottish project was always that it thwarted the ambitions which, it was widely believed, he still nursed to marry the English queen. But surely no one should have been surprised by Mary's refusal to marry the man she called Elizabeth's horse-keeper, and of whom there were so many scandalous rumours about his relationship with the English queen.

Mary's other English suitor

Despite Mary's stated reluctance, negotiations for the Dudley match dragged on into 1565 before Elizabeth suddenly informed Mary that, whomsoever she married, she would not soon be acknowledged as the English heir apparent. But by then, for Mary Stuart, there was another English husband in the wings, a possible alternative with which she might even be able to force Elizabeth's hand. Margaret, Countess of Lennox and niece to Henry VIII, had long hoped that the Scottish queen would marry her son Henry Darnley. His father's family had some claim to Scottish royalty; the Countess had boasted several times that together the couple might assume the English throne, even perhaps by displacing the Protestant Elizabeth. For speaking of such matters, both mother and son were placed in the Tower, but when released regained enough favour with Elizabeth for Darnley to be allowed to visit Scotland by October 1564.

Apparently Elizabeth, who had herself previously mentioned Darnley as a possible consort for Mary, was still confident that as his queen she could control his actions; if so, she miscalculated badly, though she could hardly have foreseen just how extraordinary that marriage would prove to be. Mary Stuart was, by all accounts, immediately attracted to Darnley, who was some three years her junior but a 'tall likely lad', and in April the Scottish queen made it known that rather than pursue a diplomatic marriage, she had decided to 'content herself with her own choice'. Elizabeth had every reason to be enraged when she learned of the sudden marriage of Mary Stuart and Darnley, although she should not have been surprised that Mary had made such a dynastically promising match to one Elizabeth herself had described in very complimentary terms. Indeed, it was likely that the marriage rendered irrelevant any decision on Elizabeth's part as to who should succeed her, unless of course she was also to marry and produce an heir of her own.

By the time of their son's birth in June 1566, however, relations between the Scottish queen and her increasingly erratic husband were already notoriously bad; one dramatic indicator of that was Darnley's involvement in the murder of Mary's French secretary, Riccio. There had been wild rumours, which Darnley chose to believe, that Mary's secretary was also her lover, even her infant's father. One evening, with Darnley present, Riccio was attacked in and then dragged from Mary's presence. Still pleading for her protection, he was then stabbed in the next room. The queen, who heard all his dying anguish, was six months pregnant at the time, with a child who would have a claim to the English throne even stronger than her own, if it survived.

A Scottish prince for England?

One of the more impressive episodes of Mary's life was the way she won back control of the political agenda from Darnley's co-conspirators against Riccio, and appeared to mend her relations with her husband. The infant, the future James VI&I, born in June 1566, had survived his mother's traumas, and his christening was delayed, most unusually, for six months to allow for a suitably magnificent Catholic ceremony. To placate the Scottish Protestants, the infant had earlier received a much more private, much less formal Protestant christening. Melville was sent again to the English court to announce the birth, and recorded that when Elizabeth was informally told the news by Cecil, the queen immediately lost her pleasure in the evening's dancing, lamenting to her ladies that 'the Queen of Scots was lighter of a fair son, while she was but a barren stock.' Perhaps she did, but neither Cecil nor her ladies seem to have mentioned her atypical outburst. Elizabeth, approaching her 34th birthday, need not have despaired of a son of her own, but must have known she should marry very soon to ensure one. That the Scottish infant's future was of some international significance was reflected in his mother's choice of godparents: Elizabeth of England, Charles X of France and the (Hapsburg) Duke of Savoy. Elizabeth, observing all the proprieties, sent her new godson a magnificent golden font by her proxy the Earl of Bedford. The infant's father, although nearby, did not attend the ceremony, reportedly for fear of yet another hostile outburst from his wife.

Given that Elizabeth's most likely heir now had a son with an even stronger claim to the English throne, she cannot have been surprised that by late 1566, when parliament met again, there were ever more anxious requests that the queen should marry or nominate an heir, or both. Such pleas echoed those from the parliament in 1559 and 1563, and were to be renewed in 1576. Negotiations for a marriage between Elizabeth and the Archduke Charles of Austria, revived between 1563 and 1567, offered the only immediate hope of some resolution, but discussions moved very slowly. The queen's primary object in those negotiations has usually been regarded as less to make a marriage, more to silence parliament on the subject and to gain the diplomatic advantage such negotiations always offered. But Cecil for one remained a strong advocate for the marriage, despite the Archduke's 'unfortunate' Catholic faith; indeed, in those years many Protestants played down the significance of Charles's religion, still seeing a Hapsburg alliance as the best protection against rising Hapsburg hostility.

Elizabeth's view, it would seem, was that prolonged marriage negotiations might well serve the same end. For the Archduke's English supporters, his religion was less important than his potential role in providing an English heir who would, it was taken for granted, be raised a Protestant. There was also another motive. For many, that marriage would also finally put an end to what was widely believed to be still the most enduring ambition of Robert Dudley, now Earl of Leicester. Cecil even drew up a table of comparisons of the relative suitability of the Hapsburg Charles and Dudley. Unsurprisingly, the former emerged the stronger candidate in every way from superior birth (that Leicester's father and grandfather had each died a traitor's death was again specifically noted) as well as enjoying a superior income, education and knowledge of international affairs. But the final sticking point for that marriage, and one which Elizabeth used to maximum effect, proved to be the Archduke's religious beliefs. After a prolonged debate at the emperor's court, the English negotiator reached a compromise whereby the Archduke would hear mass only in his private rooms, with no Englishman allowed to attend. In public, he would accompany the queen to English church services.

At this point, Dudley's more zealous Protestantism and probably his more private ambitions came to the fore, when he joined those who argued that since the Catholic mass was abhorrent to God, it should never be allowed in a truly godly realm. Preachers joined in making the same point to a much wider audience; Bishop Jewel, rumoured to have done so at Dudley's behest, preached at St Paul's, always a well-attended arena for sermons, reminding his audience that God punished his chosen people for straying from the truly religious path. He made clear that allowing any Catholic practice was a wrong path indeed. Faced with such public divisions, Elizabeth abandoned the negotiations, the council remained deeply divided, and any prospect of Elizabeth either marrying or nominating an heir was again on hold.

Because after Elizabeth's death in 1603 there was a relatively smooth transition to the next monarch, it is difficult to recapture now just how long and deeply her subjects feared who might be her successor. Thomas Norton, a zealous Protestant, parliamentarian and close ally of Cecil, prayed earnestly in his Preface to Richard Grafton's widely read *Chronicle at Large* in 1569 for Elizabeth's preservation since 'without or after [her] there is great danger and small hope'. In so doing, he voiced the deep anxiety of many of his fellow subjects. Also with the ending of those Hapsburg negotiations went, it would seem, the final hopes of Philip of Spain of recovering England for Catholicism with the present regime. Since Elizabeth's accession he had been the most important protector of English interests, but that was slowly changing. And within her realm, the situation remained that Elizabeth was still unmarried; moreover, since she had ruled out both surviving sisters of Lady Jane Grey, she had no obvious English heir and two potential foreign ones, both apparently Catholic since it seemed obvious that the infant James would be raised in his parents' religion. There was still some doubt whether a foreign-born person could inherit the English throne, but if that were the case, then there was *no* obvious heir. The future of Protestant England seemed no more secure than it had been when the religious settlement of 1559 had first been put in place.

Elizabeth, Catholics and the Protestant ascendancy

Although it was the case that after Elizabeth's accession some of her wealthier and more vehemently Catholic subjects had fled, taking refuge in Spain or joining the emergent Catholic communities at Douai in northern France and Louvain in what is now Belgium, most Catholics necessarily remained. One area in which Elizabeth had been an influential force in shaping the regime's policy was the relative accommodation shown in her early years to her formally illegal Catholic subjects. She and her more important advisers were agreed that a form of Protestantism would be the state religion, but not all agreed with her that it had to be enforced cautiously, despite the dangers of both domestic and foreign reactions. Elizabeth was, however, always able to resist the demands of the 'hotter sort' of Protestants, not least because they had no viable alternative to her as monarch.

One major consideration for Elizabeth's preferred policy was the success with which the regime of Mary I had restored a more vibrant Catholicism, and many of the Elizabethan incumbent clergy had been ordained in Mary's reign. The consequence was that by default, until significant numbers of Protestant clergy could be trained and ordained, in many places Catholic priests still followed much less than 'pure' official doctrine and ritual. Although legally all clergy were required to swear their acceptance of the 1559 Act of Supremacy, in practice many were never required to do so. There were laws requiring all subjects to attend church; in the early years, of those who did so an uncertain number were 'church papists' who publicly conformed but remained privately Catholic. Recusants, who refused to attend the parish church at all, were few in the early years and seldom punished, since they often had co-religionists in positions of local authority. And because Catholicism was practised across the entire social spectrum, including among some important nobility, Catholics were active in administration and political process at all levels, including among Elizabeth's advisers. Some, even, were elected to the House of Commons in the earlier years of her reign.

There have been plausible suggestions that it was partly in protest against what she saw as too zealous Protestant destruction of images that Elizabeth established a crucifix and candles in the Chapel Royal in 1559 and, it has also been suggested, it was for the same reason that she later ordered that rood screens should be restored in parish churches, predictably an order which was strongly resisted in the more 'advanced' Protestant areas. Despite the queen's preferences, the purging of churches of their altars, rood screens, images and clerical vestments proceeded in many places, often very slowly but proceed it did, and by the later 1560s the older religion was increasingly under attack. Although more counties further south were becoming comprehensively Protestant in practice, it was the politically conservative more distant and northern counties that were widely regarded both politically and religiously as the 'dark corners' of the land.

As many who remained Catholic came under increasing harassment from the Protestant regime to conform to the official religion, they also came under more pressure from Catholic authorities to distance themselves more clearly from Protestants. One striking example was a papal decree in 1566, confirming earlier statements which forbade Catholics to attend their parish churches, thereby increasing pressure on those 'church papists' to choose either obedience to their monarch and the secular law, which required regular church attendance, or obedience to their religious leader, But through the 1560s much of the Catholic population practised passive rather than active disobedience and made accommodation where they could.

The intensifying attention being brought to bear on Elizabeth's Catholic subjects took several forms. It was still intermittent, particularly in the parts of England more remote from London, but more frequently mass books were destroyed and religious images burned, sometimes by Elizabethan officials, often by more zealous Protestants who preached and wrote exhaustively against anything reminiscent of Catholic practice: 'the rags of the Antichrist'. One of the more important books to promote a sense of Protestant shared identity and reinforce hostility to Catholicism was John Foxe's *Actes and Monumentes of these latter and perilous dayes*. A sustained account of the many ways in which true Christian believers had always been persecuted, particularly by false believers, familiarly referred to as *Foxe's book of Martyrs*, it was first published in 1563 and went into three further editions in Foxe's lifetime. Foxe made a significant contribution to Protestant hostility to Catholicism at a time when Elizabeth was trying to reassure her Catholic subjects that, provided they obeyed her laws, their safety was assured

The gradual dissatisfaction of more radical Protestants with the queen's religious compromises is well illustrated by their shifting attitudes to the queen first hailed as a 'Very Deborah'. In the second edition of Foxe's *Book of Martyrs* (1570) the author reflected the disillusion of many other more ardent Protestants when he revised some of his previous accounts of Elizabeth's behaviour during her sister's reign, effectively to criticise her for not completing the reformation of the church begun by her father and brother.[2] On the other hand, it might be noted that she had come to the throne at a time when religious divisions between Catholic and Protestant believers were increasingly a major factor in wars, both civil and international, across Europe; to most modern eyes, one of the more remarkable achievements of her regime was that the same pattern was not established in her England despite recurrent threats, and a major factor in this relative peace was precisely the degree of accommodation that she offered. It must, however, be noted that probably few devout contemporaries shared that modern admiration for her moderate stance.

The fall and flight of Mary Queen of Scots

Meanwhile, back in Scotland, although after the christening of their son relations between Mary and her husband seemed to have improved, this soon proved to be illusory. There followed a sequence of extraordinary events, beginning with the violent death of Darnley; about the responsibility for that historians still argue, and disagree on where culpability for the several crimes within the royal circle lay.

In outline, relations worsened again between the Scottish queen and her husband – a man, it might be noted, universally agreed to be of deplorable character (excepting only, perhaps, by his immediate family). Darnley, who had been ill, was apparently reconciled with his wife, but murdered in her absence, and almost immediately the queen married Bothwell, the man most widely believed to have been responsible for her husband's death. The marriage had been preceded by Bothwell's sudden divorce of his wife, and perhaps by Bothwell's rape of the widowed queen. Many have doubted the rape, but Robert Melville, who was once again near the heart of events, always thought it had indeed occurred. Whatever the reason for the marriage having taken place, it also set off a series of battles within Mary's realm that culminated in the defeat of Mary and Bothwell, with the latter soon fleeing Scotland and Mary being taken prisoner and placed in a castle in the middle of Loch Leven. It was from such events that two feuding groups emerged: the queen's men (for Mary) and the king's men (soon promoting the abdication of Mary and the installation of her infant son as nominal king, with Mary's illegitimate half-brother, the Earl of Moray, as regent).

For the purposes of this study, the significance of those events lies primarily in the response of Elizabeth to them, above all to the imprisonment of another monarch. In general, the English councillors were delighted at Mary's disgrace, particularly by her quick remarriage to the likely murderer of her previous husband. Those who shared Cecil's views that her claim to be Elizabeth's heir apparent made Mary a potent threat to English security were particularly pleased at what was seen as her destruction of her own reputation. As one English observer contentedly remarked, Mary's fall was another example of the inevitable fate of 'such as live not in the fear of God'.

Elizabeth, however, drew no comfort from the thought that Mary's fall was a striking demonstration of divine justice. As an anointed monarch, she took very seriously indeed the admonition in Psalm 105, v. 15: 'Touch not the Lord's anointed.' She fully endorsed the common precept that if subjects suffered from harsh or ineffectual rulers, such rulers had been sent to punish the people for their manifold and evident wickedness. For her, as for her contemporary monarchs across Europe, it was a crucial tenet that all monarchs necessarily were sacrosanct, whatever their apparent misdeeds, since they were indeed anointed of God. (This was one reason that, from later in the 16th century when assassination of European monarchs became more common, it was widely regarded as a particularly, even uniquely, heinous crime.)

Despite Mary's insistence on her own innocence, and indeed on her narrow escape from the same fate as her previous husband, reports soon spread through Scotland and internationally that Mary had been fully complicit in Darnley's death. Many of her erstwhile supporters across Europe condemned both her actions and her. The French king and the pope, her most likely allies, both distanced themselves from the disgraced Scottish queen, and at first Elizabeth had also strongly censured her behaviour. But she drew a clear distinction between condemning a monarch's actions and punishing her. When her victors imprisoned Mary, Elizabeth sent a strongly worded protest. At Elizabeth's insistence, Throckmorton, now her ambassador in Edinburgh, continued to argue for Mary's release but was bluntly told that the infant James would soon be crowned king, with or without his mother's approval. The English queen's protests counted for nothing in the adjacent kingdom.

Elizabeth still refused to countenance any such move, let alone to accept what she saw as the Scots' presumption and defiance of God's manifest injunctions. But despite Elizabeth's freely offered advice to her, Mary did not help her own position when she declared that she would rather die than divorce Bothwell, whose child she believed she was now carrying. Under pressure Mary, now confined to a castle in the middle of a lake, was successfully coerced into endorsing her own abdication, and her infant was crowned in her place. That forced abdication roused Elizabeth to further fury. She told Cecil that she thought to revenge the imprisonment of Queen Mary and to set her free, presumably by force. Cecil's belief was that Elizabeth had no personal sympathy for any of Mary's recent activities but was upholding those religious teachings about the sanctity of monarchs to ensure that any such actions against their divinely ordained queen should never be contemplated by any of her own subjects. Elizabeth's commitment to those principles, however, was soon tested when Mary, still confined to her island prison, sent a plea that she should be allowed to live in England, in whatever place and manner the English queen should decree. That help was much more than Elizabeth was prepared to offer to the disgraced queen, who had, after all, also on various occasions claimed to be the true queen of England.

Perhaps to the English queen's relief, the matter of Mary's ultimate fate was taken out of Elizabeth's hands within months, for in the spring of 1568 the Queen of Scots escaped from Loch Leven and raised troops to restore her to her 'undoubted and rightful' throne. The final Scottish battle for her cause took place at Langside on 13 May and, as it went badly for her troops Mary fled the battlefield. Three days later, ignoring the advice of her companions, and ignoring the possibility of returning to France, where she had both friends and property, the deposed and defeated Catholic queen crossed into England. The threat that she posed in England was immediately emphasised when Thomas Percy, seventh Earl of Northumberland, recently returned to the Catholic faith and a prominent member of the old border nobility, offered her hospitality.

The deputy governor of Carlisle intervened to forestall that dangerous proposition, and very soon the Scottish queen, was being guarded by Francis Knollys, a relation of Elizabeth and a committed Protestant. When Mary complained to him of her Scottish treatment, Knollys reduced her to tears by arguing that there were occasions when deposition even of monarchs was justified. He is not known to have put that argument to Elizabeth. Knollys, who recognised the personal charm of Mary as much as so many others but was able to resist it, was well aware that Mary was not only an unwelcome but also a very dangerous presence in England, above all as a rallying point for Catholic opponents to Elizabeth's reign. While Elizabeth was acutely aware of the dangerous implications of any harm done to another duly crowned monarch, she still understood the threat that Mary posed.

But at much the same time Elizabeth herself made a move that increased the international threat to England's security almost as much as Mary's unexpected arrival. In 1568, French privateers (that is, 'licensed' pirates) had attacked some Spanish ships carrying freshly minted money for Philip II's armies in the Netherlands; the captains under attack took refuge in the closest safe havens, which were English Channel ports. But, following a particularly confusing set of claims and counterclaims, and perhaps misunderstandings, in January 1569 Elizabeth sanctioned the seizure of the cargo of bullion from the Spanish ships.[3] Her justification was that since Philip had not yet repaid the Genoese who had originally supplied the bullion, it was not yet his property. Relations with Philip II had been in gradual decline for a decade, but what he viewed as a straightforward appropriation of a great deal of his treasure proved to be another reason for Philip's growing hostility to his one time sister-in law, whom he had previously so often protected.

The Scottish queen as an English problem

After her arrival in England, Mary was soon seen to be a potentially useful figurehead by two quite different groups, both hoping to exploit her (always unofficial) status as heir apparent to the English throne. Some Catholics looked to her as the means whereby their faith might be restored as the official religion in England, a plan which at the very least would require a sustained rebellion and, presumably, Elizabeth's assassination. A very different group included such trusted men of Elizabeth's court as the Duke of Norfolk, Throckmorton and even Leicester, who took up Elizabeth's own earlier proposal that Mary might marry an Englishman. One she had nominated was the Duke of Norfolk, whose third wife had died late in 1567. He was England's only duke, the wealthiest peer of England, Earl Marshal and a Privy Councillor. When Mary fled to England he was still an apparently reliable Protestant, a man manifestly trusted by Elizabeth, and the most eligible man for a queen. If they married and Mary produced a child, the succession problem would, in the minds of many of Elizabeth councillors, be resolved.

No one, however, mentioned that plan to Elizabeth, not least because far from welcoming the Scottish queen to her court, her first impulse was to restore Mary to her Scottish throne, albeit with suitable conditions. Even as a figurehead, however, Mary was not acceptable to those who were now ruling Scotland on behalf of her son. Elizabeth also refused to have her anywhere near her own court, insisting that Mary must first be cleared of the dreadful charge of murdering her second husband. Above all, Elizabeth refused to countenance any suggestion she might recognise Mary as her heir, not least because, as Cecil commented, the Queen of Scots has previously openly challenged for the crown of England, not as a second person after the Queen's majesty but to replace her.

A month after Mary's flight to England, Elizabeth wrote to the Scottish exile, promising to protect her but emphasising that she could not be received at court until cleared and acquitted of the murder charge against her, in part because of Elizabeth's need to protect her own reputation. Mary, quite as conscious as Elizabeth of her own royal status, refused to be judged by any lesser beings, but finally agreed that Elizabeth, not as judge but as 'her dear friend and cousin' might hear the charges against her. An examination into those charges began in early October and culminated in the presentation of copies of the notorious Casket Letters, allegedly written by Mary to Bothwell and said to prove that she had been fully complicit in the plot to murder Darnley. But only copies of the letters were submitted, and the purported originals were destroyed in the 1580s, so no judgment could ever be reliably made about their authenticity.

From the time of her arrival in England, Mary was a cause of considerable friction among Elizabeth's advisers. Leicester and his allies were highly critical of what they saw as Cecil's provocative attitudes towards her, and of his concern to make it impossible for her to return to Scotland. Norfolk, for his part, was quite content to consider becoming consort to a Scottish queen before she inherited an English throne. But while Norfolk was considering the fresh proposals, Elizabeth's confidence in her only duke had collapsed. Questioned by her about the rumours of his intended next marriage, an account of which she had heard with all the details from Leicester, Norfolk flatly denied any knowledge of it. When Norfolk realised the situation he was now in, terrified by Elizabeth's fury and by Leicester's warning that he was destined for the Tower, he left the court without the queen's permission. In so doing he worsened his position since retiring from the court without royal permission always smacked of treason.

Elizabeth's anger at Norfolk's behaviour was compounded by her knowledge that many of the old nobility in the north, generally Catholic and resentful of successive Tudor monarchs who had reduced their regional authority, had supported the Norfolk–Mary marriage proposal. What else had been discussed among them is not now clear, but an indication of their other purposes is that as the Duke returned to court at the queen's furious insistence, he sent a message to the northern earls, begging them not to rebel since that would undoubtedly lead to his losing his head. As it was, within a fortnight of his return, Norfolk was a prisoner in the Tower of London.

There were other plotters in action at the same time and it is still difficult to disentangle their various purposes. But there were certainly moves to restore Catholicism, and for the northern leaders that was a much more important object than Mary marrying Norfolk. The conspiracy was widespread, and tentative contacts had been made with several foreigners, including one Roberto Ridolfi, a Florentine banker in London who had contacts with the Papacy; meanwhile the Spanish ambassador had been informing Philip II of his own rather unrealistic hopes of the planned uprising. There was some talk of foreign soldiers being landed at a northern port, and in the north rumours of a rising planned for October 1569 were circulating widely.

The Northern Uprising

The sudden imprisonment of Norfolk ensured that those southerners also planning to promote the marriage now dropped out of any further commitment to either project. Elizabeth, aware of the rumours of rebellion from the north, also took the precaution of moving Mary to a more secure place, thereby removing the possibility of her seizure by hostile hands. Despite having little support from the local gentry, and well before any foreign support had been organised, the northern earls, driven on by fear of Elizabeth's suspicions of them, raised their standards for rebellion although planning was seriously incomplete. Not even the restoration of Catholicism was a clear objective, though it became a major rallying point in what followed.

Years later, the Earl of Northumberland claimed that the aims included securing Mary Queen of Scots and having her named as heir; among those he named as supporters of Mary for heir was Leicester. So he had been, but never with rebellion against Elizabeth in mind. The proclamation the earls issued on 16 November 1569 made no mention of Mary, instead declaring their purpose to be the restoration of 'the true and Catholic religion'. On other occasions they proclaimed it was to promote the cause of Mary Stuart. Two days before that proclamation, the earls had marched into Durham. In Durham cathedral all indicators of Protestant worship were defaced or destroyed, and large numbers rejoiced at the restoration of the old religion and its ceremonies; in Durham itself priests said mass openly to large congregations made up from many social levels; across Yorkshire the mass was restored in some 70 churches. But there were also misgivings about pushing disobedience further, not least because of the value placed on obedience to duly ordained monarchs, an ideal which was upheld by both Catholic and Protestant traditions.

Although it was originally designed to coincide with the rebellion, the papal contribution, in the form of a papal bull (an authoritative papal utterance) *Regnans in Excelsis*, did not appear until the following year. It denounced Elizabeth as 'the pretended queen of England and the servant of crime' and, even more significantly, by it the pope declared that all who had sworn oaths of obedience to her were utterly absolved from such an oath. He went further, declaring that any nobles, subjects and others who obeyed her laws were, like the queen herself, immediately excommunicated.[4] Predictably the bull was immediately banned from England, but it is also to be noted that Pope Pius V, who issued the bull, made no provision for its distribution in England, let alone arranging for any military means of enforcing it. Nevertheless, however much it might be argued that the bull was an empty threat, it was also, in the eyes of Protestants, a fearful threat; for them, only its mistiming prevented it from becoming a seriously troublesome weapon against Elizabeth's regime. It was also troubling that one copy, of a number smuggled into the country, had been nailed to the door of the palace of the bishop of London.

In the event, because of the early discovery of the projected rebellion, there was little fighting and no full-scale battle. Indeed, the aftermath of the Northern rebellion was much more destructive than the rebellion itself, and that destruction, the evidence suggests, was explicitly sanctioned by Elizabeth. As soon as the rebellion broke out Thomas Norton, Cecil's favourite polemicist, had scolded the rebels as *Poore deceived Subiectes … Drawn into Rebellion by the Earles of Northumberland and Westmoreland.* All of them, he insisted, whatever their obligations to their lords, had erred in following them, since they had followed Percy and Neville rather than their natural sovereign lady, the queen of England. In the aftermath of that uprising, those errant subjects, who had followed their lords rather than a queen of whom they knew almost nothing, paid the highest price. It was two months after the uprising before a conditional pardon was finally offered to Northern rebels; before then some 80 of them were hanged in Durham alone, and an uncertain number – between 450 and 900 – had been hanged without, it would seem, any trial, Either figure was greater than those killed in the few clashes which had occurred, and an unknown further number died in the winter snows, having fled their homes to avoid the retribution. The harshness of those punishments was without precedent for any other Tudor rebellion, and indicates just how alarmed Elizabeth and her advisers had been by the rebellion.

By mid-February, Cecil was receiving reports that many northern places were likely to be left 'naked of all inhabitants' if the indiscriminate punishment continued.[5] Only then did Elizabeth relent enough to issue terms for pardon of the hapless followers of the earls. The leaders lived longer; Charles Neville, Earl of Westmorland lived in exile in the Spanish Netherlands until his death in 1601; Thomas Percy, Earl of Northumberland, fled to Scotland where he was finally sold back by James's regent Moray to Elizabeth for some £2,000. He was executed as a traitor in York in 1572; as was customary his head was set on a pole, but some of his hair was taken as a martyr's relic. Mary, in whose cause all that struggle had been planned, had long since been whisked away from the north to the relative security of Tutbury Castle in Staffordshire. She had been placed under the secure guardianship of the Earl of Shrewsbury and his redoubtable wife Bess of Hardwick in February 1569, months before the troubles began.

The Ridolphi plot and its aftermath

By all accounts Thomas Howard, fourth Duke of Norfolk, who derived much confidence from his status as premier English aristocrat, was not a very astute man. Even before he was released from the Tower, where he was held for denying his marriage plans and for his suspected role in plotting the Northern Uprising, he had renewed contact with Mary Queen of Scots, exchanging both rings and assurances of undying love with her. At the same time, the Duke assured Elizabeth of his allegiance to her that he had and promised to have no dealings with the Scottish queen unless his monarch so commanded him. In August 1570, he was released from the Tower but confined to his London house, where he continued to plan to marry Mary, writing to her in cipher and gradually being drawn into a conspiracy at the centre of which was the Florentine banker and conspirator in London, Ridolphi. Norfolk was once again in touch with the pope and with the Spanish ambassador in London, who in turn assured Philip II that a well-resourced invasion would soon restore England to Catholicism and install Mary, safely married to Norfolk, on the throne. Mary was equally confident that a few thousand foreign soldiers would quickly lead to the restoration of Catholicism.

The whole plot was the more dangerous because by then it was quite clear there was no hope that the current rulers in Scotland would accept the return of Mary to any position of authority. For her, it seems, the viable alternative to returning to Scotland was to take over the throne to which she regarded herself as rightful heir, and returning England to Catholicism. The scheme now looks so wild that some have suggested that it was actually a scheme of Cecil (by then Lord Burghley) to discredit Mary Stuart, but the available evidence refutes that. Once again Norfolk denied any knowledge of the conspiracy, until confronted with evidence which comprehensively refuted his denials. He went on trial in January 1572, charged with high treason, with having conspired to deprive the queen of her throne, with planning to raise a rebellion against her and with planning to change the religion of the realm. Norfolk, and indeed many others, it seems, had adopted the view that the pre-eminent peer in the land could not be treated in such a way, but the evidence against him was very strong. He was found guilty of high treason, condemned to death and returned to the Tower to await his execution.

In a pattern that was to be repeated years later with Mary Stuart herself, Elizabeth proved extremely reluctant finally to condemn to death anyone so close to her in the great hierarchy of being. Norfolk wrote to her trying to persuade her of his continuing loyalty, and insisting to her and many others that he had always been, and remained, Protestant – that claim at least was plausible, but made his other activities even more problematic. His efforts were unsuccessful, but Elizabeth's profound reluctance to confirm his execution is demonstrated by the fact that at least three times warrants for his execution were drawn up, signed by Elizabeth and then revoked by her. That procrastination hardly surprised her advisers, but their anxiety increased greatly when, in March, Elizabeth fell acutely ill, perhaps, as she said, from eating bad fish. She recovered quickly, but those about her had been sharply reminded how close they had been to total disaster.

While she was still hesitating over Norfolk's fate, Elizabeth allowed herself to be persuaded to call a new parliament. Her councillors had promoted the idea, hoping that its members might pressure Elizabeth into having both the Duke and Mary Stuart executed, something those already close to her could not achieve. Nicholas Bacon's opening address to the new parliament explained that they had been assembled because of the recent 'great treasons and notable conspiracies very perilous to her majesty's person and to the whole state of the realm'. Most in the Commons agreed that indeed Norfolk must die because the time had long passed when the Queen could have any confidence in his protestations of loyalty. Yet, given the strength of Elizabeth's reluctance to accept such advice, it was still accepted that such a view should be presented only as an informal decision. Despite unusually persistent efforts from her parliament, the fate of Mary was still treated even more cautiously, with the effective postponing of any penalty for her conspiracies. It was June before the Duke of Norfolk, the peer closest to the throne, finally went to his execution on Tower Hill.

Even then, it may be that Elizabeth only agreed to his execution as the means of saving the life of that other conspirator, Mary Stuart. Parliamentarians had been pressing their queen hard for the life of the woman who had so clearly plotted against her life and their religion. But Elizabeth's understanding of the particularly sanctified status of monarchs was so central to her own sense of security that she resisted sustained pressure from parliament, her Privy Council and less formal advisers to execute both Norfolk and Mary. Elizabeth was always pleased when she was compared with her father, but this was one issue where no such comparison was possible. Henry VIII had executed his then pre-eminent peer, the Duke of Buckingham, on very little evidence in 1521; at the end of his reign, the third Duke of Norfolk, was saved from execution only by the death of the king himself. It might be noted that Henry VIII also executed a significant number of his other peers, but the most important comparison with the man she so often claimed to admire was that one of the two queens he executed was also a crowned and consecrated queen, albeit as queen consort; she was also Elizabeth's mother. That she tried so hard to avoid following her father's example may owe something to that precedent, but also reflected Elizabeth's insecurity about her own position. Her continuing refusal to nominate an heir suggests that Elizabeth may have been still fearful for her precarious hold on the throne, made more perilous by the still-contested legitimacy of her birth, her status as Protestant ruler over a realm with many Catholics within and many more outside it, and perhaps the widespread rumours of her reported early sexual misdemeanours with Thomas Seymour and more recently with Robert Dudley. Given all that, she may well have believed that she simply could not afford to execute another crowned queen.

5 The queen and her realm mid-reign

By 1572, Wallace MacCaffrey once wrote, Elizabeth had served out her years of royal apprenticeship. She had by then been on the throne for 14 years and apparently securely so. She was well on the way to establishing her most familiar image as a queen of sartorial splendour and fabulous jewels, a long way from the demure, even plain, dress she is said to have favoured in her evangelical brother's reign. She was refining her strategies for keeping the competing religious groupings as well as her diverse Privy Councillors in some kind of balance. Her most potent rival for the throne, Mary Stuart, was in her keeping, and the English rival most frequently favoured as her heir, Katherine Grey, had died in 1568. She was developing new and important relationships with other monarchs in the shifting sphere of international relations, as well as confronting a range of older problems, and some new ones. For her subjects the two most important unresolved matters were still those concerning her marriage and the royal succession, but on neither of those matters, apparently, did Elizabeth share her subjects' concerns.

Elizabeth's family

One distinctive feature of Elizabeth's family life was the comparative absence of close relatives, exacerbated by the 11 years after the execution of Anne Boleyn during which Elizabeth's disgraced mother had been unmentionable at the court of Henry VIII. Elizabeth's father was fond of her, but was usually too preoccupied with royal business and pleasure to pay her much attention. Her elder half-sister was kind to her, but Mary was seldom with her, being much in demand at Henry's court. Her half-brother Edward was reared and educated in his own household and, apart from Christmas and other such great occasions, the family was seldom all together.

What is more remarkable is how little Elizabeth did to counter the long silence about her mother during her own reign. In 1559, during Elizabeth's coronation progress, Anne Boleyn had been included in the pageant showing the new queen's genealogy, but she was mentioned as briefly as possible in the subsequent printed report. A tradition identifying Anne Boleyn as a nursing mother of the evangelical movement had emerged, albeit tentatively, among the more reform minded in the last years of Henry's reign and during that of Edward. As queen, however, Elizabeth did nothing to promote it. Soon after Elizabeth's accession William Latymer, once Anne Boleyn's chaplain, presented her with a memoir of her mother's 'excellent virtues and princely qualities' but Elizabeth showed no interest in having the work published. It remained unpublished until 1990.[1]

Her public silence about her mother has never been satisfactorily explained, and it was some 15 years after that refusal to publish the memorial of her mother that the queen accepted the gift of a ring that had images of herself and her mother (Plate 4). Both images are visible if the ring is opened, but the ring can be closed, becoming just another bejewelled ornament; wearing it, she could still be publicly silent about her mother, while privately having her likeness close to her if that was her preference. The claim constantly reiterated at and after her accession that Elizabeth was 'mere English' did necessarily involve an oblique reference to Anne Boleyn, but its primary purpose was as another attack on Catholic Mary I for her Spanish mother and, subsequently, her Spanish husband. (Protestant polemicists in and after Mary's reign often brought together 'Catholic', 'Spanish' and 'cruel' in their critique of her rule.)

Given that Elizabeth was not yet three when her mother was executed, and that they had always lived in separate households, perhaps the closest substitutes for a mother for the young Elizabeth were first Lady Margaret Bryan and then Kat Astley, still a teenager when she entered Elizabeth's household in 1536. She remained with the queen until her own death in 1567. Once an advocate of

Thomas Seymour's flirtations and courtship with the young Elizabeth, Astley had brief periods of disgrace and detention for that and, after Elizabeth's accession, for her selective promotion of other contentious marriage projects, but she always rose again to resume her place as Elizabeth's closest female companion. Her considerable influence as chief gentlewoman of the queen's privy chamber was constantly demonstrated by her power to control access to her mistress, and she may have been a confidante to the queen in a way very few other people ever were.

After Elizabeth came to the throne, the closest surviving relations that she kept about her were all descendants of Anne Boleyn's sister, Mary. Mary had once been mistress to Henry VIII but was barred from court from 1534, ostensibly for a socially demeaning second marriage, but perhaps also because her sister, then Henry's wife, resented her presence there. Mary's two children from her acceptable first marriage to Henry Carey, who died in 1528, were William Carey and Katherine, who later married Sir Francis Knollys. It was subsequently the Carey and Knollys offspring of the second and third generations who had a unique relationship with the queen. The political significance of that relationship was well illustrated late in Elizabeth's reign, when James I requested that Elizabeth send either the second-generation Henry Carey, then Lord Hunsdon, or one of his sons to meet him. The matter the Scottish king wished to discuss was, he explained, too important to be trusted to her ambassador, but only to one of her family. Elizabeth immediately sent a Carey, as requested. Members of that family will necessarily reappear through this study. As is discussed in Chapter 9, her relatives on the Tudor side were consistently treated quite differently, perhaps because she always felt threatened by others who shared the royal bloodline.

The queen's court

Matters of government within her realm, and particularly issues of international politics with her 'brother' kings, undoubtedly occupied some of Elizabeth's time, but her advisers, above all William Cecil, saw to much of the regular work, including drafting a great deal of her correspondence. There was, however, always one function only the queen could perform: that of being the pivotal point of court ceremonial. This role carried international as well as political domestic implications since the royal court was the first port of call for any foreigner of sufficient rank to manage an introduction to it. It was also the site of all foreign delegations, and the place where actual and aspiring courtiers competed for her favour, sometimes in ways which led to occasional scuffles at court and duels outside it. Elizabeth's strategies for maintaining control included encouraging the language of courtly love, holding or withholding her approval, and the frequent display of her displeasure, which could so easily end a promising career. Another weapon in her armoury was displays of her always volatile moods which, many older observers commented, was very reminiscent of her father's temper.

In her court, Elizabeth and her entourage represented the splendour and richness of her kingdom and the good order of its social hierarchy. The visual appearance was defined by very detailed dress regulations, which were most detailed for the highest levels of the social order and included such particular details as who was entitled to wear purple silk or sable fur (only earls or above). The dress prescriptions, which were a long-standing practice, faded as they moved down the hierarchy to very little prescription for the dress of the common people, most of whom could not afford any choice at all in their attire. One exception was a proclamation ordering that labouring men should all wear woollen hats, at a time of a depressed wool trade. It was not successful, because of cost.[2]

Elizabeth's famous preference for rich dressing and spectacular jewellery, particularly but never exclusively pearls, served an important political function in an era when, at least in theory, dress defined a person's social status. In that context, it was crucial that the queen should represent visually her role as apex of the whole social hierarchy, and Elizabeth dressed to achieve that throughout her reign. Her success was the more remarkable because, from the time of her accession, there were repeated complaints of her acute shortage of money with which to manage all her realm's affairs. One of the ways she managed to maintain her regal appearance was that she made it known that gifts of rich fabric and jewels were always welcome. The traditional courtly exchange of gifts, particularly at New Year, were as carefully graduated as all other expressions of the hierarchy, and the queen received many rich gifts then.[3] She also had many of her garments fashioned and refashioned (and, as time went on, widened) to refresh her wardrobe and keep up with prevailing fashions. So, although impressive, her magnificence was achieved with considerably less wardrobe expense than, for example, that of her successor.[4]

But, as ever, there was another side to the court presented in that visual display. Gatherings with the queen were also sites for approval or humiliation for individual courtiers. Robert Carey, of the third generation of her relatives, once described how she 'knew but would not know' that he was at court while he was in disgrace. She often practised the art of 'seeing' but 'not seeing' those who had incurred her displeasure. Catching her eye as she moved through a gathering was a cause for celebration, but even the most eminent of her court could be, and were, cast into despair by her refusal to see. That was only part of a political and social process at the upper social levels that was still dependent on a complex compound of personal, political and social patronage.

The rivalry inherent in the whole process has been aptly described as the politics of royal jealousy, often revolving in the earlier years around Dudley, in the later years of her reign around Essex, but always a potent force at court. Access to the more important people around court was always complex, requiring support from patrons current or potential, although sometimes a sufficiently handsome appearance could attract the queen's attention. Sir Christopher Hatton, who went on to exercise considerable influence in her reign, may have attracted her attention that way in 1562, but the ability he subsequently demonstrated amply justified that choice. Even his acknowledged skill in the language of courtly love, much appreciated by Elizabeth, was only part of his ability.

The queen and her people beyond the court

For her subjects more generally, there were several other ways in which Elizabeth reached out beyond the court. There was a range of traditional royal functions for lesser subjects that Elizabeth observed, such as the rituals of Maundy Thursday. For some centuries the day before Good Friday had been marked by Christian monarchs washing the feet of selected 'deserving poor' and distributing 'maundy money' to them, in imitation of Christ washing his disciples' feet at his last supper. A more unusual royal function was the power claimed only by two monarchies, of France and England, of the 'royal touch', the capacity to heal 'the king's evil'. (That condition is now recognised as a form of scrofula, which unpredictably sometimes goes into remission.)

That healing power of the ruler was believed to come from the form of consecration used for crowning French and English monarchs. In the 14th century, French leaders confronted with the possibility of an English monarch through his French inheritance, argued against allowing female transmission of royal authority in part because of the significance of that 'royal touch'. That sacral power was, they argued, so close to the priesthood that it was denied to women. In England, however, Mary I ignored that argument and maintained the practice of the healing royal touch (with apparently as much effect as any other monarch). Elizabeth then continued the practice of touching for the king's evil.

This royal capacity to heal was one more reason among many for the attraction of crowds to the monarch's entourage when she was on progress, though there were also specified days when the healing was practised at her royal residence. (The last monarch to practise the royal touch was Queen Anne, who died in 1714.) Given that it was Catholic Mary who set the precedent for a female monarch to exercise the healing touch, there is a certain irony in the fact that late in Elizabeth's reign, when her right to rule was again challenged by some Catholic critics, one of her chaplains published an argument that Elizabeth was indeed a rightful monarch and ordained of God, as irrefutably demonstrated by her effective exercise of that healing touch.

Elizabeth, like all early modern monarchs, moved around her kingdom a great deal for various purposes. One basic reason was that, given the number of people at court, it was necessary frequently to move the entourage so that the palace could be 'sweetened', a process by which the accumulated waste of various kinds was removed and the whole cleansed. The royal sport of hunting was another reason for the court moving, as was the intermittent need to inspect fortifications, visit friends and strengthen loyalties. One of the unusual aspects of Elizabeth's travels was that she never travelled outside England and, after she was on the throne, she never met another crowned monarch. These limitations may have owed something to the consideration that, as a female monarch, she was never expected to lead an army, and she never undertook the face-to-face negotiations that other monarchs still sometimes practised, although it was becoming more common for all to rely on diplomatic representatives.

The Queen on progress

Despite the attention many scholars have paid to Elizabeth's travels through her realm, many parts of it remained quite unknown to her. Certainly she travelled frequently, but she visited only some 25 of her 53 counties. She never visited Wales and never went near Ireland. Given that Wales had been fully incorporated into England only by 1543, that may not be particularly surprising, but Devon and Cornwall, also not visited, were crucially important for her sea-faring people and contained the homes of many of her better-known subjects. She never ventured further north than Lincolnshire and Staffordshire, and always stayed well away from the more troublesome and more Catholic northern counties. Her more frequent progresses were made within the Thames Valley as she usually stayed in relatively close proximity to London. One reason may well have been that, although at least some of her leading advisers usually travelled with her, as well as favoured ambassadors, the greater part of her business was always transacted in London and communication between the travelling and the permanent court needed to be maintained. Another explanation for her not travelling far from London was that the usual distance her entourage (and baggage train) managed each day was 12 miles.

In the age-old manner of monarchs, Elizabeth's travels across her realm had several purposes: to reinforce her authority across her territory, to show herself to her people, to honour local leaders whose status was greatly enhanced by her presence, to encourage loyalty from some, to honour loyalty in others, and to ensure the practice of her preferred religious forms. On at least one occasion, indeed, and possibly with the queen's connivance, her host was publicly exposed as a practising Catholic, whose religious icon was publicly burned in the queen's presence.[5] One constant was always the crowds her entourage attracted for a range of reasons, and another the care she usually took – as she did in London – to ensure that she was visible to as many as possible. Whether she was visiting a university, a town or one of the increasing number of great houses appearing across the landscape, the demands on her hosts were considerable indeed. The journeys she undertook had certain common features, including the huge train of wagons carrying all her luggage, including, some claim, her bed, which was dismantled and reassembled at each move.

One much-noted factor was her acknowledgment of her subjects gathered to see her pass, although there was careful vetting of those allowed to come close to her. Such colourful spectacles as she provided were rare outside London and always attracted crowds, only in part because it was customary to distribute some coins among the poor. Early in the next century, Robert Burton included watching a royal procession among the cures he listed for that endemic condition, melancholy. And, for those who were deemed socially acceptable, there was always the possibility of submitting a petition, the addressing of which was, in principle, a central concern of any monarch.

But there were also many variations in the details of her progresses. They could last for a week or two or, as on one occasion, for 139 days. Sometimes she had few hosts, but on one progress she managed to stay with some 35, admittedly an unusually large number. As well as visiting close companions, particularly Cecil but also other leading advisers like Nicholas Bacon, she frequently visited significant towns like Rye or Norwich.

Welcoming her appropriately, for private as for more institutional hosts, was always a challenge, even for those most closely associated with her. Working out how to accommodate, let alone feed, what was always a large entourage was even more challenging, even for those who had built houses specifically designed to accommodate her and much of her entourage. There were also those such as Hatton, who spent huge amounts to build Holdenby for her accommodation but which she never visited, despite her high estimation of him. Sometimes she visited relatively unassuming houses, such as that of the Norris family at Rycote; having known her since the time during her sister's reign when Elizabeth was confined at Woodstock, they were almost as close to the queen as the family of the first Baron Hunsdon.

At the other end of the scale from such almost familial visits were the great spectacular welcomes which the queen sometimes received from her courtiers. Two of the most spectacular, and now most studied, entertainments arranged for the queen were probably those at Kenilworth, a Leicester residence, in 1575 and at Elvetham, belonging to the Earl of Hertford, in 1591. Those two occasions offer intriguing insights into the possibilities and uncertainties of entertaining the queen. Leicester took advantage of her two-week stay to renew once more his plea for their marriage, as well as mount arguments for policies he preferred. His several failures in this were marked by Elizabeth's refusal to watch a masque designed to promote his marriage ambitions, and her disregard of other appeals. Leicester subsequently abandoned all hope of marrying her, and three years later finally married a woman rumoured for several years to have been his mistress, Elizabeth's kinswoman Lettice Knollys. For that marriage, Leicester was soon forgiven by the queen, although, as previously indicated, she was much less forgiving to his second wife.

The festivities at Elvetham were designed to serve a quite different purpose from those at Kenilworth. Edward Seymour, Earl of Hertford, was the eldest son of Edward Seymour, Lord Protector in Edward VI's reign, and in 1560 he had secretly married Katherine Grey. That was a dangerous move since his wife was sister to the ill-fated Lady Jane Grey and, by the will of Henry VIII, next heir after Elizabeth. The marriage became public only when Katherine, then a maid of honour at Elizabeth's court, became pregnant. By law, members of the royal family required the crown's permission to marry; this marriage was the more offensive to Elizabeth since Katherine gave birth to a boy in 1561, thereby increasing the already considerable pressure on Elizabeth to acknowledge the Grey lineage as her heirs.

That acknowledgement, however, the queen would not give, having never forgiven them for the argument Edward VI made for Jane Grey's claim to the throne, that like her elder sister Elizabeth was illegitimate and therefore ineligible for the throne. The married couple had been imprisoned separately in the Tower and forbidden to meet, but Katherine produced another boy-child in 1562. Elizabeth had already ensured their marriage was declared invalid, and penalised the pair further for the second child, whose legitimacy she also denied. Katherine died in 1568, still in custody and always kept separate from her husband. Finally released from custody, the Earl increasingly took his place at court, but never achieved any position of real importance, perhaps because he several times tried to have his sons declared legitimate. (Elizabeth's resolute stance against those attempts is yet another reminder of her consistent opposition to the possible identification of any heir to her throne.)

In 1591, however, he was apparently forewarned that the queen intended to visit him and, because of the limitations of his own house, he constructed a wood-and-canvas palace to provide accommodation for her and her retinue, and constructed a lake on which to stage a mock sea-battle. The queen was reported to be equally pleased by those actions and by the quality of the music, the entertainments and the hospitality she was offered. In brief, the Earl of Hertford was demonstrating, even to Elizabeth's satisfaction, the expenditure and the splendour a truly loyal subject would apply to providing a suitably rich occasion for her. It did not, however, save him from later being sent to the Tower again, when his surviving son tried once more to establish his legitimacy. By implication, such a move would renew his claim to the throne, and even after nearly 40 years on the throne, Elizabeth was still not prepared to countenance any discussion of her likely successor. She was, it may seem, always uncertain of her continuing tenure of the throne even after decades of rule.

'Love' and a female monarch

By the 1570s the habit of referring to the common people's 'love' for Elizabeth was pervasive. It was, however, quite a different concept from the more familiar 'chivalric love' commonly used by Elizabeth's courtiers in their relations with her. The popular idea of the love Elizabeth attracted owes a great deal to her own and others' image making. In November 1558, in the eyes of most of her subjects, Elizabeth was a rather suspect heir to the throne. But as Mary, England's first effective queen regnant was dying, her heir insisted that when she was suspected of treason and sent to the Tower, her life had been saved not as the Spanish ambassador would have it by her brother-in-law Philip II but by the 'love' of the English people. That was a mantra constantly invoked in the published account of her coronation progress through London, and in a multitude of subsequent accounts of her activities, both public and more private. It was, in short, part of a comprehensive publicists' drive to highlight the people's accepting the legitimacy of this relatively unknown new queen, of dubious birth to an even more dubious mother and whose own reputation had been already marred by the widespread reports of her relations with Thomas Seymour in her brother's reign.

It is hardly surprising that there has been considerable confusion about just what was denoted by the word 'love' which recurs so often in accounts of her activities. Some historians have even written of Elizabeth's 'romantic wooing' of her subjects. There are several problems with that interpretation, only one of which is that almost all Elizabethans regarded romantic love as a dangerous and socially disruptive passion. Poets and playwrights frequently wrote of it, but when it came to marriage, particularly among the upper levels of the social hierarchy, property arrangements and political connections were at least as significant, although there was an understanding that the pair should at least 'like' each other. Indeed, the more intense and passionate 'love' might be, the more destructive of the family marriage business it was at the elite level, as Shakespeare's *Romeo and Juliet* illustrated.

The political language of 'love' was quite another matter. It had its origins in monastic communities, and denoted the relationship central to the ideal of 'communal perfection'. It then was invoked to describe the proper relationship between subject and monarch, and had become widespread in the reign of Henry VIII. It recurs so often in the correspondence between that king and Cardinal Wolsey, for example, that at the accession of Elizabeth there was nothing gender-specific about using 'love' to describe the bonds between subject and ruler. Rather, what it signified was the ideal of 'civility', that is a compound of good citizenship, good order and sociability.[6] That ideal relationship was demonstrated by, among other means, displays of good will, or even of interest, as overtly displayed between monarch and subjects. But the term, applied to royalty, was much more about a display of proper deference on the one side and its acknowledgement on the other, much less about the kind of more frenzied adulation which, for example, the late Princess Diana was able to attract.

It was an ideal which was much more widely invoked by Elizabeth and her loyalists, particularly as the explanation when great crowds gathered near the queen's entourage. It was, as previously discussed, much used in the published account of the Elizabeth' coronation progress. By April 1559 loyalists explained crowds gathering round the queen in those terms of civility. On one such occasion, the queen had gone up the Thames to supper with the Earl of Pembroke, and on her return was rowed up and down the river with, it was reported, 'hundreds of boats' and 'thousands of people' to see her, because of their 'love' for her.

That it was truly a prolonged and spectacular occasion, with many flutes, drums and trumpets at work, and many guns set off, might suggest other reasons also for so many to flock to the riverside. Indeed, whenever she and her magnificent train were on the move, as in other reigns before and after her, the magnificent and colourful spectacle itself, and the money distributed, were seen as significant attractions. For Elizabeth, however, that deferential 'love' was central to the construction of her public image; insistence on her ideal relationship with her people, from her accession, was an important part of sustaining her image as the embodiment of political good order. And so it continued for much of her reign.

More problems abroad and more marriage proposals

Elizabeth's rather reckless seizure of the bullion intended for Philip's armies in 1569, discussed in the previous chapter, had proved to be just one more indication of growing tensions in the Low Countries. Antwerp had long been the primary outlet for the English cloth trade, and was also where a growing number of Protestants were challenging the established Catholic hegemony. Philip, now permanently based in Spain, sent a large army to restore Catholic good order in his troubled domain. In principle, as ever, Elizabeth supported the right of a monarch to define and uphold the royally preferred religion, but, like her advisers, she was nervous that Philip's larger project was to use those forces against 'heretic' England. It did not improve Hapsburg relations with Elizabeth that many of those Protestants under attack fled to and were given refuge in England, where they proceeded to plan for their return to their own lands, by force if necessary.

As relations with Spain deteriorated, the French royal family made several gestures towards improved relations with England. It seems likely they took the initiative in opening a tentative discussion of a marriage between Elizabeth, now 37, and the French king's 19-year-old brother. A similar proposal some years previously had never been serious, but now the proud, ambitious and religiously zealous Henry, Duc d'Anjou, was proving something of a problem for his family. The French proposal was renewed in late 1570, when England's rulers were still concerned about the implications of the late Northern Uprising, the Spanish support which had been part of the larger plan, and the papal bull excommunicating Elizabeth. The French purpose was to ensure that England and Spain were not reunited by their common interests in the Low Countries.

As ever, a preferred means of demonstrating improved relations was a royal marriage. One significant difficulty, however, was that Anjou, a devout Catholic, consistently rejected the idea of marrying even a queen regnant if, as he believed, she was also a 'heretic bastard'. On the other hand, Elizabeth approached that marriage proposal with some interest since it had potential to nullify several problems. Those included ending the French royal family's support for Mary Queen of Scots. Anjou himself was particularly close to the very powerful Guises, who were rumoured to be planning their niece's rescue and, perhaps intervening on her behalf in Scottish affairs. Moreover, as Spanish control of the Low Countries seemed to be waning, there was growing English fear that the French would move in, threatening the vital English commercial interests there. For such reasons, the current marriage proposal had the support of not only Cecil and Bacon, who were often in agreement, but also of Leicester, itself probably an indicator that he believed Elizabeth's aims were essentially diplomatic rather than marital.

The French, however, also had several reservations, despite it being their initiative. Catherine de Medici, the powerful mother of the king, doubted Elizabeth's commitment to *any* marriage. When tentative negotiations began, the first problem to arise was again the English prohibition on any Catholic royal husband practising his own religion. But because of the mutual benefits for both parties, the negotiations were remarkably prolonged. Elizabeth even briefly contemplated allowing Anjou to hear mass privately, provided no Englishmen attended. Nevertheless, negotiations continued until Anjou himself flatly refused to proceed unless he was allowed to attend full Catholic services in public places, a request which served its probable purpose of putting an end to the whole process.

Mary Stuart: the continuing problems

But the failure of those negotiations also underlined the fact that the problems that had encouraged Elizabeth to consider the proposal were all unresolved, for both parties. Mary Stuart, for one, continued to pose an insoluble problem. The earlier possibility that she might be returned to Scotland had manifestly become an impossibility by 1573. Not only had it become obvious that the then Scottish regime would never take Mary back, but also her supporters in Scotland were increasingly on the defensive. The Battle of Carberry, after which Mary had fled into England, had confirmed the battle lines already drawn between those Scots who were the queen's men, and those who were the king's. The infant James VI had become the figurehead for mainly Protestant forces, and the queen's men were primarily but never exclusively Catholic. Those lines of demarcation were further confused by pre-existing tensions between some clans, and the whole was rendered even more complex by English interventions. When, for example, Moray, the first regent for James VI, returned from the York enquiry into Mary's possible role in the death of Darnley, he also brought £5,000 with him. Scottish suspicions of his too-close relations with England, still widely regarded as the 'auld enemy', increased when he seized the Earl of Northumberland, who fled to Scotland with the failure of the Northern Uprising, and returned him to a certain traitor's death in England.

As late as 1570, Elizabeth hoped that the Scottish queen might yet be restored to her throne, albeit with restrictions, but as the struggles between contending Scottish groups continued, Moray was killed. Elizabeth then sent English forces north to support her recommendation that the Scottish Earl of Lennox, father of the murdered Darnley, should act as regent, but he soon died after another brawl between the queen's and the king's men. Nevertheless the intervention of the English forces probably saved the king's men from total defeat. One of the last strongholds of the queen's men was Edinburgh Castle itself, not won by the king's men until 1573, and then only with just enough help from Elizabeth's resources to destroy the defences.

Elizabeth's own position had also changed. Previously, her plan had been to open negotiations for Mary's return, either to rule jointly with her son or to rule within carefully prescribed limits. But after the 1570 papal bull was issued against Elizabeth, and followed by the discovery of the Ridolfi plot, not even Elizabeth was prepared to allow Mary any free movement; all negotiations for her return to Scotland apparently ended. That left Elizabeth with the prospect of an anointed and crowned queen, who had already proved herself willing to plot a foreign invasion for the English throne, permanently on her hands. And any residual hopes among the Scottish 'queen's men' of French help waned as the intermittent civil and religious wars in France between Catholics and Huguenots continued.

The English parliament of 1572 had an apparently simple solution for the problem of Mary Stuart. As one member of the Commons expressed it, they should just 'cut off her head and make no more ado about her'. Others agreed that no one, not even a queen, had the right to commit treason with impunity. The series of civil and religious wars that had raged – and would rage more – in France and the Netherlands were just one more reminder to the parliamentarians of the extent to which religious divisions and a disputed crown could ravage formerly stable communities. Many Old Testament examples were cited for Elizabeth of the numerous wicked rulers justly put to death. But Elizabeth was adamant in her refusal to consider even a parliament bill explicitly excluding Mary from the line of succession, let alone considering a bill of attainder for treason, since she flatly refused to consider the execution of an anointed queen. That, she still considered, was a precedent which would be altogether too dangerous.

Since Mary was a Catholic queen with close connections not only to the French royal family but even more closely to the Guise faction, themselves of the most zealously Catholic persuasion, it was predictable that the Massacre of St Bartholomew's Day in August 1572, of which more later, would undermine her standing in England even further. But her life was by no means intolerable. Still guarded by the Earl of Shrewsbury and his formidable wife, better known in modern times as Bess of Hardwick, Mary spent much of her time agreeably enough in malicious gossip and superb embroidery with Bess, entertaining visitors and various forms of hunting. Much of Mary's correspondence from these years was filled with descriptions of her ill health, with a depressing range of ailments and symptoms, some of which became markedly worse when she received the news of the execution of the Duke of Norfolk. On the other hand she was still treated like a guest of considerable distinction and had her own household, albeit reduced, to attend to her needs. She was still free to order elaborate and rich clothing in the latest fashions and even, on occasion, to carry out such regal functions as observing all the rituals of Maundy Thursday with some of the local poor.

Inevitably, she also resorted to secret correspondence, some of which was discovered; that simply served to ensure that she remained under the closest possible supervision. But she was far from being completely isolated. One of her visitors in 1574 was Margaret, Countess of Lennox, niece to Henry VIII and the Scottish queen's mother-in-law during Mary's marriage to Darnley. That might seem a remarkable gesture, since Margaret probably shared the general view that Mary had been implicated in the murder of her elder son. Be that as it may, Margaret brought her younger son Charles Stewart, now Earl of Lennox, with her and they stayed for five days. That proved to be time enough for Bess of Hardwick to make a match between Margaret's son Charles and Elizabeth Cavendish, her daughter from a previous marriage. In so doing, Bess failed to consult either her current husband or her queen, as such a marriage manifestly required. The significance of that 'oversight' became clear when the young couple's daughter, Arabella Stuart, was born in 1575; with significant Tudor blood in her veins, she was, and remained, a potential successor to the English throne even, for a time, after the accession of her cousin, James VI&I.

Changes at home, tensions abroad and another marriage proposal

In the years since Elizabeth had come to the throne Robert Dudley's standing had shifted from favourite (though he always retained something of that) to councillor by the early 1570s; by then Earl of Leicester, he seldom challenged Cecil's pre-eminent role. Nicholas Bacon's fortunes fluctuated more, but he was usually in good standing with the queen until his death in 1579. Sir Francis

Walsingham, best known now for his later part-time role as the spymaster of her regime, was made principal secretary and a Privy Councillor in 1573, and was to become one of her most trusted men. Among the many other changes during those years, both domestic and foreign, the most problematic were the increasing tensions across the European continent as the Protestant denominations grew in numbers and posed ever-increasing challenges to the Catholic hegemony which had defined European Christianity for so long.

As religious differences spread across Europe, there was very little room for religious toleration; Elizabeth's approach to religious difference was more tolerant than most, but seldom honoured for that by her contemporaries. Elizabeth's most private religious views were and are notoriously hard to identify;[7] she is better understood for giving priority to her subjects' conformity to the legal requirements for public worship rather than to exploring their beliefs. In that, she was more permissive than many of her own subjects, including a number of her councillors.

Many more believers in each of the major Christian denominations saw those who did not accept *their* central doctrinal truths as actual or potential 'soul-killers' leading their gullible followers to eternal torment in the afterlife. The intensity of feeling between different groups of Christians is grimly illustrated by an incident at the 1552 marriage of King John III of Portugal to a daughter of Charles V. A Protestant English trader present, one William Gardiner of Bristol, was so outraged by the 'popish idolatry' of the nuptial mass that he snatched the consecrated host from the priest and ground it underfoot. He was immediately seized, to be tortured, stoned and burned alive – as he must have known would be his fate. The deeply shocked young king, on the other hand, went into profound penitential depression, never recovered, and died within a year.[8]

As religious difference spread across Europe the two most powerful monarchies of the later 16th century, those of Philip II of Spain and of successive French monarchs, faced more challenges to their religious authority, Spain in the Netherlands and France from the Huguenots. In France, after several outbursts of civil warfare, the most notorious confrontation broke out with what is now called the Massacre of St Bartholomew's Day of 1572. It began with the attempted assassination, perhaps with Catherine de Medici's connivance, of the Huguenot leader, Coligny, and rapidly spread to a much wider attack on Huguenots more generally across the country; the death toll has never been agreed, but certainly rose well into the thousands within a few days. The shock of those attacks had a lasting impact on Protestants across Europe and in Elizabeth's England; as many Huguenots took refuge there, Protestant fear of Catholicism was given a whole new impetus with the tales of their sufferings.

Before that massacre, however, Catherine de Medici and her son Charles IX of France had achieved some improvement in their relations with Elizabeth in two ways. One was a treaty between the two kingdoms, providing that if either were attacked the other would provide some support. In itself that marked an important shift in relations between the two countries, consistently at loggerheads since medieval times. The other initiative was the transfer of Elizabeth's marriage negotiations from Henry of Anjou to his even younger brother, Francis Duke of Alençon, born 1555. In early 1572 Elizabeth *may* briefly have considered seriously a marriage with him, but even before and certainly after the events of the Massacre of St Bartholomew's Day the negotiations became a series of political manoeuvres, punctuated by lengthy periods of inactivity.

Elizabeth's reasons for continuing the French negotiations, even after the Massacre, included the political aims of strengthening the position of England against possible Spanish hostility and of discouraging any incipient French intervention in the Netherlands. She also found those marriage negotiations useful to ward off renewed pressure from both her councillors and her parliament, since a new parliament had been called in 1572. She was still resisting, as adamantly as ever, all requests to name a successor, as indeed she was resisting all calls to 'resolve' the succession problems (and the Catholic threat) by finally addressing the threats Mary Stuart still posed. The Scottish claimant to her throne was still a focal point for plots to restore Catholicism, drawing on and being pursued by both domestic and foreign forces. Perhaps Elizabeth even hoped a French alliance would help quieten the Guise support for Mary Stuart and their continuing interest in Scottish affairs.

Trouble in the Spanish Netherlands

There were several good reasons for Elizabeth to continue negotiations with another French prince after the first candidate withdrew and, after a decent pause, even after the St Bartholomew's Day Massacre. One reason, rapidly becoming more pressing, was the deepening crisis in the Netherlands. The campaign of Philip II against his heretic subjects there had not succeeded as he had hoped when he first despatched Alva and his unusually large army there in 1567. The harsh suppression of the rebels and the execution of two of their most prominent leaders had temporarily silenced the Protestants. But in 1572 local resistance groups, now known as the Sea Beggars, were sufficiently successful in taking over a large number of Dutch towns to install William of Orange, once a close Hapsburg ally but now the pre-eminent leader of resistance to Philip's authority.

By 1573 Alva had been recalled in disgrace because of his failure to recover the lost areas, and English volunteers were going in large numbers to support the Protestant rebels. Although the cost of the wars saw Spain go bankrupt in 1575, throughout Elizabeth's reign there was little understanding of just how strained Spain's resources were. Most English observers remained fearful that after Philip had reconquered the Netherlands and destroyed Protestantism there, he would move on to conquer heretic England as well. When English volunteers went to fight with the Protestant forces in the Netherlands, Elizabeth carefully (and mendaciously) explained to the Spanish that they went despite her explicit instructions to remain in England.

There were several reasons to fear King Philip's intentions, beyond the most obvious consideration that with the accession of Elizabeth England had once again turned away from the Catholic faith and papal jurisdiction. It had also become a major supporter and refuge of what Philip perceived as a new and very dangerous heresy; both Huguenots and Protestant refugees from the Netherlands had fled to England in considerable numbers. Once there they often found the means (and assistance) to plan counter-attacks on their Spanish overlords. Elizabeth, however, continually resisted the calls of such men as Leicester to be allowed openly to lead English troops in support of William of Orange. Formally she still insisted that all monarchs had the right to define their subjects' religion, and, moreover, in the early 1570s she still distrusted French intentions in the Netherlands. This was so much the case that Leicester suffered yet another rebuff during her 1575 visit to Kenilworth; one more of the magnificent staged events Elizabeth refused even to watch was a mock battle designed to restate Leicester's case for being allowed to fight with William of Orange against the Spanish Catholic forces.

Renewed pressure against the Elizabethan settlement

It is likely that by 1572 there were more Protestants than Catholics among Elizabeth's subjects. But by that time Elizabeth was facing renewed pressure against the accommodations she had made in the religious settlement of 1559. There had always been those who deplored the apparent lack of truly Protestant zeal of her preferred official religion. By 1561 a range of differences in practice were creeping into some church services, disregarding the uniformity of forms and ceremonial she had decreed. Her protests against the variations, and the actions taken by Matthew Parker, her Archbishop of Canterbury, had little effect at the parish level among the disaffected. Elizabeth's own view was that uniformity in the reformed religions was an absolute necessity if her Church of England was to survive the critiques posed, particularly by Catholics. It was not only clergy who dissented from Elizabeth's preferred uniformity; many among all levels of the landed gentry, who controlled many parish benefices, felt free to pursue their understanding of a purer reformed religion. Parker, for example, regarded Leicester as one (but only one) of his more consistent and powerful opponents as the Archbishop struggled to enforce the queen's preferred order.

One remarkable attempt to influence the queen's own position was made in 1570. Edward Dering, a notable scholar and one-time chaplain to the Duke of Norfolk, had been chosen to preach before the queen, always a promising opening for a cleric seeking preferment. His sermon, however, now known often as the 'Unruly Heifer' sermon, because of a scriptural analogy clearly referring to Elizabeth, rebuked her strongly for her continuing use of the cross and candles in her chapel, as well as for sitting idly by while many abuses, which Dering enumerated at great length, continued to corrupt the English church. For the many offences Dering gave her, Elizabeth cancelled his right to preach, but perhaps the more interesting aftermath of that event was that the sermon had appeared in 16 editions by 1603, making it the most printed sermon of her reign. This illustrates just how difficult was her search for her preferred uniformity.

That difficulty, of course, was considerable before even mentioning the continuing Catholic presence in her realm. In 1570, after the Northern Uprising's threat had been defeated, Elizabeth had issued a statement reiterating her lack of interest in investigating individual conscience in religious matters, and asserting the Uprising was the work of those who had flouted the laws by refusing to attend church. But, whatever many of her subjects thought, she and – perhaps more reluctantly – her council showed little interest in several anti-Catholic bills discussed in the 1571 parliament. Only one, designed to prevent the importation of any more papal bulls after the scandal of *Regnans in Excelsis*, declaring Elizabeth an illegitimate monarch, was treated seriously.

Other proposals included a bill to punish those who left the kingdom without royal permission, one to penalise 'massing' priests who travelled the country disguised as serving men, and one aimed at fining those Catholics who attended church, as legally required, but failed to take communion. It is suggestive of ongoing religious divisions as well as indicating Elizabeth's reluctance to push for more conformity that most of those bills disappeared in the House of Lords. The one to pass all processes was that condemning any person who reconciled another with the 'Bishop of Rome' but even it was not invoked before 1577. By then, that inclination to accommodate those Catholics who made some gesture towards conformity with the law had come increasingly under question as missionary priests re-entered England and a new Catholic evangelism began.

6 Old problems and new in the queen's middle years

Catholic Elizabethans and continuing problems

The successful restoration of Catholicism in the reign of Mary I posed serious problems for Elizabeth. Although a number of Catholics had fled after her accession in 1558, usually to Spain, many more had remained in England, in what was to become an increasingly suspect environment for them. Despite the 1564 Council of Trent's decree that Catholics should never attend Protestant services, many continued to go to their parish church, but over time recusancy (refusal to attend church) became more common, and fines for non-attendance were increased. In 1571 Elizabeth had protected the right of Catholics to be present at church services without being required to take communion. Her policy of passive toleration of quiescent Catholics was always one which more zealous Protestants deplored, but the queen's religious pragmatism was accepted, if not always admired, by her advisers. Her policy preference, however, for tolerating her Catholic subjects seemed much more dangerous after the 1570 papal bull that no Catholics should obey the English 'pretended' queen, or her laws.

At the same time, government officials became aware of an increasing number of Catholic works being smuggled into England. One response came in July 1570, with the first of a number of royal proclamations against importing, distributing or reading any Catholic works. Other proclamations soon followed, ordering the destruction of any such seditious (i.e. Catholic) books. In 1574 the English seminary established at Douai in 1568 sent its first Catholic priests back to England; by 1578 there were 20 new priests from Douai. Many more young men went there for training, and in 1579 a second seminary was opened, this time in Rome. All these seminary priests came officially not as missionaries but to renew the faith of existing Catholics, with explicit instructions against trying to convert Protestants. This relatively passive approach meant little to the Protestant authorities, given the earlier papal attack on Elizabeth's rule and the missionary priests' insistence that their Catholic followers defy Elizabethan requirements for regular parish church attendance. However limited the returning Catholic clergy claimed their objectives to be, Elizabeth and her regime viewed them as a serious threat to the political stability of the Protestant ascendancy.

By 1580, there were about a hundred seminary priests in England, and that year the first Jesuits, Edmund Campion and Robert Parsons, also arrived. Their instructions again were to focus on recovering Catholics; they were again explicitly forbidden to interfere in matters of state, or to speak against Elizabeth. They also brought a statement from Pope Gregory XIII that the now infamous papal bull *Regnans in Excelsis* was suspended until such time as it could be enforced. Given the increasing tensions between Elizabeth's regime and Philip of Spain, however, English Protestants did not find that qualification reassuring, not least because, with Philip's acquisition of the Portuguese crown that year, Spanish sea power and resources had been greatly enhanced. There was much more English hostility towards Catholics, and increasingly torture, particularly on the rack, was used to extract confessions from suspect offenders. The first execution of a seminary priest was carried out in 1577, and in the following years the authorities repeatedly called for the capture of Jesuits and seminary priests. Pressure on existing Catholic subjects was also increased. From punishment by fines and imprisonment, penalties for Catholic activists were increased to include torture and increasingly, particularly for Jesuits, death. By 1582 all Jesuits, the most feared of the Catholic orders, were declared to be traitors, and three years later all seminary priests were included in that category. As one proclamation explained, given a choice between supporting the Pope and supporting Elizabeth, however much they prevaricated, in the end these people usually declared a higher loyalty to the Pope. That choice made them subject to the traditional traitor's death of hanging, drawing and quartering.

Elizabeth's last Catholic suitor

It was in that increasingly tense religious context that the courtship of Elizabeth and a French Catholic prince was resumed. Her wooer was again Francis, previously Duke of Alençon but now also Duke of Anjou, since his brother, the previous duke, had assumed the French throne as Henry III in 1574. When the negotiations were reopened in 1578, they were still directed to addressing the international situation, with little personal inclination on either side. Anjou's wooing of Elizabeth was always related to his search for more aid in the Netherlands against the Spanish; in 1578 he was in a parlous position, short of money, losing the trust of his most important Dutch allies and faced with a new leader of the Spanish interests in Don John of Austria, Philip II's illegitimate half-brother. Don John was celebrated throughout Europe for his devastating defeat of the Ottoman forces at the Battle of Lepanto, and thereafter had a formidable military reputation.

There were rumours that Philip had promised Don John both the hand of Mary Stuart and the English throne if he restored complete Spanish control to the Netherlands. Those rumours had some plausibility since it was widely known Philip had backed the 1570 Ridolfi plot, but in 1574 Philip and Elizabeth had signed a new treaty, which saw Philip expel from the Netherlands not just, as Elizabeth had requested, English exiles but all English Catholics. For a time Elizabeth's hopes for the restoration of a 'peaceable, quiet and well-ordered kingdom' seemed well founded. Although Don John had died in October 1578, before he could make significant headway, Anjou had not achieved much military success and, as importantly, he was mistrusted by William of Orange, the pre-eminent leader of the Dutch revolt. Moreover, although English interests welcomed French support in the Netherlands, they were also concerned to forestall any French ambition to replace waning Hapsburg power there by their own.

In that rather confused international context, it was not surprising that Elizabeth's marriage negotiations with Anjou were initially rather desultory. But they assumed more significance with the arrival in England of Francis of Anjou's representative, Jean de Simier. Elizabeth soon gave him the nickname 'Ape', presumably for the 'simian' connotations of his surname; that was a hopeful sign since nicknames were usually a mark of her approval. She still had serious reservations about the marriage proposal, not least because of her suspicion of Dutch intentions, her strong belief that monarchs had an indisputable right to define the religion of their subjects and her anxiety about deteriorating relations with Spain. Observers did, however, suspect that all those concerns soon gave way to the flirtatious pleasures of discussing marriage with Anjou's envoy. Those delights may have seemed even more compelling after some worrying reports in May 1579 that significant parts of the Netherlands were improving their relations with Philip II, but even before that news was known, Elizabeth had approved renewed discussion of formal marriage negotiations among her councillors.

Their responses were as varied as ever. One obstacle was still the issue of how much religious freedom the Catholic prince should be allowed. But there were new problems, above all anxiety about the dangers of any pregnancy for the queen, now well into her forties. Another issue was the increasing possibility of Anjou himself inheriting the French throne, given that Henry III had produced no heirs. That prospect opened up the unwelcome possibility of a French king married to an English queen, and even, perhaps, a union of the crowns by their putative heir. There was, however, enough support for the proposal that Elizabeth decided to proceed, a decision perhaps made easier for her when she learned that the previous year Dudley had secretly married Lettice, Countess of Essex, a Knollys cousin of hers; as noted elsewhere Lettice was never forgiven for that offence.

For a while it seemed that any reservations about the queen's marriage had vanished, at least on the part of the queen herself. Anjou arrived in England on 17 August 1579, ostensibly travelling incognito. Elizabeth named him 'Frog', reportedly for his bandy legs and husky voice. If the visit was ever secret, it did not long remain so; he was in England for some ten days, and Elizabeth reportedly found him not only sensible in political discussions but also most agreeably attentive to her. There was some romantic role-playing on both sides too, but there is no consensus among historians about the extent to which Elizabeth ever seriously contemplated marriage to him. Her Council was still seriously divided on the matter and, predictably enough, wider protests

increased when it became known in and beyond England that
Anjou was at Elizabeth's court.

Some London preachers, quite probably with encouragement
from their more vociferously Protestant noble and Council patrons,
inveighed against the prospect of such an ungodly union, and in
that they were soon joined by other opponents. This time, Elizabeth
responded with unexpected ferocity to her critics. Thomas Norton,
inveterate pamphleteer and parliament man, was one opponent
committed to the Tower, apparently for a speech made in the 1576
parliamentary session against the Anjou cause. Soon there was a
much more dramatic demonstration of Elizabeth's rage at public
opposition to a marriage. At Anjou's coming to England one
pamphlet particularly hostile to the marriage was printed,
apparently in the thousands, and distributed across much of
Elizabeth's realm. The author, John Stubbs, was a lawyer with
connections at court and even stronger ones with radical Protestants.
His work, the title of which begins *The discoverie of a gaping gulf
whereinto England is like to be swallowed by another French marriage* ...,
was a comprehensive assault on the whole idea of the marriage,
repeating many of the issues once raised at Council.

It did not help Stubbs' defence when the time came that he also
doubted the strength of Elizabeth's commitment to Protestantism.
Elizabeth was finally dissuaded from her first impulse, which was to
have him and two associates summarily hanged. She was persuaded
to allow the matter to go before a jury, and finally accepted that
Stubbs and a major distributor of the pamphlet should 'only' each
have their right hand cut off. The printer of the offending material
was excused that part of the punishment because of his extreme old
age. It reportedly took three blows to remove Stubbs' hand, but
surgeons were present to prevent either victim bleeding to death,
After that the three men were committed to the Tower, where
Stubbs remained for well over a year. An unusually lengthy royal
proclamation was also issued, roundly condemning *A gaping gulf*,
defending the French prince against a range of aspersions, and
reiterating the queen's concern to 'retain betwixt her and her
subjects that devotion of love which hitherto by God's goodness she
hath possessed'.[1]

Several historians have argued that the ferocity of Elizabeth's
response, which was indisputably *her* response rather than that of

her advisers, demonstrated that she did indeed feel a strong emotional attraction to Anjou. This may well be the case, but she also suspected that some of her Council had been feeding arguments against the marriage to Stubbs; she was unable to prove her case, but among those who were mentioned as likely suspects for that leak were both Leicester and Walsingham. That behaviour was the more remarkable since both also knew that while Anjou was in England, Catholic forces with Spanish and papal support had landed in the southwest of Ireland to stir up rebellion there, all of which made the French alliance ever more important. As a further complication for Elizabeth, while some of her advisers could never accept a Catholic marriage, the French court apparently saw her purpose as being to draw them into a full confrontation with Spain while she planned to remain on the sidelines.

England's unmarried queen regnant

For Elizabeth, however, her last credible marriage opportunity had passed, an occasion that may have given rise to another emotional crisis. Some reports described how, as the prospect of that marriage disappeared, she had raged against her councillors' opposition. They all, she said, had families and domestic comforts to support and love them (well, most of them did), but she had none. She may well have seen herself facing a lonely old age, but she always carried much of the responsibility for her continuing single state, having resisted so many possible candidates, some of whom even her councillors had thought eligible. It may, of course, be a sign of her endemic insecurity that she never married or publicly named an heir. Urged from the earliest days of her accession to marry, she had prevaricated and delayed until her age meant that childbearing, even if she could achieve a pregnancy, would be very dangerous. If, as some argue, the reason she never married was because her council could never agree on a suitable candidate, this might suggest she felt less secure as a monarch than her predecessors. Certainly neither Henry VIII nor Mary I ever accepted that their councillors had any role in determining their marriage partners.

That Elizabeth did not marry has been variously explained. One reason may have been the early warning from several of the older nobility that if she married Dudley, to whom she was strongly attracted, there would be an aristocratic revolt. Many nobles always viewed him as a social upstart whose father *and* grandfather had both been executed as traitors. But there were always many other candidates within and beyond Elizabeth's realm. Even if, like her sister, Elizabeth was reluctant to marry a subject, there were good reasons for a foreign marriage, reasons indeed often exploited by Elizabeth in her various failed negotiations. Diplomatic marriages were the norm for royalty rather than the exception, and there was widespread agreement that the marriage treaties of Mary I and Philip II provided a good starting point for future negotiations to ensure England remained fully independent after any foreign marriage of a queen regnant.

But it is perhaps the most familiar feature of Elizabeth's reign that all her marriage projects failed, perhaps because of Elizabeth's affection for Dudley in her earlier years, and in her later years because of the problem of finding a suitable consort of comparable age and status. And always, there was the self-interest of those councillors reluctant to make way for another and likely pre-eminent male at court. Why Elizabeth never married remains an intriguing question, which has given rise to wildly varied verdicts on her queenship but for which there has never been a fully persuasive answer. One factor, not often considered, is what has been described elsewhere in this study as the queen's endemic insecurity, and her related repeated reluctance to make irrevocable decisions.

Refashioning Elizabeth

By the middle years of Elizabeth's reign, there had been significant developments in the images of her and of her reign projected by both her supporters and her critics. Given the widespread and consistent propaganda in support of the Protestant queen from her accession onwards, it is hardly surprising that her religious opponents countered with their alternative accounts. That material often began with the character of Elizabeth's mother, an attack which had the advantage of also drawing attention to the problematic circumstances of Elizabeth's own birth. The widespread speculation about Elizabeth's own sexual adventures, reportedly with Thomas Seymour and later with Robert Dudley, was another feature of hostile gossip, including those reports that she had borne an uncertain number of children. Later, ever more improbable rumours of her sexual adventures with others, including Christopher Hatton, also circulated. Perhaps this was in part the price Elizabeth paid for remaining a single woman. Whatever the reasons, as Catholic resistance to her religious order grew, Elizabeth was increasingly the subject of scurrilous reports published in Europe.

To counter such attacks, from her accession the propaganda *for* Elizabeth was at least as widespread. In what might now seem an ironic touch, many of the terms in which Elizabeth was praised were borrowed from the lexicon of praise for her predecessor and sister, the Catholic Mary I. One example, already touched on, was the moment in Elizabeth's coronation procession when she identified herself as 'Truth, the daughter of Time'. That had been Mary's much-repeated motto, particularly in the Latin form, *Veritas Temporis Filia,* which was used on her 1553 Great Seal, among other places. Many familiar biblical models were cited and proved adaptable for them both. The grounds on which the two queens were praised were, however, mirror images, particularly in religious matters. Officially Mary was exuberantly praised for restoring the Catholic religion, while Elizabeth was constantly praised as the Lord's chosen instrument in saving her realm from Catholicism.

There was, however, at least one quite new way for Protestants to celebrate Elizabeth, and that was by celebrating her Accession Day as marking the (hopefully) final establishment of reformed religion. The practice may have begun, as Helen Hackett suggests, with some Elizabethan official making an inspired career move in the first decade of her reign,[2] but it took time for the innovation to spread across England. Records from 1567 show that Elizabeth's accession day was marked by bell ringing within some London parishes. Oxford and Cambridge also both adopted the practice relatively early, but the practice spread much more slowly in the north.

By the 1580s, however, the Accession Day celebrations had widened to include tilts and festivities at the royal court and, gradually, bonfires, beer and often feasting as well as music and church services at the parish level. Formally, it apparently became a 'national' celebration for Protestants, combining the accession of their queen, the triumph of their religion and the miraculous repudiation of popery, as preachers that day often chose to emphasise. And so it became a festive day in which all levels of English society, if not all Christians, could share. The celebrations continued in some places decades after the death of the queen whose accession day they marked, despite attempts by subsequent monarchs to appropriate the celebrations for *their* accession day.

The long-standing tradition that Elizabeth was effectively the first English female monarch and had to invent the modes of successful female rule has been significantly qualified in recent years, since more historical attention has been paid to the reign of Mary I. Mary's rule was closely observed by her younger sister, and many precedents set by the one are now understood to have been adopted and adapted by the other. But one means Elizabeth used to enforce her authority with the men about her that Mary never encouraged was the courtly use of the language of chivalric love. Used by many of Elizabeth's courtiers and advisers, that language, ostensibly of erotic but sublimated desire, could easily become a compelling metaphor of political loyalty. But as historians suggest, that language had provided some grounds for executing Anne Boleyn, which demonstrated graphically the extent to which the use of erotic metaphors could invoke other dangers. That may be the reason that Elizabeth willingly received such language as appropriate, but seems to have avoided reciprocating in comparable terms. The most obvious exception was some of her letters to Robert (Robin) Dudley. The undoubted affection they reflect marked a particularly close friendship, but almost certainly no more than that.

When, on the other hand, Christopher Hatton wrote to Elizabeth 'I love yourself. I cannot lack you. I am taught to prove it by the wish and desire I find to be with you,' such language could indeed be easily misinterpreted, perhaps even explaining the (very improbable) rumours of a sexual liaison between him and his queen. But as demonstrated by the extent to which he used the same language about the queen when writing to fellow courtiers and advisers, the language carried at least as many connotations of worship and adoration as of lust, and was a discourse Elizabeth reportedly expected from her courtiers of all age until her dying days, in her eighth decade.

Elizabeth, the Virgin Queen

As a female monarch Queen Elizabeth was unusual; as an unmarried monarch she was unique in post-1066 English history. As the negotiations for the Anjou marriage faded, Elizabeth was increasing described in the language of a Virgin Queen, even as the traditional cult of the Virgin Mary came under ferocious official attack in England. One benefit of addressing her in such terms was their formal erasure of those still-current scandalous rumours of her relations with Dudley, although for her enemies those tales never entirely disappeared. By 1578 some poets had begun praising Elizabeth for her virginity, often in terms reminiscent of the attributes of the Virgin Mary and of that classical iconography that celebrated women who, by their chastity, had acquired remarkable authority over men.

It could be no surprise that the implied references to Elizabeth echoing the Virgin Mary led to increased hostile Catholic attacks on the queen. Her parentage came under more ferocious attack, particularly her mother who, as her husband had publicly insisted, had had sexual relations with her own brother as well as several other men. What sort of person, the writers rhetorically asked, could possibly result from such parents? But the counter-attack to those Catholic polemics was very strong, and increasingly focused on Elizabeth's unique position as unmarried queen. Not only did those printed polemics continue for the rest of her reign, but portraits of her were deployed to the same end. The most impressive portraits for this purpose were the series known as the 'Sieve Portraits', the earliest of which may have been painted in 1579, and the most spectacular of which is the version held in Siena (see Plate 7). The sieve itself had become a familiar symbol for chastity, popularised by Petrarch's version of a classical Roman myth, and the painting also shows Elizabeth with her councillors well behind her.

The transition from urging a queen to secure the safety of her realm by marrying and providing an heir to praising that queen for rising above conventional expectations of marriage and child-bearing took many forms. One of the more consistent forms of praise was that which John Lyly, also cited in *Euphues and His England* (1580), used when he wrote of:

this chaste Virgin Elizabeth ... who by the space of twenty and
odd years with continual peace ... with sundry miracles, contrary
to all hope, has governed that noble Island. ... What greater
marvel has happened since the beginning of the world, than for
a Virgin to make the whole world ... to honour her, and [that]
with her sword in the sheath, with her armour in the Tower,
with her soldiers in their gowns.[3]

Similar themes were repeated for the rest of her reign, as illustrated
by Lady Russell's welcome for the queen to her place at Bisham in
1592. A woman of limited means, she made no effort to rival such
spectacular welcomes as the Kenilworth or Elvetham celebrations
for the queen discussed previously, but she did reiterate what had
become common themes for praising the queen. The theme for the
occasion was set by a 'wildman' who saluted her with the observation
that her virtue conquered his fierceness and her beauty his madness.
She was also that day celebrated as, 'the wonder of the world and
nature's glory, leading affection in fetters, Virginity's slave;
embracing mildness with justice, Majesty's twins'.[4] The welcome
reiterated that by her complete subordination of her passions,
Elizabeth had indeed become a profoundly rational ruler, as great as
any male, ensuring peace and plenty for her realm – as well as
upholding true religion. But few were prepared still to confront the
most obvious consequence of the queen's permanent virginity,
which was the manifest failure to provide a plausible heir who
could be an appropriate alternative to the imprisoned and ever
more discredited Mary Stuart.

England and European troubles

Despite the idyllic description of Elizabeth's realm with which
Lady Russell had welcomed the queen, by 1592 the political and
social realities were actually much more difficult in both foreign
and domestic spheres. The international situation became more
threatening in the years after Elizabeth neither married Anjou nor
established a formal alliance with France. Her realm had been left
more vulnerable to Catholic and Spanish hostility, and, briefly,
there had also been renewed tensions with Scotland. In late 1579,
Esmé Stuart, related to James VI through his father's line but raised

in France, had returned to Scotland and quickly gained influence over the young king, then 12 years old. Fears that Stuart had arrived in Scotland with the backing of the Duke of Guise to overthrow the Protestant order and restore Mary to the Scottish throne faded when Stuart refused to challenge James's rule and publicly converted to Protestantism. He did, however, support another scheme, also devised by Guise in 1582–3, a scheme with which the young James VI briefly flirted. That project, to invade England and place Mary Stuart on the English throne, was aborted only when Philip II refused to support it. For Philip, apparently, restoring Catholicism was not worth pursuing if the price was strengthening French influence in Scotland, a view reinforced by Anjou's continuing involvement in the confused religious and political struggles of the Spanish Netherlands.

Whatever his concerns about French international ambitions, Philip was no better disposed to heretic England. This was partly because of his knowledge that Elizabeth had made significant financial contributions to Protestant forces in France in the first wars of religion there, and had also sent large amounts of money, as well as the men she insisted were volunteers, to the Netherlands as Philip fought for complete control of his territories. His growing hostility to Elizabeth, whom he had defended from French enmity when she first came to the throne, was increased further by Elizabeth's tacit support for the growing number of raids on Spanish possessions by English privateers, private citizens with a royal commission to attack the ships of hostile countries. John Hawkins, one of the first Elizabethan privateers, had begun his career by attacking French ships with the full support of Mary I and Philip. But after Mary's death in 1558 he widened his range to include slave trading, which meant flouting Spain's declared spheres of influence. And indeed Spain was then by far the wealthiest and most powerful contemporary realm; king of Portugal from 1580, Philip then ruled an empire which had conquered the Philippines, asserted control in Peru and extended its authority into India, Indonesia and China. Even the Ottoman Empire had declared a truce with the mighty Spanish king. It is hardly surprising that privateers such as Francis Drake found their assaults on Spanish trade and Spanish possessions in the following years frequently lucrative.

Drake, in his remarkable three-year voyage around the world, raided numerous Spanish settlements in the Caribbean and Pacific, assuring his hapless Spanish captives that he had his queen's approval for his actions. However dubious that claim, when he returned to England in late 1580 Elizabeth was among those who made an excellent profit on their investment in his voyage. Just how much the Spanish had lost to Drake's activities may never be known, because Drake and Elizabeth agreed that if the total was never made public the Spanish could not seek accurate restitution. It was indeed a realm of vast resources, and Drake clearly took his share of it. The Spanish ambassador, Mendoza, reported that from Drake's ships vast quantities of gold, silver and pearls were taken to the Tower for safekeeping. Observers valued the loot's worth at somewhere between one and two million pesos. It is also clear that for her own part Elizabeth did well out of that enterprise.

In May 1583, therefore, the Spanish ambassador in Paris was hopeful when he reported to his king another scheme against Elizabeth which Philip might choose to support. As already mentioned, the Duke of Guise had turned to working with the English Catholics to restore their faith as the official religion. Once again, however, other events deflected that threat to Elizabeth, at least in the short term. In early 1584, her one-time suitor, Anjou, died, a death which threatened the future of the Netherlands, where he had recently been having a more successful campaign. But the implications of his death for France were even more serious, since he was the last of the sons of Catherine de Medici and Henry II. The next heir to the throne was the man who would become the first Bourbon king, Henry of Navarre, who had long been a committed Huguenot. Faced with the possibility of a Protestant king of France, Henry of Guise, like all his family devoted to the Catholic interest, turned away from foreign intrigues and placed himself at the head of the French Catholic League. By December 1584, he concluded a formal treaty with Philip of Spain, and within months religious wars had broken out once more in France. That, in turn, left Elizabeth's England relatively isolated, and Spain freer to concentrate on the struggles in the Netherlands, which now could look only to England for any hope of external support for the anti-Spanish forces. Elizabeth's priority was, as ever, to avoid provoking outright war with Spain; she therefore continued to resist all attempts to involve her officially in any foreign wars. It was, however, becoming clear that the English volunteers 'unofficially' fighting in the Netherlands were most unlikely to have any significant impact on the experienced Hapsburg forces there.

More of Mary Stuart's plight, plots and problems

Hopes of restoring Mary Stuart to her Scottish throne, albeit as co-monarch with her son and with careful restrictions, did not immediately die with the failed attempt of 1582–3. The project, however, became ever more difficult after what is now known as the Ruthven Raid. Protestant leaders of a counter-coup in Scotland seized James's person in August 1582, took control of his government and forced the return of Esmé Stuart, now Duke of Lennox, to France. The new leaders also barred any further communication between Mary and her son. Nevertheless, when Guise signalled his continuing interest in attempts to restore Mary to Scotland, she assured her Spanish contacts that her main aims were to convert her son to Catholicism and to secure an alliance between him and the king of Spain. As always, to Elizabeth's representatives she declared her overriding wish to 'serve her good sister', but with the proviso that she could, of course, commit to nothing until she had discussed with her son her future status. But any such discussion had been rendered impossible by the events of the Ruthven Raid.

It is easy to mock Mary's undoubtedly duplicitous accounts of her hopes and purposes, but she had been in English hands for some 15 years, with worsening health problems and with the irritation of knowing that her Guise relatives were appropriating much of her French revenues. The chances of the woman who had been a queen all her life ever regaining her freedom, let alone her throne, were steadily diminishing. Having no power base of her own, she was entirely dependent on others, whose interests were never straightforwardly hers. Her final chance for release may well have been the project which Elizabeth had promoted for Mary to return to Scotland with appropriate assurances from her son of her security there. That project, however, had been abandoned in 1583, not least because of James's own reluctance to accept any responsibility for his mother or to contribute any expenses to supporting her.

Even before that scheme had been abandoned, Elizabeth's principal secretary Walsingham, by then enhancing his skills in intelligence gathering, had uncovered Guise's recent plan to invade England, an invasion to be backed by financial support from Philip II and the pope. In 1583 he also uncovered a number of English supporters prepared to do whatever it took to rescue the imprisoned Scottish queen and place her on Elizabeth's throne. From the start Mary herself was a willing player in the conspiracy, and presumably accepted the implied assassination of Elizabeth with equanimity. One lesser player involved in those far-reaching plans was Francis Throckmorton, who was implicated by plotting with the Spanish ambassador, Mendoza, and with English and Scottish Catholic sympathisers as well some Jesuits. Walsingham was soon well informed about the plan which, despite the numbers involved, resulted in the execution only of Throckmorton, the temporary imprisonment of several prominent English Catholics and the expulsion of Mendoza. Since the Spanish ambassador was not replaced, communications between Mary and Spanish interests became even more difficult. But the most important consequence of the Throckmorton Plot was that Elizabeth was finally forced to acknowledge Mary's untrustworthiness, and abandoned all hope of being able to return her to Scotland, let alone as co-ruler with her son. James was at least consistent in his preference to have Mary remain in England, entirely at Elizabeth's expense.

Mary's isolation increased, in part as a result of the final and acrimonious collapse of the marriage of Shrewsbury and Bess of Hardwick, her keepers since 1568. One result of that long guardianship is some superb needlework which the two women worked on, including three magnificent hangings still on display at Oxburgh Hall, but it ended in mutual acrimony. In 1584 the elderly Ralph Sadler was ordered to take over responsibility for the Scottish queen's safe keeping, but any improvement in her circumstances was soon undermined by another attempt to assassinate Elizabeth on behalf of Catholic interests. One William Parry, once a member of parliament, in the 1580s working either as a spy or a traitor, and always a confusing character, apparently plotted to kill her and was duly executed in 1585. Parry claimed his plot had been intended to entrap others, but whatever his real purpose, his apparent conspiracy fed the already widespread

Protestant anxiety, itself heightened by the assassination of William of Orange which was believed to have been ordered and/or rewarded by Philip of Spain. Political assassination was becoming, it seemed, a more common international strategy, and Englishmen were particularly nervous since, if Elizabeth was assassinated, her next heir was still assumed to be Mary Stuart.

After the two assassination alarms, from Throckmorton and Parry, Elizabeth's councillors promoted a Bond of Association for her loyal subjects to sign. Those who signed the Bond thereby swore to obey their queen, to defend her against all enemies and, above all, to never accept as her successor anyone in whose interest any attack on the queen was made. The Bond of Association, signed by many thousands of Elizabeth's subjects, was designed to avert the threat that Mary Stuart could gain Elizabeth's throne by treacherous means, whether she was demonstrably involved in a conspiracy or simply the 'pretended successor'. Elizabeth resisted accepting the proposal until the wording was altered to exclude James VI from such provision, the first indication perhaps that she deemed him an acceptable successor to herself. The most explicit aspect of the Bond's final form in the Act 'for the Surety of the Queen's most royal person' (1585) confirmed that any possible successor to Elizabeth who was found to be implicated in any way in an assassination attempt on her was liable for judgment and execution within the terms of the Act in the same way as any other conspirator.[5] That provision was directly aimed at Mary Stuart.

Given her refusal to name any heir for almost three decades, the wording of the Act is significant in part because Elizabeth finally, and however privately, indicated her likely heir, although she refused ever to acknowledge her decision openly until she was on her deathbed. And in 1586, during the negotiations leading to the Treaty of Berwick, signed in July as a 'league of amity' between England and Scotland, Elizabeth again privately indicated James VI was her preferred heir. Publicly she agreed to pay him an annual pension, albeit one rather less than he had hoped for and delivered only spasmodically. Although many understood reports of that pension to be an acknowledgement of his new status, for many more the question of who was to succeed the present queen remained dangerously open. When James's mother heard rumours of Elizabeth's acceptance of James as her heir, Mary assured some English supporters that hope was what made her imprisonment endurable. To others, however, she soon insisted she would leave her succession rights to the English throne to Philip of Spain, particularly if James had not converted to Catholicism by the time of her death.

Whatever may have been her private plans, Mary's conditions became more trying when her next and final keeper, Amyas Paulet, took over duties from the aged Sadler. But still Elizabeth's regime, at the insistence of the queen herself, continued to maintain Mary with considerable dignity. Elizabeth met some of the costs of Mary's food and fuel, and ensured she still dined under a cloth of estate. Her high status was also reflected by the fact that two courses of 16 choices each were still presented to her at every meal. However deprived she regarded herself as being, Mary's household numbered over 40, and Paulet found great difficulty in keeping them all isolated from the wider world, forbidden to talk even to members of his household except in his presence, or to leave Tutbury (where Mary had been returned) unless with a guard. Mary still complained of the inadequacy of her accommodation and furnishings, but admitted to enjoying the hunting she was allowed, albeit always with some 40 or 50 servants, some armed, to prevent any attempt at escape or rescue. And gradually Paulet managed to establish what he hoped would prove a comprehensive system to prevent any secret communications whatsoever between anyone within Mary's household and any conspiracy-minded supporters within or beyond England.

Mary may have suspected that Elizabeth had privately acknowledged James as heir to the English throne. There were suggestions at the time that Elizabeth had done so in order to separate him from his mother's interests, but that is to assume he had previously protected her. Whatever the relations between the previous and the current Scottish rulers, however, Mary continued to plot for the death of Elizabeth and her own accession in England. It may be a mark of her growing desperation that she did so while fully aware that by recent legislation any such conspiracy, if discovered, would result in her own death.

The growing pressure to open warfare

While the presence of the dethroned Scottish queen was proving to be a recurrent threat to Elizabeth's life, her regime was also facing increased dangers internationally, because of the deepening hostility between Catholic and Protestant forces across many parts of Europe, most forcibly expressed, perhaps, by the events of the 1572 St Bartholomew's Day Massacre across France. Ever since her early interventions in France and the humiliating results of that in 1563, Elizabeth had avoided any official declaration of war. Instead, as already noted, for several years when Spanish authorities complained about the many English fighting for the Protestant cause in the Spanish Netherlands, Elizabeth declared that such soldiers joined the wars against her express will. But religious difference between Christians was becoming an ever more important component in the changing reasons of European wars. They were increasingly fought less for the traditional causes of chivalric battles for royal honour or dynastic aggrandisement, and more on the grounds of religious difference and competing regional commercial interests. One practice which violated all the traditional chivalric values was that of assassinating political leaders, but assassination was now gaining at least some religious sanction. The codes of war were indeed changing.

For England, the Hapsburg wars now represented a deepening crisis in the Netherlands, given the death of Anjou in June 1584 and the assassination of William of Orange. Elizabeth and her council above all feared the probability that, should Philip recover full control of that region, he would use it as a base from which to attack England. In his eyes, England was ruled by a heretic queen and had become not only a bastion of heresy but a commercial irritant because of the recurrent English raids on Spanish trade and settlements. But despite the imminent threats of Spanish control being restored across all of the Netherlands, Elizabeth was still reluctant to face the expenses and uncertainties of war, still resisted open warfare, still was reluctant to sanction what would be the first English-declared war with Spain since the 14th century. It was not just the final break with such a long-standing alliance which concerned her. She knew she was likely to get little help from other erstwhile allies, since on the one hand the French Wars of Religion had resumed, and on the other Antwerp was in imminent danger of falling to the Spanish forces. Elizabeth's England, the next target of Philip's 'mortal enmity' against all non-Catholics, was apparently without viable support.

And still relations between England and Spain continued to deteriorate. In May 1585 Philip had seized a number of English ships in his ports (which were there at his request, importing grain). He later released them, but Elizabeth had already responded by sending Drake to attack ports in the Caribbean. He did some damage, but his plunder brought less profit than had been hoped; it did, however, reinforce Philip's view that an attack on England (for which preliminary plans were already in place) was essential both to restore true religion there and to secure his position in the Netherlands. Reports of his intentions were circulating in England, and the situation was deteriorating to the extent that, despite her consistent reluctance to be embroiled in warfare, Elizabeth was forced to recognise the dangers facing her and her Protestant realm.

Elizabeth was finally persuaded that she should formally side with the enemies of Spain in the Netherlands, if only to forestall a direct attack on her own realms. But again she prevaricated and hesitated, hoping that some other option would appear. While she still hoped that France would again come to the aid of the Netherlands, it soon became clear that would be impossible given the ongoing religious conflicts in France. After other diversionary attempts, she finally agreed in August 1585 to sign the Treaty of Nonsuch. By the terms of that treaty, she agreed to help defend the Netherlands against Spanish forces, promising them financial aid, 6,000 soldiers and a large number of mounted men.

Her support for the revolt of the Netherlands against their lawful ruler was, in her mind, a contradiction of her own repeated description of the royal authority, including the right to define the realm's religion. Moreover, as she well understood, her formal intervention thereby transformed the struggles in the Netherlands from what Philip had regarded as a purely domestic affair to a formally declared international military confrontation. Leicester was finally granted what so much of his entertainments at Kenilworth had been aimed at in 1575, and put in command of the expedition. Nevertheless Elizabeth, according to the earl's own account to Walsingham, was most reluctant to let him go, worried by a recurrence an illness she suffered, and by a fear that in his absence she might die. Leicester had several other problems with his queen, most of them now arising from the consideration that he had recently, and secretly, married the queen's cousin.

Nevertheless Elizabeth did send him to rescue the Netherlands, where he was soon offered and accepted the appointment as their governor-general. He may have seemed an obvious candidate for that position as a known backer of the Netherlands' cause since the early 1570s, as Elizabeth's favourite and an earl. But he failed to consult Elizabeth before accepting the position; Elizabeth was enraged by his elevation to official leader of the Netherlands against their Spanish overlord. There were reports that the queen was particularly affronted that Leicester's new wife was welcomed with almost royal splendour. In the event, his appointment had little longer-term impact. Despite his long commitment to their cause, most historians now agree that Dudley was probably too old and certainly too seriously lacking in military experience when he took over the command he had so long wished for.

But he also faced many difficulties. Even after she accepted his new position, Elizabeth displayed her usual reluctance to meet anything like the full costs of the expedition. At least Leicester avoided direct responsibility for one humiliation, even if that was more from good luck then good management. He left his post to return for England at the end of 1586, thereby avoiding direct responsibility for the disastrous defections of Sir William Stanley, whom he had placed in charge of Deventer, and of Rowland York, in charge of Zutphen. Both men handed their commands to the Spanish early in 1587 and took with them some 700 English soldiers, many of whom then fought for the Spanish. Although there has never been agreement on why either leader did so, both men were branded by English observers as Catholic traitors and their actions used to illustrate once more how easily English Catholics would betray both their country and their monarch. Nor did it allay the resultant anxieties of the States General that, as Leicester left for England, Elizabeth was known to be negotiating with the Duke of Parma for a settlement which might return the condition of the Netherlands to the more accommodating and tolerant days of Charles V. In brief, she was still, as ever, seeking to avoid a state of formal war with Spain. But it was becoming increasingly hard for the queen to avoid being confronted with some very difficult choices indeed, both at home and abroad, not least because of the deepening religious divisions across Europe.

7 Killing a queen and facing invasion, 1585–9

These were the years when Elizabeth faced two of the greatest crises of her life. The first was when she was finally forced to accept that as long as Queen Mary lived, her own life would be in danger; the second was when the Spanish Armada of 1588 came so near to achieving the ambition of Philip II of Spain to replace Elizabeth by a Catholic monarch (something he could much more easily manage after the execution of Mary, the strongest Catholic claimant to the English throne.)

Mary Stuart's last conspiracy

Soon after Amyas Paulet assumed her guardianship in 1585, Mary Stuart asked that she be removed from the increasingly dilapidated Tutbury Castle, and from there she was moved to Chartley, a moated manor house. That move suited Paulet's plans very well, for there he was able to establish ever more tightly controlled access to the household. Above all, he was able to examine all messages exchanged between Mary and the world beyond Chartley; indeed, the Scottish queen's guardian openly inspected such correspondence before it was handed to her. Paulet's procedures proved so effective in isolating Mary from any would-be conspirators that finally Gilbert Gifford undertook to find new and more secret lines of communications with her. Gifford, one of the numerous Catholic exiles on the continent, had the added advantage of being a native of Staffordshire, where Mary was being held,
    Perhaps Gifford was already a double agent when he undertook that task. The official account had it that he was arrested as he

returned to England, where he was taken to England's spymaster; he soon accepted Walsingham's suggestion that they should cooperate in allowing and recording secret communications for Mary in and out of Chartley. By their plan, secret messages were to be hidden in the barrels of the weekly beer delivery to the Chartley household. By that arrangement, Walsingham's men would copy all those ostensibly secret messages before they went in and as they came out. From January 1586 the system apparently worked well as a backlog of secret messages up to two years old went through, and were all carefully copied by Walsingham's men. When the brewer understood the value of his cooperation, his charge for his services increased considerably. The information that was uncovered was worth the money, at least in the eyes of all those who understood that the Scottish queen was still a serious threat to Protestant England.

In June 1586, Mary received a letter (already carefully copied) suggesting she should write 'kindly' to one Anthony Babington, whom she had known as a page when she had been in Shrewsbury's custody. Babington responded to Mary's first rather general letter of goodwill with a letter which addressed her as his 'sovereign lady and Queen'. As he reminded Mary, they had all been freed from obedience to Elizabeth by the papal excommunication of 1570. He set out his plans for her rescue, including the information that six friends would undertake 'the dispatch of the usurping competitor' as a necessary part of the scheme. In her reply, she showed no hesitation in accepting the plan and offered her own advice on how to proceed in several ways.

Walsingham's men followed the usual practice, and carefully copied each communication before returning it to the appointed place in the beer barrel. It may have been that while Mary's reply was being copied, a postscript was added, asking for the names of the six men who were Babington's proposed assassins. That possible interpolation has been used to argue that Mary was framed for apparently condoning Elizabeth's assassination but, if so, it was hardly a necessary addition. Nowhere else had she shown any resistance to plans involving the queen's likely death. That, after all, had also been the necessary corollary for earlier schemes to install Mary on the English throne and restore Catholicism to England. Moreover, copies were made of Mary's subsequent letters to Mendoza, by then Philip's representative in Paris, and to other supporters on the continent; they also proved to be full of optimism and good cheer about the 'design' under way. Mary, still with no suspicion that every word she received or dispatched was being copied, was finally arrested in August, when Walsingham had decided he had all the information he needed and that it would be dangerous to allow further development of the plot.

Mary had been invited to a hunt on a nearby property but was arrested on the way, as were her two secretaries; then her rooms at Chartley were searched for further evidence of her plots. Elizabeth's response to the conspiracy was to write to Paulet in terms of righteous distress and outrage. 'Let your wicked murderess know how ... her vile deserts compel these orders; and bid her from me, ask God for forgiveness for her treacherous dealings toward the saviour of her life many a year, to the intolerable peril of my own.'[1] But, whatever her outrage, in the weeks, indeed months, that followed, the English queen showed deep reluctance to even contemplate the obvious response to Mary's role in planning her assassination.

For Babington and his co-conspirators, events moved quickly and lethally. His first letter to Mary was dated 6 July; her response was sent on 17 July and received by him on the 31st. When his co-conspirator Ballard was arrested on 4 August, Babington's first response was to order another co-conspirator to go immediately to court to kill Elizabeth, but by then the information gathered was so complete that all the conspirators were immediately rounded up. They were tried in mid-September, and all executed on 20 and 21 September by the traditional traitors' death, although the 'lesser' conspirators hanged on the second day were not disembowelled until they were dead. Some say this relative clemency was at Elizabeth's command, others that it was because of the crowd's reaction to the live disembowelling the first day. It may well have been both, given the sight of so many suffering the full penalty the previous day.

Elizabeth as reluctant regicide

The speed with which those conspirators met their fate was in marked contrast with the pace of events which led finally to Mary's execution. The reason for that was Elizabeth's profound reluctance to be seen to execute a dethroned monarch, even one so active in yet another plot to assassinate herself. Mary Stuart also did what she could to delay proceedings against herself, adopting the argument that as a foreign monarch she could not be judged in England since she was subject neither to English law nor to an English monarch. But after the plot was exposed, she had to submit to being moved again, this time from Chartley to Fotheringhay Castle, a grim and secure castle of Norman origins in Northamptonshire. There, over 40 Commissioners assembled on 11 October, many of them members of the House of Lords and at least one a Catholic. When she was brought before them, Mary refused to accept their jurisdiction, being, as she reiterated, a queen herself. She consistently denied all knowledge of the Babington correspondence, all of which was read to her from the surviving copies, and insisted that she would respond to questions only if she appeared before either Elizabeth or the parliament.

After several attempts to dissuade her, and despite a promising line of argument from Hatton encouraging her at least to clear her name of such heinous charges, the commissioners had made no progress with the charges against Mary. They were probably relieved to receive Elizabeth's urgent instructions not to pronounce sentence before they returned to London. There they met again on 25 October. This time Mary's two secretaries Nau and Curle appeared before the Commissioners. Both confirmed, as the record reports, 'without hope of reward' that the Babington correspondence transcripts were indeed a true account of the plans for assassination and invasion, and a true account of Mary's response.

That was deemed grounds enough for the commissioners to declare Mary guilty of seeking the death of Elizabeth, and therefore subject to the penalties of the Act for the Queen's Safety. Parliament met four days later, and both houses confirmed that Mary, having been found guilty, should suffer the punishment prescribed by law. Only Elizabeth, it would seem, continued to resist, even asking the Commons to suggest some penalty other than execution. They replied that they had no alternative suggestion. And still Elizabeth sought some resolution other than confirming Mary's execution. Her hesitations were never simply due to squeamishness on her part, for among the alternatives she pursued was one in an indirect message to Paulet that perhaps he might find another, less public way to 'ease her [Elizabeth's] burden'. To Elizabeth's considerable irritation, Paulet who was a staunch Puritan with a firm belief in legal process, refused to be involved in any furtive murder of Mary.

Elizabeth had good political reasons to prevent Mary's judicial execution, quite apart from the difficult fact that they were both crowned monarchs. One followed from the recently improving relations with James VI. Indeed the Treaty of Berwick had been under negotiation even as the Babington plot was taking shape in July 1586. It was an important agreement for Elizabeth, primarily because of English concern to secure Scotland's alliance as relations with Spain worsened, ensuring that Scotland would not provide any access for a Spanish attack on England. As the nature of the Babington plot emerged, and its likely consequences for his mother became clearer, James deplored the prospect of one crowned monarch executing another. Formally, he also protested, as had his mother at her trial, that no English monarch had the right to try a Scottish one, and that such an event would undermine his own royal status. That, however was apparently all he felt he could do without endangering the tacit agreement that he was Elizabeth's preferred successor; those around him said that he resented deeply the slur on his mother and the implied insult to the Scottish crown but it was left to other Scots to protest more vehemently against the English killing their rejected queen.

Elizabeth had often demonstrated a deep reluctance to make irrevocable decisions, frequently to the frustration of those around her. But in the case of the fate of Mary, she had particularly strong reasons for that hesitation. Mary was indubitably once rightful queen of Scotland. For Elizabeth at least, the psalm's injunction 'Touch not the Lord's anointed' was a sacred command, quite apart from any consideration of the appalling precedent that would undoubtedly be set if one anointed monarch had another executed. She must also have been well aware that the death of Mary Stuart would ensure an easier path for Philip to invade England. Free from any obligation to support the claim of the French-backed Catholic Scot for the English throne, he would now be free to establish his own preferred candidate.

So Elizabeth delayed the whole issue. More than a month after parliament had confirmed Mary's death sentence even, that verdict had still not been published. Elizabeth finally agreed to the necessary proclamation of Mary's guilt on 4 December, and within days of that the formal warrant for Mary's death was drawn up. Mary wrote her final letter to Elizabeth on 19 December, with all her last requests. But still she lived on. In January both Henry III of France and representatives of James VI again warned Elizabeth against the execution of Mary, warnings which served only to infuriate her and feed rising tensions in England. Nor did James's suggestion that his mother might be sent to some other (unspecified) country where she should could be safely contained strike her as helpful.[2] Rumours of imminent foreign invasions on Mary's behalf emerged in several parts of the south, and Elizabeth's councillors remained frustrated.

The queen finally seemed to change her mind in early February and signed Mary's death warrant, then handing the document to William Davison, a principal secretary of state. Davison took it immediately to Elizabeth's councillors; they sent the signed warrant post-haste to Fotheringhay, where it was quickly acted upon before Elizabeth could create any further delays. All of those involved acted with the utmost speed, precisely to forestall any attempt that Elizabeth might make to halt proceedings again. Elizabeth's subsequent rage must have been in part because of her understanding of just how many of her 'servants' had connived to frustrate her known profound reluctance to agree to Mary's execution. It was indeed a remarkable display of her male advisers acting in the queen's 'best interests' against the queen's known inclinations.

At her execution, Mary was denied a Catholic chaplain, and she refused the services of Richard Fletcher, Dean of Peterborough. When the executioner had completed his task (it took two blows), Fletcher led the cry, 'So perish all the queen's enemies.' As the executioner, following a widespread tradition, held up her head, only Mary's auburn wig remained in his hand as the skull, close cropped with grey hair, fell away. Mary Stuart had first claimed the English throne when Mary I died in 1558, and continued to seek to make good her claim, increasingly with some foreign and Catholic support, for almost 30 years. Now, at whatever cost to herself, Elizabeth had finally silenced her most dangerous rival.

The aftermath of Mary's execution

However enraged many Scots were at the execution of their repudiated queen, many of Elizabeth's more loyal subjects rejoiced at her death. Londoners rang church bells, fired guns and lit bonfires in their pleasure, and such demonstrations were repeated across many parts of the realm. Elizabeth, on the other hand, continued to insist that Mary's execution came as a complete shock to her; perhaps she was genuinely astonished that the signed warrant had been sent on without her explicit approval. When she was told that Mary had been executed, she retired to her private chambers and remained there, reportedly weeping profusely. Whether that was because of distress or fear of possible repercussions it is impossible to know. Always anxious about her own security, she was well aware what a dangerous precedent for removing an unwanted monarch she had set, as well as violating her own deeply held view of the nature of monarchy.

There may also have been some display directed at soothing the Scots. Her court was ordered to follow her example and go into deep mourning for the late queen; the hapless William Davison was sent to the Tower for passing on the signed warrant she had given him. That was at least more lenient than her first reaction, which reportedly was to have him summarily hanged. Cecil, now Lord Burghley, at least dissuaded her from pursuing that, but still even her longest-serving and most trusted councillor was sent from court and forbidden all forms of communication with Elizabeth for several weeks. Walsingham fared only slightly better. Leicester, while still in the Netherlands, received messages from his colleagues advising him how fortunate he was to be elsewhere during the uproar occurring at court. He returned to England during the queen's rage against her councillors, but his timely absence from court meant he escaped her direct fury.

In brief, Elizabeth made the period following Mary's execution a very difficult time for many leading people at her court. To silence those of her subjects who might mourn the Catholic queen, there was a rush of printed material aimed at all levels of society. That consistently reiterated what an unreliable and murderous woman Queen Mary had been, and how committed to trying to restore false religion, and repeated the details of her various plots. One event, which Elizabeth herself must have found galling but apparently endured in silence, was a sermon preached before her only days after Mary was executed. The preacher was the same Richard Fletcher who had been in attendance at Mary's execution, and his message was substantially an elegantly phrased rebuke to the queen for resisting Mary's execution, and an exhortation, drawing on numerous biblical instances, that rather she should 'rise from her bed of foolish grief [and with] her scattered elders ... pursue their newly scattered enemies'.[3] In other words, a mortal blow had been struck against the false religion, and the queen should rejoice in that instead of mourning a worthless denier of religious truth.

Elizabeth understood that the international situation was far too tense for any such celebration but, probably because of the elegance with which the sermon was delivered, Fletcher's career was in no way harmed by his criticism of the queen's reactions. By July, court affairs had settled down again and the queen no longer spent so much time in her own quarters. At the end of the month, Mary Stuart's body was finally moved from Fotheringhay to the nearby Peterborough Cathedral where, after a Protestant funeral service with a very cursory sermon, she was buried near that other queen who had been repudiated by Protestants, Katharine of Aragon. There Mary remained until after her son came to the English throne. Then, as detailed in Chapter 9, in 1609 James VI&I, had his mother reburied much closer to Elizabeth than she ever managed to be during her life. He had, apparently forgiven her for her various attempts, discussed in previous chapters, to will away his rights to the English throne.

Foreign reactions to Mary's death

Elizabeth's concerns about international responses from other monarchs to Mary Stuart's execution were proved to be well founded by subsequent events. If she herself had so long resisted accepting the need to execute a fellow monarch, others found it just as offensive, but also foresaw future benefits in Mary's death. Pope Sixtus V, for one, was clear that it was now the duty of Philip II to invade England and take the throne; although that was a project primarily designed to restore Catholicism to England, part of its rationale was Mary's frequent claim that she was about to will her

English succession rights to the King of Spain. One problem was, however, that no evidence could be found that Mary had ever done so; moreover Philip was at the time more immediately concerned with regaining full control of the Netherlands from his still rebellious subjects there.

Although both James VI and the French king Henry III had written to Elizabeth before the execution pleading that Mary's life should be spared, neither could offer satisfactory alternative solutions for the problems posed by that consistent conspirator. Elizabeth had more reason to be concerned about the reactions of Scotland than about those of France, caught up as it was with struggles between the monarchy and the Guise-backed Catholic League. She had written several times to James after Mary's conviction and sentence of execution, and there had never been any suggestion that the Scottish king was prepared to take any responsibility for his deposed mother. Elizabeth's responses therefore focused more on her lasting friendship with James and included several indirect reminders of his English succession prospects.

In her first letter to James after Elizabeth learned of Mary's execution, she insisted, one might well think implausibly, that she was entirely innocent of that death. On 14 February 1587, she wrote to the king she styled her dear brother an almost incoherent letter which insisted on the extreme grief she felt for that 'miserable accident' which she had never intended to allow to take place. Much of her message was committed to the carrier of the letter, but the letter itself made clear how concerned she was to conciliate Mary's son. There was some anger at Mary's execution in Scotland, but it was soon apparent that James himself would not risk his future prospects for the memory of a mother he had never known. His response to her agitated messages was that he fully accepted what she said, and indeed that he 'dare not wrong you so far as not to judge honorably of your unspotted part therein'. Mary's son then reiterated his hope that Elizabeth would satisfy his desire that he could in the future 'strengthen and unite this isle', establishing the true religion throughout it.[4] That is, he still wanted the English throne rather more than he wanted revenge for his mother's death.

Burghley also prepared careful arguments for foreign consumption in justification of the execution. He denied that Mary was killed for her religion, insisting instead that she died because of her treason. Furthermore, having abdicated her throne and fled her realm, she was no longer a monarch (itself an argument Elizabeth never accepted). Above all, Mary's repeated involvement in conspiracies against Elizabeth meant that the English queen had, finally, no alternative but to agree to the Scottish queen's death. The French reaction was always of less concern, but for Elizabeth the reaction of Spain was more important.

In 1585 Philip had still believed it was preferable to reconquer all the Netherlands first, but by January 1586 he had asked for a detailed plan for the invasion of England. Indeed, the death of the Scottish queen with close ties to the Guise interests made such an action more attractive, with the removal of the strongest Stuart claimant to the throne. Philip's claim might seem tenuous, but his own lineage did go back directly to John of Gaunt's marriage to Constance of Castile and was impeccably legitimate, whereas the legitimacy of Gaunt's Tudor descendants who had occupied the throne for three generations since 1485 was always disputed; this was in part because the 1397 Act which finally legitimated the Beauforts, from whom the Tudor line descended, had also explicitly debarred them from claiming the English throne. But for the time being, Philip seemed content to forego any such claim for himself.

Elizabeth's favourites

Despite the threatening approach of war in these years, life at Elizabeth's court continued much as usual. Ever since Dudley had first leapt to prominence at her court, Elizabeth had always had favourites among her courtiers, and their friendships frequently took such forms that, particularly in the earlier years of her reign, there were (it must be said, always improbable) rumours about her sexual relations with them. She always retained a particular affection for Robert Dudley, and no one else achieved such a close, enduring and explicitly affectionate relationship, but the younger men who followed after Dudley were all expected at least to practise the language of courtly love. As mentioned in a previous chapter, Christopher Hatton had done so, and rose to be a Privy Councillor and, in 1587, Lord Chancellor. Edward de Vere, Earl of Oxford, noted for his poetry and for gambling away his considerable inheritance, as well as for his strikingly erratic judgment in matters of love, religion, politics and courtly behaviour, was for a time another favourite.

Then there was Walter Raleigh. Born in 1554, his early advantages included being the nephew of Elizabeth's closest female confidante, the late Kat Astley, and half-brother to Sir Humphrey Gilbert, already a successful soldier and explorer. His other advantages included his appearance and his ability to address pleasing poems to the queen, always another desirable attribute for a favourite, a position he was enjoying by 1581. From his relatively impoverished condition, Elizabeth ensured he soon became quite wealthy, being granted some of Babington's estate in 1586, and later some confiscated Irish lands.

Raleigh was still the pre-eminent favourite when Robert Devereaux, Earl of Essex, first appeared at Elizabeth's court. Essex had been a promising scholar at Cambridge, and became an experienced soldier in the following years when he sailed with his godfather (and, more recently, stepfather), the Earl of Leicester, to the Netherlands in September 1585. He reappeared at court in October 1586 and, with the added benefits of being schooled by Leicester at how to behave to his queen, he quickly became a great success, frequently playing cards and gaming with her late into the night. By 1587, at the age of 19, he had emerged as a new favourite, even though his mother was Lettice Knollys, Elizabeth's relative whose second marriage, to Leicester, had so annoyed the queen. Some said that his company was a pleasing distraction for Elizabeth during the fraught final months of the other, Scottish queen. At one point he fell out with Elizabeth over her treatment of one of his sisters, and left court to rejoin his stepfather in the Netherlands, but Elizabeth's relative Robert Carey was sent after him to bring him back to court. Rivalry between Raleigh and the newcomer was still apparently muted, and both received considerable financial rewards, though such benefits seldom if ever came from Elizabeth's own resources.

Almost all favourites aspired to follow the example of Dudley and Hatton, and become significant decision makers. Essex and Raleigh both became involved in the current debates about the best way to handle the looming contests with Spain. Essex argued for land battles, supporting the Netherlands and France. Raleigh backed the naval option, raiding the Spanish coastline and plundering those Spanish fleets carrying silver from the New World.

The maritime strategy was also the preference of both Burghley and Elizabeth, not least because it was the cheaper option. Indeed, it has been suggested that one reason Burghley dominated English politics for so long was precisely because he always shared his queen's reluctance to undertake expensive military campaigns. Despite losing that argument, Essex continued high in the queen's affection, surviving even the discovery that he had begun a secret correspondence with James VI in late 1589, apparently in the expectation that neither Elizabeth nor several of her most valued councillors, particularly Burghley, could live much longer. That was only one of Essex's many actions which defied or challenged the queen's decisions; but apparently her affection for him and her tolerance of his repeated disobedience and defiance only became more pronounced in later years.

Equipping the Spanish Armada, and English responses

As previously mentioned, Philip II's tentative plans to invade England received fresh support, including from the pope, following the execution of the Catholic queen. From Philip's perspective, a successful invasion of England would have a number of most satisfactory results, including restoring the true religion there and ensuring the security of his Spanish, American and Netherlands possessions. Moreover, if Philip had been able to land his troops as intended, England would have found it extremely difficult to repel the invaders. The Armada which set sail in 1588 was impressively equipped. Somewhere between 130 and 140 ships of varied size carried some 7,000 seamen and 19,000 soldiers, almost all of whom carried firearms. The expectation was that they would be involved in close combat with the English fleet when they finally met. But the most important task was to gather up some 27,000 troops to invade England; they were to be led by the Duke of Parma. They were all from Philip's forces in the Spanish Netherlands, and if they had been able to land there was little in the way of military preparedness to block the invading troops. Moreover, all involved had the added benefit of knowing that Pope Sixtus V had granted every participant a plenary pardon for their part in this holy crusade.

He had, however, prudently delayed paying his considerable share of the costs of the whole enterprise until he had firm confirmation that the Armada troops had indeed landed in England.

Elizabeth and her advisers well understood that a Spanish attempt to invade England was imminent in 1587; it was certain that an actual assault was in final preparation in 1588. One reason for the year's delay was Drake's raid on Cadiz in 1587, for which he had the use of six royal ships and rather more 'private' ones, and during which he destroyed a considerable amount of Iberian shipping and stores which were already being gathered for the projected Armada. But Drake acted in such a way that Elizabeth, still hoping to avoid open warfare with Spain, was able to respond to their protests that she was greatly offended with him for his pre-emptive strike. Nevertheless she celebrated Drake's return; he had attacked several ports on the Iberian coastline before taking a large ship carrying a vast amount of Spanish treasure. In brief Drake had enjoyed a thoroughly rewarding voyage and fulfilled his ambition to 'singe the king of Spain's beard'. The destruction of so much Spanish shipping and supplies also ensured the postponement of the Spanish attack for a year.

Meanwhile, within the realm, Cecil had long been hard at work, identifying the most likely spots for treasonable activities which he anticipated from disaffected Catholics. He had been a major sponsor for Christopher Saxton's enterprise in mapping all the English and Welsh counties, a project completed by 1578. The maps Saxton produced were invaluable for helping Cecil track precisely where leading Catholics were located. To a modern eye, one interesting feature is how much those familiar county maps, when put together, still emphasise the identity of individual counties rather than the totality of the English realm.

The primacy of individual counties was reflected in several ways, not least because defensive works and military needs were primarily dealt with at the local level. Regional rather than 'national' interests often prevailed, as when the Earl of Huntingdon, then President of the North, reported that the northern gentry were reluctant to pay for new weapons to resist the Spanish, although if they should be used against the 'ancient enemy' the Scots, there would be no objection to meeting the costs. Coastal defences were also largely a charge against the local community, with the exception of such major fortifications as those at Dover, where Elizabeth met the expenses from the royal coffers.

As well as having the use of other vessels, Elizabeth had inherited and maintained some very large ships, and had several more built, giving her 34 'movable forts' by 1588. Ironically enough, some of them had been comprehensively overhauled during the reign of Philip and Mary, who had done much to restore a neglected fleet. But, although Elizabeth's navy was impressive, should Philip's plan to land a large and experienced army succeed, then her regime would be in serious trouble indeed.

In late July 1588 when the Armada arrived in the English Channel, preparations for the defence of England against a likely invasion were still seriously incomplete. In London there had been orders to mobilise some 10,000 citizens, but as the Armada approached few of them had received any training, and many were armed only with bows and arrows. Elsewhere the county militias, the main source of English soldiers, were similarly underprepared. It has been argued that Elizabeth and at least some of her advisers had been lulled into a false sense of security by Parma's prolonged peace negotiations from the Netherlands. But those negotiations, Philip had made clear to Parma, were never intended to achieve a peaceful outcome, only to buy time. That, it might be argued, was also what the depredations of Drake and others on the Iberian coast and Spanish fleet were also intended to achieve.

The English problems in preparing for war were the more serious because of a shortage of money which was partly due to the decline in the country's international trade resulting from their tensions with Spain, and partly to the fact that most European bankers were confident Spain would win the coming wars. Elizabeth's advisers also had worries about the outcome, since the available experienced soldiers were mainly veterans of the Netherlands battles, and a significant number of them were Catholic and therefore expected to be more sympathetic to the Spanish – and papal – cause. Moreover, it could not be assumed that all Englishmen hated the Spanish. Rather, reports were still coming to the court that many of the common people continued to describe Elizabeth's church settlement as 'the new religion'; reluctance to support either Elizabeth or her new religion could reasonably be expected from some northern areas, as Huntingdon's report indicated, but there were reports even from Kent of men openly rejoicing when they heard of Spanish success, 'and sorrowing for [news of] the contrary'.[5]

English victory and its aftermath

However ambivalent the view of Elizabeth's subjects, the English strength on that occasion lay with the fleet, but their ultimate 'victory' over the Armada owed much to the appalling weather the Spanish fleet encountered. The first encounter *was* won by the English, when English fire ships broke up the Spanish formations in the English Channel and prevented them joining up with Parma's troops awaiting embarkation. There were other brief encounters between the fleets until early August, then the Armada disappeared. While the English navy's commanders prepared for the return of the Spanish ships and a renewed battle, the Spanish fleet was being blown northwards up the east coast of England and Scotland, and then down the west side of Ireland, with many shipwrecks on the way and surviving crews running out of food and water.

Some sailors from the Armada ended up in Scotland, then a neutral country. Scottish sympathisers helped some of the earlier arrivals on their way to the continent, although James, always careful of his prospects of inheriting the English crown, soon pursued a less tolerant attitude. Those who were wrecked along the Irish seaboard met with much more mixed reactions from the local people. Many drowned, died or were killed on the beaches, some were allowed to live but robbed of all they had on them, others were completely protected and helped on their way. Three months after the shipwrecks one report described more than 1,100 Spanish corpses scattered along the Sligo coast. In all, it has been calculated, perhaps half of all those who sailed on the Armada died on the voyage, almost all because of the storms they had encountered. But the great Spanish galleons had suffered less damage, and Philip therefore still had the resources from which to launch another attack if he so wished.

The English government was slow to learn the full extent of the Armada's failure. The Spanish fleet had been seen off the English coast in late July 1588. The pursuit was abandoned on 2 August, but it was not until 8 August that her advisers thought it safe for

Elizabeth to visit the rather makeshift defensive fort Leicester had prepared at Tilbury on the Thames, and to speak to the assembled troops. There, tradition has long insisted, on the second day, wearing armour and mounted on a white horse, Elizabeth delivered a brief speech which has gone down in history as one of her memorable achievements, above all for the sentence which assured her soldiers that 'I know I have the body of a weak and feeble woman, but I have the heart and stomach of a king, and a king of England too.'

There are, however, several problems with that account, starting with its origins. The first known text of the speech was published in 1654, ostensibly based on a letter written some time after 1624. That, it must be said, is a long time for an accurate memory of a speech to survive. Those sources and subsequent elaborations have been carefully traced by Susan Frye; they make interesting reading, and as she argues, cannot be read as substantiating that version of Elizabeth's visit to Tilbury.[6] That has not prevented the much-quoted sentence shown above from being widely hailed as a heroic and novel declaration in which, by describing herself as a 'king', Elizabeth transcended all the traditional limitations of being female. Unfortunately, that is also a problematic claim. What it ignores is that from 1553, when Mary Tudor became monarch of England, there had been a problem in comprehending the language of 'queen' since that was normally indicator of the lesser royal position of a king's wife, the queen consort. A queen regnant, ruling in her own right, was a quite different authority. One strategy adopted in Mary's reign and continued in that of her sister was to refer to a female monarch as both king *and* queen, although Elizabeth at least once in Mary's reign referred to her sister simply as 'king'. Indeed, in the original version of what became known as Elizabeth's 'Golden speech' of 1601, she referred to herself as a 'king' twice, a 'prince' twice and a 'queen' twice. So if Elizabeth did indeed utter those words, or something like them, at Tilbury, she was making a relatively conventional rather than an innovative argument about her tenure of the royal office. Regrettably, the tradition that Elizabeth wore armour on that or any other day has even less to support it, partly because if there had been any possibility of any fighting breaking out, she would not have been there at all.

Celebrating a mighty victory?

Given the circumstances in which they lost sight of the Armada, it is not surprising that it took a little time for the English to recognise that they were the victors. And before that realisation sank in, the English seamen were enduring hardship on board their ships almost as much as did the Spanish. Their fresh water supplies ran out and they began suffering from typhus from which, it was said, so many died that some ships lacked enough crew even to raise the anchors. One ship lost 200 of its 500 crew in the first month at sea. By early September, some of the commanders were expressing great distress at the conditions the seamen were enduring. Howard of Effingham, lord admiral of the fleet, was appalled that after the service they had rendered, those men should be left to starve.

But Elizabeth was apparently unmoved by such reproaches, or by Howard's more pragmatic warning that such treatment would make it harder to persuade other men to serve when next the need arose. By one account Burghley even expressed hopes that such fatal sickness would reduce the costs of discharging the seamen. Many of Elizabeth's other advisers were apparently no more concerned, for when the final accounts were prepared for the costs of defending England, of the nearly £400,000 tallied only £180 had gone to those who had been injured. Rather, it was left to such commanders of the navy as Drake and Hawkins to establish a fund from their own and others' resources to help those who had been injured in the war. That indifference from the triumphant Elizabeth and her advisers looks even more callous when a comparison is made with the Spanish response. Defeated as they were, Philip insisted that it was part of his Christian responsibility that before any of the survivors were dismissed from either his army or navy, their service record should be examined to ensure that each discharged man received his complete entitlements.

However parsimonious the English authorities were to those who had borne the brunt of the fighting, they had much less hesitation in celebrating their great victory, once they knew of it, with church services and festivities. On 24 November Elizabeth made a magnificent progress through the city, with a large number of courtiers and nobles, to a thanksgiving ceremony at St Pauls. Leicester had, as previously noted, returned to England from his leading role in the Netherlands when the court was in a state of high tension over the execution of Mary Queen of Scots. He remained to play his part in the preparations against the coming of the Spanish Armada, and was responsible for placing a boom across the Thames above London and erecting a fort at Tilbury on the riverbank, which may well be why Elizabeth was ever there.

Repelling the attempted invasion had apparently gone well, and Leicester was at Elizabeth's side as they watched her new favourite, his stepson the Earl of Essex, jousting as part of the victory celebrations. Shortly after that he left court, with the queen's permission, and wrote to her from one of her favourite places, Rycote, the home of perhaps her most long-standing friends, the Norris household. That was the last letter she received from him, since he unexpectedly died on 4 September. Elizabeth annotated his most recent message as 'his last letter' and kept it by her until her own death.

Elizabeth undoubtedly mourned for Leicester, but it is less clear who else did. Even for Elizabeth there were many diversions. The rapid rise of Essex to take a position comparable to that of his late stepfather was one, and the widespread preoccupation with the continuing celebrations of victory over the Armada was another. Some three months after the victory was first celebrated, Elizabeth went in an elaborate chariot, accompanied by a crowd of courtiers and nobles, to attend a thanksgiving service at St Paul's Cathedral. A range of commemorative medals were struck with triumphant mottos; one, reworked for the Spanish, echoed Caesar's famous comment 'I came, I saw, I conquered', but this one, also in Latin, ended: 'I fled'. The best-known medal carried the message, 'God blew upon the waters and scattered his enemies.' Another, more private, way of commemorating the victory was the 'Armada' portrait of Elizabeth, probably originally commissioned by Drake. (One version is reproduced in Plate 10.)

There are now three versions of this portrait. As was customary, there was little pretence of representing Elizabeth's facial features accurately; in each version, her face is effectively a mask which disguises the appearance of a woman well into her fifties, with the more important messages transmitted by the richness of her dress and the backgrounds. It is in essence an allegorical painting, showing two stages of the sea battles, one the fire ships wreaking their havoc and the other the storm-tossed Spanish ships being driven on to the Irish coast. The imperial crown beside her, and her hand resting on the Americas on the globe, represent possible burgeoning imperial ambitions. If the first version was commissioned, as has been suggested, by Francis Drake, the references to the Americas as coming under Elizabeth's hand are less surprising in this record of triumph over Spanish might and of increasing imperial ambitions for England.

Elizabeth's problems with her putative heir apparent

However much it was advisable for young English courtiers hoping for advancement to present themselves as conscious of Elizabeth's accomplishments, the young James VI presented quite another problem. He seldom expressed gratitude for the pension Elizabeth had granted him following the 1586 Treaty of Berwick. Rather, he often felt he deserved more and deeply resented Elizabeth's habit of subtracting from it sums paid for other purposes. Moreover, she paid it intermittently and seemed not to understand that his need for those payments was the more pressing since Scotland levied no regular taxation. Often during their exchanges in subsequent years, James felt the need to remind her that he was also a free and independent monarch, because of her inclination to withhold payment on occasion as a mark of her disapproval of some policy decision. That it should be a female who raised such difficulties may have been the more irritating for him, given his dismissive comments in his 1599 *Basilikon Doron* where he suggested a realm with a woman or an infant on the throne was equally disadvantaged. Once on the English throne he made clear his belief that as a male he was a more complete ruler than either of the two women who had preceded him.[7]

That, however, was in the future. In the years immediately following the Treaty of Berwick, relations between the two kingdoms were threatened only by the execution of Mary Queen of Scots; it was after all, the king's mother who had been executed by a foreign power. Elizabeth's sustained insistence that she had no part in the final decisions may have assuaged James's hostility, but it did little to satisfy some of his more important subjects. While England faced the threat of the Spanish Armada, James ignored the pleas of powerful and pro-Spanish Catholic Lords to intervene on Spain's behalf; that was hardly a surprising position for him, since James knew that the pope was urging Philip to seize the English throne, and that Philip himself was already considering the claim of his daughter through her descent from John of Gaunt. But James was also calculating the benefits of maintaining friendly relations with Spain. His title of *Rex Pacificus* may have been acquired later, but he was already demonstrating a marked distaste for going to war if it could possibly be avoided.

As the fate of the Spanish Armada was being worked out, several hundred Spanish sailors had ended up in Scotland. Elizabeth and her advisers, anxious that they might join up with Scottish Catholic and pro-Spanish forces, put pressure on James to expel them, pressure which included sending three English warships to hover near Edinburgh in mid-1589, as protection against any uprising. The queen was, however, also slow to grant the Spanish the safe-conducts through English waters which were essential for their safe passage back to the European continent; one major reason for the delay became clear when the unarmed ships carrying the Spanish to Dunkirk were set upon just before they reached there. Their attackers were Dutch ships which had been advised of their coming by the English; more than half of those Spanish survivors were drowned or killed before they could reach land.

If James had been grateful for Elizabeth's intervention in helping remove the Spanish sailors, he was less compliant when Spanish issues rose again. English sources had intercepted letters to Philip II from several eminent Scottish lords in early 1589; all regretted the defeat of the Armada, and promised their support should he try again. An outraged Elizabeth once again scolded James, insisting that permitting such behaviour was intolerable to any monarch. James did demote the offenders, including his favoured Earl of Huntly, but made clear how much he resented the admonitory tone which Elizabeth so frequently used to him. He was, after all, now fully monarch in his own kingdom.

In 1590, as James returned from his marriage to Anne of Denmark and his lengthy stay at the Danish court, Elizabeth wrote to him again warning him of subjects plotting against him, and once again without receiving a response she considered satisfactory. Although always anxious to preserve his implied status as

Elizabeth's heir, James was never prepared to seem subservient to her. In January 1592 Elizabeth wrote a particularly agitated letter, reminding him of the care she had taken of him 'since you first breathed' and warning him against 'those wicked conspirators of the Spanish faction'. The reference was to some Scottish Catholic lords who had joined a Jesuit plot to land Spanish troops in Scotland as a preliminary to another attempt by Philip II to invade England. James had once more been scolded for his apparent negligence but, as an independent monarch, continued to pursue his own foreign policy.

Not only did he wish to avoid being involved in England's wars, but he also kept an eye on preserving all possible means of acquiring the English throne. That included him contemplating the possibility of invading England himself if his succession rights were ignored. He was, it would seem, prepared to do whatever was needed to assert his regal rights by whatever means would do it, and canvassed potential support, including military support, at several European courts. Elizabeth could perhaps be forgiven for doubting whether her Scottish royal godson would, after all, be a satisfactory heir, although she never indicated any idea of a more satisfactory alternative.

1. The Family of Henry VIII, c.1545 (oil on canvas), English School, (16th century)/The Royal Collection ©2011 Her Majesty Queen Elizabeth II/The Bridgeman Art Library

2. Elizabeth I when Princess, c.1546 (oil on panel), Scrots, Guillaume (fl.1537-53) (attr. to)/The Royal Collection ©2011 Her Majesty Queen Elizabeth II/The Bridgeman Art Library

3. Queen Elizabeth I by Nicholas Hilliard ©National Portrait Gallery, London

4. Locket ring belonging to Queen Elizabeth I, c.1575 (gold with enamel, rubies, diamonds & mother-of-pearl), English School, (16th century)/By kind permission of the Chequers Trust/Mark Fiennes/The Bridgeman Art Library

5. Portrait of Queen Elizabeth I. Zuccaro, Federico (1542-1609). c.1557-1609

6. Robert Dudley, 1st Earl of Leicester by unknown artist ©National Portrait Gallery, London

7. Portrait of Queen Elizabeth I (1533-1603) in Ceremonial Costume (oil on canvas), Zuccari, or Zuccaro, Federico (1540-1609)/Pinacoteca Nazionale, Siena, Italy/Alinari/The Bridgeman Art Library

8. Lord Burghley (1520-98), English School, (16th century)/Burghley House
Collection, Lincolnshire, UK/The Bridgeman Art Library

9. Mary Queen of Scots, portrait miniature by Nicholas Hilliard. England, late 16th century ©V&A Images/ Victoria and Albert Museum, London

10. Elizabeth I, Armada Portrait, c.1588 (oil on panel), Gower, George (1540-96) (attr. to)/Woburn Abbey, Bedfordshire, UK/ The Bridgeman Art Library

8 An ageing queen and the difficult later years of her reign

Changing conditions for Elizabeth's regime

As the rule of Elizabeth, in her 67th year, entered the last decade of the 16th century, her realm was strained by a series of bad harvests, and she had been driven into wars she had no wish to wage. Those wars imposed a heavy personal cost, as well as a serious financial drain. Elizabeth's surviving female friends of long standing included Lady Margery Norris, whom she had long since nicknamed her 'Black Crow' and whose family history indicates the price Elizabeth's elite could pay for their status. In 1597, Elizabeth wrote a moving letter of condolence after the death of Lady Norris's most renowned soldier son, who died in the queen's service in Ireland. By late 1599 another four of Lady Norris's six sons had died in Elizabeth' service; that year their mother also died.

Elizabeth was also losing many of her most familiar councillors. Leicester she always missed, but others soon followed. Francis Walsingham, who died in 1590, had been a more recent adviser than many, but had been much relied upon as both Elizabeth's 'spymaster' and principal secretary. Sir Christopher Hatton may have originally caught the queen's eye by his dancing, as legend has it, but he went on to become a particularly trusted adviser well before he died in 1591. William Cecil, later Lord Burghley had been her most trusted man of business even before she came to the throne; he died in 1598, but through the 1590s his work had been shared with his son Robert, who became secretary of state in 1596.

In brief, by the end of the decade there were few of her own generation still alive and at her court. The newer men were of a quite different generation, raised in a predominantly Protestant environment and even promoting the almost continuous wars in Ireland, the Netherlands and on the continent. Moreover, shaped by very different assumptions, the new and younger often showed less tolerance for Elizabeth's foibles than had those who had matured with her. The impact of the many changes was political as well personal for the queen, not least since Elizabeth proved reluctant to appoint new advisers to fill the gaps the deaths had left. Her first Privy Council had consisted of 20 advisers of a range of opinions, but by 1597 it was reduced to almost half that number, most from families she knew well, and three related to the queen herself. The only fresh blood was that of Robert Devereux, Earl of Essex, one of the more ambitious members of that much younger generation.

There are many signs of the damaging impact of this relative atrophy among her advisers, which compounded the ever-greater complaints about the demands the queen made on her people in money and resources for the wars; at the same time she allowed, by default, her close advisers to accumulate great personal wealth. One ever-growing grievance was her increased reliance on monopolies (that is, giving an individual a licence, most often to control some trade in foreign goods or in domestic manufacturing). The outcome of that practice, which other Tudors had also used, but more sparingly, was effectively to shift the cost of rewarding courtiers from the royal court to Elizabeth's subjects. Late in Elizabeth's reign her use of monopolies became a major source of complaint but, despite her golden words to her 1601 parliament on the subject (to be discussed more fully in the next chapter), Elizabeth did little actually to limit the practice. As ever, she was much attracted to a strategy which saved her from further royal expenditure, for she was always aware of how limited were her resources.

If the personnel of her court had changed over the decades of her reign, the wider context in which she ruled was even more significantly different. England's cloth trade, still the dominant export sector, was in continuing decline, not least because of the ongoing wars in the Netherlands and the consequent damage to those traditional outlets for the trade. That England remained at war with Spain also meant that considerable amounts of money were being spent on both naval and land-based defences, costs which were about to increase substantially because of looming expensive campaigns in Ireland.

In domestic matters, her realm was also troubled. It was a time of rapid population growth in an essentially agricultural economy, which offered only mainly seasonal employment. That coincided with a series of poor harvests, as well as widespread underemployment. Indeed there was only one year in the 1590s when the harvests were productive enough to be described by modern historians as 'abundant'; four harvests of that decade were described as 'bad' and two others defined as resulting in 'dearth'.[1] Local authorities, urged on by the queen's advisers, did what they could to provide for the poorest as food prices rose, but there were several periods of widespread hunger and an uncertain number of deaths by starvation, particularly in the more remote areas.

One consequence of the greater anxiety among her advisers about a range of 'social disorders' in the later decades of her reign was a series of attempts to control 'masterless men', primarily those itinerants defined as 'rogues and vagabonds'. A parish-based Poor Law system was established for the local impoverished, which provided the basis for the system which survived, with modifications, until the 19th century. The older values of hospitality for all comers were giving way in the face of increased demands from a growing population to a sharper distinction between the 'deserving' and the 'undeserving' poor, with much stronger control of the latter. Individuals were still expected to practise charity, at least in their own communities, but there were also quite new conversations about those defined as 'surplus population'.

In the context of chronic food shortages, high prices and widespread underemployment, it is hardly surprising that there was a good deal of muttering against the rulers, including the queen herself, across the realm. There was even a grumble from Kent that Philip II cared more about the English than did the queen, and that, unlike her, *he* would ensure that the people had food, drink and clothes. The old rumours about the queen's imputed sexual adventures also resurfaced as another slur on the monarch. As ever there was also uncertainty about who would succeed the aging queen. But that issue Elizabeth would allow no one to address in public; those who did were liable to severe punishment. The 1590s indeed proved a difficult decade for very many at Elizabeth's court and beyond.

Religious challenges and religious conformity

As discussed in Chapter 3, from the time Elizabeth took the throne there were disputes among 'reformed' groups about their preferred form of Protestant worship. Even many of the men closest to her, including Robert Dudley, had openly encouraged a more advanced Protestantism than Elizabeth had established. But there were other, more pressing problems for her church, such as the inadequate numbers of Protestant clergy even across southern England, let alone in the 'dark corners' of the north. On many matters, the queen's religious position was more conservative than, for example, that of either of her first Archbishops of Canterbury. They were Matthew Parker, archbishop from 1559 to1575, and his successor Edmund Grindal, who died in 1583. It has been well said that her motto *Semper Eadem* (Always the Same) was particularly apposite for her attitude to the religious practices she had established after her accession.

As one example of the several difficulties, Elizabeth's settlement had required clergy to wear stipulated church vestments according to their position, beyond those prescribed in the final Edwardian settlement. The more advanced Protestants always considered such clerical vestments the 'rags of the antichrist' (that is, remnants of 'ungodly' Catholic practice), and many of Elizabeth's advisers agreed with them. But for Elizabeth the dispute about vestments also reflected her strong commitment to upholding and visually enacting the hierarchical order which underpinned the whole social order. She had no sympathy for those who argued that such distinctions of dress among the clergy and between them and the laity echoed the ethos of a separated priestly caste, as in the false Catholic church.

After he became Archbishop of Canterbury, Grindal differed from his queen not only on the vestments issue but also on the widespread practice of religious meetings known as 'exercises' or 'prophesying'. Those exercises, commonly sanctioned by the relevant bishops, were meetings of clergy who preached sermons which both honed their own skills and instructed the lesser members of the gathering in the skills they needed to qualify as preachers, much needed at this time. Since almost all members of the Church of England shared the typically Protestant view that preaching was a crucial means of instruction and salvation for their congregations, such prophesying was widely approved in the mid-1570s. Elizabeth's opposition to the 'exercises', however, was in part because such less formal meetings challenged her insistence on ensuring the proper hierarchy in all proceedings, and also because, as she said, she had never explicitly approved them.

Elizabeth was sufficiently concerned by so much preaching by so many people that in 1576 she instructed Grindal to end the exercises and reduce the number of preachers in each county. Grindal, with rather more religious zeal than political tact, protested to his queen against her attack on a crucial means of promoting true religion. He went even further, suggesting that Elizabeth should follow the examples of those ancient rulers who had consulted with their divines on religious matters. Deeply affronted by his resistance, she was even more affronted by the implication that she might be mistaken in her opposition. Burghley and others of the Privy Council who sympathised with Grindal finally managed a compromise settlement on the matter of the 'exercises', but Grindal himself became a permanent victim of the queen's displeasure. She could not remove him from his consecrated office, but at her insistence Grindal spent his final years as Archbishop of Canterbury in enforced retirement.[2]

This confrontation about what Elizabeth manifestly regarded as *her* Church of England did not end recurrent clerical as well as lay pressure for the English Church to become more like many of its continental Protestant counterparts. One Thomas Cartwright came to prominence soon after joining another attack on Elizabeth's preferred religious order. He was a leading proponent of the argument that the primitive church, which had no bishops, was the true model of Christianity and the model which the Church of England should adopt. He was soon embroiled in printed debate with John Whitgift, created Archbishop of Canterbury after Grindal finally died in 1583. Cartwright's was a widespread and widely followed debate which argued the merits of a Presbyterian vis-à-vis an Episcopal (i.e. bishop-based) organisation of the Church.

Elizabeth always viewed a Presbyterian order, with its greater equality among the clergy and a stronger commitment to the view that defining religious truth was a matter for clergy rather than the monarch, as another serious attack on the divinely ordained hierarchical order of all things. But a yet more serious controversy was to follow in 1584 when Archbishop Whitgift issued new requirements for proof of conformity to the Church of England. Some of his proposals were not contentious, but many clergy were outraged when they were required to agree that the 1559 Book of Common Prayer included nothing contrary to the word of God and should be the sole form of public worship. This demand effectively renewed debate about every aspect of the 1559 church settlement that had ever been questioned, but for Elizabeth it demonstrated that she had at last a prelate who shared her view of how the church should be ordered, and was prepared to enforce it.

Whitgift's position was attacked in parliament in 1584–5; at least one petition then was supported by several of Elizabeth's councillors. (It will be remembered that since the innovations of Henry VIII in the 1530s, all religious changes had required parliamentary sanction.) The petition proposed a modified version of Presbyterianism which retained some functions for the bishops, but even this more moderate set of propositions was quite enough to bring about Elizabeth's intervention. She announced that there would be no parliamentary debate about it; some aspects of the petition would be considered by the relevant clergy and others by Elizabeth herself, while those parts that the queen believed attacked the Book of Common Prayer were declared to be beyond any discussion. Two years later, there was another, more explicit attempt in parliament to abolish both the Book of Common Prayer and the episcopacy. That bill Elizabeth simply confiscated; in her reign there would be no further religious changes by parliament.

Debate about the religious order in parliament had indeed been silenced, but in a society where print was becoming a more common medium and tight print censorship was proving difficult, there was also a widespread, less official war of words for changes within the church, and against the episcopacy. The most notorious of those publications were the racy pseudonymous tracts written by 'Martin Marprelate'. The 'author' strongly defended Cartwright's well-known position on the issue and mocked the existing church establishment. The origin of those pamphlets was never identified, although there has long been much speculation.

More usually the legal system and the official print medium were both means by which the powerful supporters of Elizabeth's religious status quo discredited and silenced all those seeking change. In the final years of Elizabeth's reign, the men promoted within the church not only maintained her preferred orthodoxy, and her royal supremacy, but established a new orthodoxy that not only monarchs but also bishops governed by divine right (*iure divino*). In brief, the religion of the final years was defined by Elizabeth's exercise of royal authority rather than by any attempt to find a consensus, and the more fervently Protestant church fostered by many her most trusted councillors was under challenge.

The further rise of Essex

Among the many changes at court during these later years, Essex maintained and even enhanced his standing as Elizabeth's preeminent favourite, replacing Raleigh, but he frequently proved much less of a conventional courtier than previous favourites. Elizabeth's attraction to and affection for Essex was partly in appreciation of his combined high culture, chivalric behaviour and ambition, and probably also for the pleasure in having such an attractive young man pay court to her. Essex had the extra advantage of being the stepson of the late Leicester, the man for whom she had most cared and some of whose offices had gone to his protégé. Whatever the explanation, however defiant Essex was, for years he consistently managed to assuage whatever royal wrath he brought upon himself.

Essex always sought power for himself as well as royal favour, and he had a particularly strong interest in – and firm opinions about – how Elizabeth's foreign policy should be conducted; indeed he frequently demonstrated little respect for alternative views. Above all, his primary ambition was for his own military glory, and his restless seeking for it and for a stronger voice in foreign policy frequently led to tensions at court. An early indication of just how independent he could be came in 1589 when he defied Elizabeth's express wishes and secretly joined a seafaring expedition led by Drake and Sir John Norris in the first significant response to the Spanish invasion attempt the previous year.

The attraction for Essex may have been the greater because one passenger whose voyage Elizabeth did approve was Dom Antonio, briefly Antonio I of Portugal before Philip II took his throne in

1580. The one-time king's years of European exile led finally him to London, but his presence on the voyage failed dismally in its aim of causing a Portuguese uprising against Philip. Indeed, despite the military bravado of Essex, the assault in Portugal was an abject failure; Essex had no option but to return to the court and face Elizabeth's fury at his serial defiance of her commands.

He was, however, once again quickly restored to the queen's favour, which he retained until he secretly married the daughter of the late Walsingham some time in 1590. Secret marriages of courtiers were always offensive to monarchs; they expected to be always in control of the alliances of their most important subjects since these always carried political implications. The secret marriage of a favourite was an even worse offence, and Essex's wife was never welcome at court. (A brief digression here: More generally, it is worth noting that several women were barred from Elizabeth's court for the same offence; royal women, like women in other large households, traditionally arranged suitable marriages for their attendants. Despite the popular myth, it was not that Elizabeth was always jealous of other women at court; on the contrary she had many good and enduring female friendships among the women about her, but secret liaisons and marriages directly challenged her authority.)

In 1591, partly at the urging of Essex, Elizabeth agreed to send another army as limited support for the French Henry IV (previously Henry of Navarre) in his wars against the Guise Catholic League and their ally, Philip of Spain. Then, despite Essex's many breaches of royal protocol, at the age of 23 and with minimal military experience, he was given command of some 4,000 troops to aid the French king. The Earl ignored the advice of often more experienced leaders, defied the queen's orders and was finally ordered back to England, where he so effectively faced down the queen's rage that he briefly returned to France. There the siege he was leading failed, but he successfully transferred blame to the French for that, at least in the eyes of the queen.

Then he returned to England and began a new campaign for his advancement, this time to become a member of Elizabeth's Privy Council. Again Elizabeth gave way to his demands and his admission to that most important body had a significant impact of the sphere of high politics in the following years. How often his was sound advice is a matter of historical dispute, but he undoubtedly added a fresh perspective to Council discussions, having few doubts about his preferred policies, and considerable persistence in voicing them. His relations with more experienced councillors such as Burghley, once his guardian, were generally calm, but his relationship with Robert Cecil, whom he saw as his rival for higher office, was more problematic. His primary ambition, however, was still to win military renown, and his main project was to form a Protestant alliance of England, France and the Netherlands to resist the Spanish drive to restore Catholicism across Europe. He promoted this frequently, despite his clear understanding that such an expensive and fraught policy was always anathema both to Elizabeth and to Burghley.

Beyond his military and Privy Council activities, Essex played an intriguing role in one rather mysterious episode of Elizabeth's later reign. At the centre was one Roderigo Lopez, who was executed on the (highly improbable) grounds that he plotted to assassinate the queen. Born in a Portuguese family of 'New Christians' (forcibly converted Jews), he became a medical doctor in London, attending both Leicester and, from 1581, the queen herself. After Dom Antonio also ended up in England, Lopez was active in encouraging Elizabeth to support his claim to the Portuguese throne. By 1590, however, Lopez was also in contact with the Spanish ambassador in France, almost certainly at the suggestion of Walsingham, to pursue two objectives: to prepare the way for peace negotiations and to end English support for Dom Antonio.

But Walsingham died in 1591, the same year that Essex, whom Lopez had also treated, learned that his physician had told others of a 'dishonourable' medical condition that Lopez had treated him for. In 1594, Essex uncovered Lopez's secret communications with Spanish sources through his own information networks, and also uncovered his secret reversion to Judaism. Without Walsingham to protect him, Lopez was left facing Essex's fury and was subsequently charged with seeking to poison the queen. Elizabeth herself always doubted that charge, but the trial organised by Essex focused almost as much on his Judaism as on the putative plot and Lopez, with two others, died the full agonizing traitor's death. Later, when his widow petitioned the queen for the restoration of her late husband's property, her request was granted, a strong indication of

Elizabeth's belief in her late physician's innocence. Essex, however, became even more of a popular hero as Lopez's fate fed into popular hostility to Jews. It has also been suggested that the Lopez affair provided the 'inspiration' for Shakespeare's *Merchant of Venice*.

But Essex worried that he was still being marginalised by the rise of men like Robert Cecil who, despite his complete lack of military experience, had risen to offices that Essex had failed to achieve. Always believing his military prowess was not sufficiently appreciated at Elizabeth's court, Essex also sometimes blamed the queen's reluctance to follow his advice on the fact that she was a woman. Elizabeth, in turn, suspected that he would much rather serve a male monarch. As well as knowing of his particularly close relations with Henry IV of France, Elizabeth understood that Essex had re-established contact with James VI, with a mutually satisfactory arrangement whereby Essex promised to support the Scottish king as Elizabeth's successor and James promised Essex sufficiently gratifying rewards.

More war in the Netherlands, France and at sea

English support for the struggles in the Netherlands against the Spanish forces had continued long after Leicester had returned to England, and their forces had even won an early victory against the Duke of Parma, universally recognised as Europe's pre-eminent commander. But by then Elizabeth's own attention was drawn away from the Netherlands to events in France. In August 1589, a young Jesuit had assassinated the childless Henry III in revenge for the king's part, the previous year, in the assassinations of both Guise brothers, the Duke and the Cardinal. With that death of the last Valois king, the heir to the throne was Henry of Navarre, long a prominent Huguenot leader. Since few Catholics found his religion acceptable, and the Catholic League was actively hostile, the wars of religion soon broke out again. Philip II, who had always backed the Catholic League, continued to do so, to the extent that Parma was to intervene twice on behalf of Catholic and Spanish interests, to relieve Henry IV's second siege of Paris in1590 and of Rouen in 1592.

Elizabeth had no choice but to support the new French king, since she understood that otherwise Spanish interests could soon dominate France, thereby gaining an ideal launching site for further assaults on England. Her first intervention was to send 3,600 soldiers to aid Henry at the first siege of Paris in September 1589, but she limited her costs by agreeing to pay only for the first month of their service. The soldiers proved relatively successful, but the winter fighting and the scarcity of supplies meant that the 800 or so who lived long enough to return to England in late December did so in an appalling condition.

Somewhat reluctantly, and partly at the urging of Essex as well as Burghley, Elizabeth again joined in with Henry's battle plans in 1591, not least because his campaign included a siege of Rouen, the capital of Normandy and a major port on the River Seine. Elizabeth's costs, it was agreed, were to be met through the rich customs revenues of that city and, as previously noted, she appointed Essex to lead the English troops for his first independent command. The siege, however, had made little progress by the time Parma successfully moved to relieve it, leaving Elizabeth with heavy losses of men and money, with no customs revenue from the campaign, and with a renewed suspicion that Essex would prefer to fight for Henry IV, in part because he was male, in part because Essex would be allowed more action against the Spanish.

The Queen's always mistrusted Henry IV, and her reluctance to support him was the greater because of the French king's lack of interest in supporting her English troops in Brittany, where they were fighting off a Spanish attempt to establish yet another bridgehead for further English assaults. Her mistrust was only reinforced when, in 1593, Henry converted to Catholicism (reportedly explaining 'Paris is worth a mass'). That conversion by Henry IV, and a growing French concern that Philip II was eyeing the French throne primarily as a trophy for a member of his own family, resulted in many French Catholic subjects turning away from Spanish support and acknowledging their new and newly Catholic king. That, in turn, left Elizabeth's regime again exposed to danger from likely further Spanish attempts at invasion. It also meant that again Elizabeth had lost a great deal of money and thousands of men, with little to show for either, by her support for the seemingly ungrateful but triumphant and, to her, annoyingly independent French king.

English tensions with Spain continued, and in 1595 further

reports were circulating that another Spanish invasion was being planned to achieve what the 1588 Armada had failed to accomplish. An unusually ambitious English plan was hatched in response, whereby Drake and Hawkins were to attack Spanish strongholds in the West Indies in what was also designed as yet another fundraising set of raids. As ever, the financial prospects were a major reason for Elizabeth's support. In fact, the expedition proved to be another serious failure, foreshadowed by the death of Hawkins even before the fleet, mainly provided by Elizabeth, had taken any action against the Spanish bases. Those attacks that were made proved disastrous in terms of English losses; moreover, before the generally unsuccessful fleet could return to England, Drake had also died.

The loss of two such eminent commanders and of several ships greatly alarmed Elizabeth, who still believed there were plans for an imminent Spanish strike against her. A minor Spanish attack in Cornwall in July 1595 helped persuade her that an attack on Spain itself, perhaps with the chance to capture a Spanish treasure ship or two, would be a suitable response. That expedition, originally led by Lord Admiral Howard, was later joined by Essex, this time by Elizabeth's decision, although Essex had little maritime experience. The queen's instructions for the expedition were clearly defined, but in a letter he left behind on his departure Essex set out his quite different plan, which he considered much superior and which, he argued, could have the added benefit of freeing all Christendom from the tyranny of Philip II.

The fleet's first target was Cadiz, which was indeed quite easily taken, although there were reports later that, in the ensuing scramble for loot in the city, the English had overlooked the fact that in port was a fully loaded fleet for the Americas. At the initiative of Essex, and contrary to the queen's instructions, the soldiers captured the town, destroyed several large vessels and set fire to whatever they could. Pleased with their loot, most of the forces were only anxious to return home, despite the queen's clear instructions to focus on further destruction of Spanish ships and supplies. Once they were safely home, they learned that the queen, quite unimpressed by their 'triumph' at Cadiz, suspected, indeed accurately, that much of the booty was being concealed from her officials, leaving her with many costly bills to pay and very little to show for all the expenses incurred. Few from that expedition ever received thanks for what they did achieve, a fact that Essex particularly resented, despite his flagrant and repeated disregard for the queen's instructions to the expedition.

Moreover, there were fresh reports that a new Spanish Armada, based in Lisbon and therefore unaffected by the Cadiz raid, was being prepared for yet another attack on England. It seems likely that Philip's determination to launch that attempt had been strengthened by the new anti-Spanish alliance, confirmed in October, between England, France and the Netherlands. At the same time Elizabeth was particularly concerned that a Spanish landing in Ireland was likely to have a much more enthusiastic welcome than in previous years, given the parlous state of Irish–English relations by then and the successes of rebels there. But once again England was saved by stormy weather in the Bay of Biscay in November, which destroyed most of Philip's new fleet. Without such good fortune a second time, Elizabeth would have found it almost impossible to repel a Spanish attack, since her land defences were hardly stronger than a decade before. The queen's relief at that second Spanish disaster would have been the greater since at the same time her government faced serious problems at home, with food riots in London in the mid-1590s and widespread social discontent.

Troubles in Ireland

Beyond the discontents in England, there were pressing needs for many more men and much more money in her Irish domains. Following Elizabeth's accession in 1558, and despite the strength of Catholicism in Ireland, the Irish parliament had quietly adopted Elizabeth's preferred form of Protestantism in 1560. The transition may have been easier because the final wording of the Elizabethan form of worship left some room for the traditional Catholic belief in the real presence at the consecration of the wafers. There were also some modifications to the English forms for Ireland, including one which allowed those clergy who knew no English to conduct services in Latin. Indeed, in its earlier days the Elizabethan Irish church proved flexible enough to accommodate not only the future Jesuit and Catholic martyr Edmund Campion, who was executed in 1581, but also the future arch-Calvinist Presbyterian Thomas

Cartwright, whose opposition to Elizabeth's church settlement has already been discussed.

One factor in the always slow progress of establishing Protestant religion there was the reluctance of many English clerics to go to Ireland or, once there, to remain. Elizabeth herself made only one recorded gesture towards advancing the Protestant religion in the vernacular when she sent money to Ireland specifically to ensure that the New Testament could be printed in Irish. That particular project failed. In its place, in 1571 the first Gaelic book did appear in Ireland, containing both the Church of England catechism and the English articles of faith, but with only 200 copies printed it could have made little if any impact on the populace at large.

More generally, however, Elizabeth followed the policy of her predecessors in trying to establish more royal control across Ireland. Accordingly, she was, as ever, reluctant to make any concessions to rebellious subjects, as indeed she had demonstrated in the aftermath of the Northern Uprising. From 1570, one Elizabethan response to uprisings in Ireland had been effectively to plant colonies of Scottish and English settlers in appropriated lands. But another problem, as religion became a more contested matter, surfaced publicly first in 1579 when James Fitzgerald appealed for Spanish support against the English heretical queen who claimed to rule them. For Catholics, that was a legitimate position, ever since the 1570 papal bull denying Elizabeth's right to rule. But Fitzgerald's appeal had little success, since Philip then had more pressing concerns, particularly in the Mediterranean. In later years, however, he was to prove more responsive to his Irish co-religionists.

But religious difference was only part of Elizabethan problems in Ireland, and by the 1590s conditions there had become much more difficult for the English rulers. Elizabeth herself had never shown much interest in that part of her realm, preferring to leave administration there to her officials. She showed even less interest in meeting the costs of bringing the more troubled parts of Ireland more completely under royal control. Nevertheless she was finally forced to acknowledge the need for greater expenditure, as an ever more dangerous situation emerged, and more Irish nobles when exercising their traditional rights were being frustrated by minor English officials whose own concerns included creating better opportunities to enrich themselves. Their official duties prescribed introducing ever more English law and custom, in accordance with royal policy; one result was that Elizabeth herself was seen as directly complicit in the fracturing of the traditional order in Ireland.

Irish issues had always cost Elizabeth some money, but by 1594 resistance to the English and the effects of Spanish subsidies to Irish Catholic leaders resulted in a struggle which was to become the most costly of all Elizabeth's wars. Her first response to further unrest had been to transfer her forces in Brittany to Ireland, thereby effectively turning her back on Henry IV's continuing struggles in France. For that reason Essex, always an enthusiastic supporter of Henry IV as part of his wider vision for English expansion, was particularly disturbed by her decision. In part that was because he thought it bad policy to distance England from France, but it was also partly because, concerned for his own and his supporters' military prestige, he viewed Ireland as a field of war offering much less glory than the wars on the continent.

Elizabeth, however, had been particularly dismayed by the French king's explicit declaration of war against Philip II, a declaration she had always meticulously avoided even in the face of his attempted invasions. Essex continued to press for further action against Spain, particularly through more support for Dutch resistance to Spanish forces. He still planned for a time when Spain would be destroyed and England would have easy access to all the Iberian imperial riches. Elizabeth's preferred policy, however, was informed by her anxiety at the ongoing heavy demands of warfare on her limited financial resources. As a monarch, her gender left her unusually free of any imperative to pursue personal chivalric glory; more commonly her goal was to extricate herself as far as possible from any continental entanglements.

The ongoing Tudor strategy to suppress traditional Irish practice was made more difficult in the later years of the century by the emergence of Hugh O'Neill, Earl of Tyrone, as dominant leader of Irish resistance. In his younger days he had been a royal ward at the English court, and had learned English methods of fighting; in 1588 he had still been sufficiently loyal to the English administration to execute some 500 Spanish castaways from the Armada. But by 1595 Tyrone had been declared a traitor in London, in part for promoting a petition on behalf of other Irish lords against further English innovations. He waged war intermittently for several years, and as late as 1598 the Irish Privy Council was uncertain whether to sue for peace with him or to prosecute war against him. Its decision finally to continue the fight against him resulted in some significant victories for Tyrone; indeed some victories were sufficiently impressive for him to hope for meaningful Spanish support from the new Spanish king, Philip III (Philip II having died in September 1598). One mark of Tyrone's success was the number of Irish volunteers who joined his ranks, replacing the more costly and less reliable mercenaries who had been a feature of earlier outbreaks of resistance. He proved indeed an unusually successful opponent of English rule after the Elizabethan regime alienated him.

Essex in Ireland

In 1598, there was a scandalous scene at court after Essex failed to win support for his candidate as the next lord deputy in Ireland. Told of his failure, Essex immediately and publicly challenged the queen about her decision, and when she abruptly rejected his preferred candidate, he turned his back on her, a serious violation of court protocol. Later reports added that she boxed his ears and he put his hand on his sword. Forcibly restrained, he was said to have told Elizabeth he would not have accepted such an indignity even from Henry VIII. That confrontation had occurred in late June or early July, and it was September before he returned to Elizabeth's court.

By then affairs in Ireland had become even more worrying, and as the pre-eminent English military commander, Essex was the obvious leader to send. There were still delays, for it was December before he was formally appointed lord lieutenant of Ireland, and April 1599 before he finally set out with the largest army Elizabeth had ever sent abroad, and with very clear instructions about how he was to use it. By then, even Essex had accepted that his plans for greater English imperial expansion had been foiled by the decision of Henry IV in 1598 to make peace with Spain. And by then, both the need to reassert control across Elizabeth's whole realm and the fear that Ireland would provide a launching pad for a fresh Spanish attempt to invade England were taken very seriously.

Because of the extent to which he delayed in other parts of Ireland, and despite the clarity of his instructions to confront

Tyrone immediately, Essex did not reach his base in Ulster until, as he could argue, it was too late in the season to fight. In such circumstances it may well have seemed sensible for Essex to agree to a parley with Tyrone rather than seeking immediately to destroy him, but their private conference – on horseback in the midstream of a river – was easily used by Essex's many critics at Elizabeth's court as tantamount to treason. Subsequently Tyrone spread damaging reports, never verifiable, that Essex had contemplated defying Elizabeth's command to fight him. What is certain is that Essex agreed to a six-week (renewable) truce with Tyrone in defiance of his queen's instructions, and that the whole enterprise had been costing Elizabeth some £1,000 a day. Essex then set sail for England, having disbanded most of his unprecedentedly large Irish army and having disregarded the queen's orders in so many ways. By then, he was well aware that his behaviour had outraged the queen – whose letters were explicit on the subject – and her advisers, but he may have relied on his considerable popular support in London to protect him, at least to some extent, from what would undoubtedly be an uncomfortable reception by Elizabeth.

Relations with the probable heir apparent

It was not until October 1594 that Elizabeth could express any satisfaction with James VI as her prospective heir. Before that, particularly irritated by James's refusal to take her advice on controlling his pro-Spanish lords, Elizabeth had threatened to break the terms of the Treaty of Berwick. An equally exasperated James had even made tentative moves towards renewing Scotland's 'Auld Alliance' with France, an alliance traditionally threatening for England. In the end, cooler heads prevailed, once again not least because of James's enduring concern to ensure he inherited the English throne.

He explained away one letter, which had given Elizabeth great offence by including a reference to Virgil in which he seemed to allude to Elizabeth as a 'seduced queen'; he abjectly sought to explain the reference away, and as abjectly begged her pardon for any offence he had given. A placated Elizabeth responded by renewing his pension grants; James also finally took steps against at least some of his troublesome Catholic lords. The gesture did something to please Elizabeth, who seemed never to understand just how difficult it was for James to assert complete control in a society so different from her own, let alone that it was not in his interests ever to appear subordinate to her. What was to prove ultimately more significant was that, like Essex, several of Elizabeth's leading councillors had also established lines of communications with the man they saw as their future king.

There was another brief period of tension in 1597, when English sources thought that James had complained too strenuously in the Scottish parliament of his treatment by Elizabeth. He had attacked her in his parliament both for the execution of his mother and her refusal publicly to acknowledge him as her heir. Her response was to suspend his pension again, but other possibilities were also raised. As Burghley reminded the Scottish king, the English parliament had the power to alter the line of succession. He might well have added that there was no shortage of other contenders for the English throne, and arguing just who had the strongest claim had become a widespread – if always perilous – activity.

One particularly unnerving discussion of alternative contenders to the English throne was the Jesuit Robert Person's *Conference about the Next Succession to the Crowne of England,* a work printed abroad in 1595 and circulated secretly in England. Persons cast doubt on the legitimacy of all English monarchs since Henry II (died 1189) and, in apparent contradiction of that listed a number of possible contenders and declared Isabella, daughter of Philip II of Spain, the most likely claimant to the English throne. He based that argument on her lineal descent from John of Gaunt (died 1399), on her religious preference and on her being the most likely victor in the inevitable battles for the English throne. His most potent point, which concerned many others as well, was the number of possible contenders for the English throne, given the lack of an indisputable successor. As previously discussed, Henry Hastings Earl of Huntingdon paid a high price for his Plantagenet descent and always tenuous claim to the throne. But there were many other claimants. Arabella Stuart had a similar lineage to that of James, but with the added advantage that she was born in England. Indeed, the objection most consistently raised against James was his foreign birth; some argued from (probably irrelevant) legal precedents that was an insuperable barrier. Others were more straightforwardly hostile to any foreigner as monarch. In his unpublished discussion in 1601, Thomas Wilson listed his candidates as the 12 most likely competitors for the English crown, a discussion which ended with the grim comment that the crown was 'not like to fall to the ground for want of heads that claim to wear it'.[3]

James therefore had reason enough to be anxious about his status as unofficial heir apparent to the English throne. His anxiety was particularly evident in the case of one Valentine Thomas, sometimes described as a border thief, who had been arrested in the north while plotting to aid the return of the Earl of Westmoreland to England. That earl, it may be remembered, had fled into exile after his involvement in the abortive Northern Uprising of 1569; he was subsequently a serial participant in plots to rescue Mary Stuart as a means of rallying northern recusants. Years later, when Thomas was captured by the English as a thief, he pleaded guilty to that charge of plotting, but also claimed that James himself had urged him to kill Elizabeth. No one in England believed that improbable claim, but James struggled for several years, from early 1598, to have the English government issue a public repudiation of the slander. He was particularly concerned because the terms of the Act for the Queen's Security could mean that Thomas's charge of the king's complicity in an assassination plot against Elizabeth might debar him from the English throne. English authorities always made it clear that no one believed Thomas's claims against James, but he was held in the Tower until 1603 where, after James became king, he was executed.

From May 1598 the ever-anxious James appealed to other Protestant rulers to support his inheritance claim, and even asked them to provide him with military support if he needed to fight for the crown after Elizabeth's death; no ruler he approached agreed to the military proposal, however much they were prepared verbally to support his claim and however anxious some of them were not to have a Catholic monarch of England. Nor did it help his position in relation to Elizabeth that he sent an envoy to Philip III asking him not to support the candidacy of his half-sister Isabella for the English throne. Elizabeth found this particularly offensive, not least because, she wrote, such questions might wait at least until she was dead, which as yet, she acerbically noted, she was not.

The ceremonious queen

Despite the many tribulations and problems of the early 1590s, Elizabeth's court retained its primary function as the spectacular epicentre of high politics and royal spectacle. Well-born foreigners on their tours of Europe and delegates from foreign powers continued to appear there; their reports of the court rituals surrounding the queen reflect a well-established theatre of authority and magnificence, which effectively defied the many problems facing the regime. What could not be disguised, however, was that the queen herself was ageing. By 1597, when she was 64, she was described by the French ambassador as having a long, thin face, with yellow teeth, and many of them missing. (The next year, another foreigner observer described her teeth as black, a common English defect, he thought, resulting from their love of sugar, then still an unusual and expensive luxury.) Her figure, the ambassador reported, was fair and tall and graceful; there were very few hints ever that she was growing stouter, a feature which was also never reflected in her portraits. Her clothing, which records show was significantly altered over these years to accommodate her broadening frame, remained magnificent as many ambassadors reported; they often dwelt at some length on details of the richness of both her dresses and her spectacular jewellery, which she always regarded as an important signifier of her majesty.

In summer, she still liked to stay at Greenwich, where each Sunday her councillors and courtiers gathered. That was a place where many foreigners of sufficient importance also went as part of their English tour; they observed the courtly rituals and the many ways of enacting the pre-eminence of the queen, the procession of her officers and councillors, the train of ladies accompanying her, the gentlemen pensioners protecting her, the people falling to their knees as her eyes passed that way, each person who had been addressed speaking to her from a kneeling position. Sufficiently well-credentialed foreigners were sometimes able to address her, albeit with varying fortune. Some delivered a complete speech, others found themselves raised to their feet and thereby silenced before they could complete their oration.

After she had passed through the presence chamber to the chapel, those present were able to observe preparations for her dinner. The relevant ceremonies were again performed with great reverence before some 24 separate dishes were brought in, each tested for poison by offering a portion to her guards. In those years, despite the abundance of food, the queen herself ate sparingly and privately, with the rest of the food going to other members of the court.[4]

Although the splendours of court protocol were always maintained, the practice of the queen going on progresses had been curtailed during the fraught years of 1588–9. In the early 1590s she resumed her visits to councillors and others she wished to honour. Although in these years she seldom ventured far beyond the home counties, the rituals of her progresses remained much as they had been. She still drew crowds, attracted by the uniquely magnificent and colourful retinue, and by the money traditionally cast among them. She still caused much activity for those about to be visited, as they contemplated finding sufficient accommodation for the entire royal entourage, followed by problems of finding sufficient food and devising elaborate and pleasing welcomes for the queen. By this time, however, she often visited her more intimate friends, such as Lady Elizabeth Russell, to two of whose children Elizabeth was godmother, and trusted councillors such as Burghley, so the splendour, although always required, could often be of a more familiar kind. In all, the queen may have been ageing in those years, but she made as few significant concessions to that disagreeable fact as possible in the early 1590s. What was the case, however, was that she was making fewer political decisions herself, leaving more to her trusted councillors as the problems confronting her realm still proved so demanding.

9　Elizabeth's final years

Elizabeth and her relatives

There was at least one feature of Elizabeth's reign that remained constant throughout her reign. Although Elizabeth often invoked the memory of her father, her references to her mother were very few indeed. Yet throughout her reign she consistently promoted her relatives on her mother's side, in marked contrast to her treatment of the descendants of her father's two sisters. That attention was particularly the case for the offspring of her mother's sister, Mary Carey, and, as several examples in Robert Carey's *Memoirs* illustrate, she also demanded that they always behaved in a manner befitting their connection to the throne. Carey's detailed account of her sustained fury when he married, for love, a woman of little fortune offers a typical account of the treatment Elizabeth meted out to those who had fallen short of their worth as her relations. When she finally agreed to see him again, her interview with him was, he wrote, 'stormy and terrible, which I passed over in silence', and he simply refused to get off his knees until he had her pardon.[1] More generally she made good use of her mother's relatives. She always had at least one Carey relative on the Privy Council, and family members were several times entrusted with very secret tasks and communications with other royalty.

Towards the relatives on her father's side, however, Elizabeth's attitude was quite different. Since they shared the Tudor bloodline, she regarded them all as potential threats to either her security on the throne or to the choice she might make of her successor. If that was one reason for the hostility she showed to them, it was also one consequence of her own failure to marry and produce her own indisputable heir. The descendants of Henry VIII's elder sister

Margaret included her daughter, Lady Margaret Douglas, and *her* son Darnley, briefly husband of Mary Queen of Scots and father of James VI. In the case of Lady Margaret, Elizabeth's dislike may well have been fed by her knowledge that she had been not only a close confidante of Mary I, but also that in the reigns of both Henry VIII (after he had declared both his daughters illegitimate) and of Mary I, Lady Margaret, undeniably of legitimate birth, had been suggested as preferred successor.

Margaret Douglas's other son, Darnley's brother Charles, had one daughter, Arabella Stuart, who was therefore a cousin to James VI. She was for some time at Elizabeth's court, before being sent away, as gossip had it, for being too friendly to the Earl of Essex. The tragedy of Arabella's life was that although she wanted very much to do so, she was repeatedly prevented from marrying, first by Elizabeth and subsequently by James. Both monarchs, apparently, feared that she might complicate the line of succession by producing an alternative heir. The same anxiety explains the disastrous consequences in Elizabeth's reign of the secret marriage between Katherine Grey (younger sister to the nine-day Queen) and Edward Seymour. Katherine and Jane were granddaughters of Mary Tudor, the younger sister of Henry VIII, by her second marriage. Elizabeth had Katherine's secret marriage to Edward Seymour – which produced two male children – declared null and void, and the children illegitimate. The details of the queen's prolonged resistance to recognising either the marriage or the children is more fully discussed in Chapter 5.

Perhaps even more curious is Elizabeth's continuing failure to make a serious effort to restore her mother's reputation. There were many admirers in England who believed her to be entirely innocent of the charges which brought about her death. They wished to rehabilitate Anne Boleyn for her significant role in furthering a Protestant religion. Elizabeth might well have been concerned to avoid any implications her mother's rehabilitation might suggest for the gullibility of her father, whom she so admired. But her permanent silence about her mother now seems even more poignant because by the last decade of the century the reputation of Katharine of Aragon, Henry's first wife whom he had discarded in favour of Anne, was showing a marked recovery. This was despite John Foxe's many attacks on Katharine in successive editions of his widely read

Actes and Monumentes. One indicator of the first queen's rise in popularity can be seen in the publication history of Vives' *Instruction of a Christian woman,* initially written at Katharine's request for her daughter Mary. Early editions included a glowing tribute to Katharine, but such praise disappeared in the following decades, only to reappear in the 1585 and 1592 editions. But Anne Boleyn's reputation showed no sign of such recovery, despite some efforts to defend her by Foxe; Elizabeth's effective silence about her mother in the face of such developments stands in marked contrast to the honour – and pride – that she so frequently displayed for her father, and indeed her favour towards her mother's relations.

The decline and fall of Essex

Unlike her constancy in depending on her mother's relations, other relationships were changing. One example by 1598 was the queen's attitude to her favourite. Elizabeth was well aware that Essex, still her pre-eminent favourite despite his frequent defiance of her orders, was ever more inclined to pursue his own interests and was now corresponding with James VI, promising him both men and support against his enemies in England. James was the more gratified when Essex first made contact with him because he was seriously concerned that Robert Cecil, rapidly assuming much of his father's authority, opposed his accession. For his part, Essex had no reason to dissuade the king from that view of the man he had always regarded as his most serious rival for political promotion. Elizabeth, then well into her seventh decade, understood that Essex was anticipating her own death soon, and was ensuring for himself a more satisfying military career under a younger and male monarch. That way lay the glory he had so long sought.

But Essex was soon to offend in more serious ways. Well before he was sent to Ireland, the Earl had a wide popular following, particularly in London; he had also developed a coterie of well-born friends who shared his discontent and supported his ambitions. Above all, he feared the activities of those he regarded as his enemies, and just before he left London he had described himself to Elizabeth as 'Her Majesty's exiled servant'. Once in Ireland, he had become progressively more discontented, primarily because he believed even more strongly that powerful enemies at court were plotting against him. If that was indeed the case, he provided them with ever more reasons to attack him as he repeatedly ignored his instructions for the conduct of the Irish campaign; he was, as ever, convinced that his preferred strategy for victory in Ireland was better. Correspondence from London, including some from he queen herself, frequently reminded him of Elizabeth's growing anger at his disregard of her instructions and those of her Council. That knowledge only reinforced Essex's conviction that back in London hostile groups, particularly within the Council, were scheming against him.

When he first decided to return from Ireland, Essex had considered a landing in Wales with some 6,000 of his remaining soldiers (he had lost about 10,000 of the original force through warfare, disease and malnutrition). He was, however, dissuaded by those around him from such an openly rebellious project. Instead, in September 1599, he landed in England and took horse immediately to Elizabeth's court, finally finding her at Nonsuch, in Surrey. Still muddied from the ride there, and defying all royal protocol, he burst unannounced into the room where she was dressing. He arrived so early in the day and so precipitately that she was still without her cosmetics, her wig and her outer garments. She had every reason to be affronted, even alarmed by such an incursion; there were even reports later that she briefly suspected a rebellion was already under way. Reassured on that point at least, she did see him twice more that day; the first of those meetings was relatively amicable, but the second ended with her instruction that he explain himself and his actions to the Council. She was angry about his conduct in Ireland and even angrier about the cost of his failures in both money and men. His unprecedented eruption into her rooms only increased her annoyance.

Essex had more than a year to live, but he never saw the queen again. Banned from court, he was confined to his own house and examined by members of the Council. He did briefly win his freedom from house arrest in August, but by then his finances had become very strained. In September the queen refused to renew a major source of his income, his monopoly of sweet wines. Her explanation was that Essex still needed to be brought further under control, but her decision ensured that he now faced complete financial ruin. Although ever more resentful, for several months Essex took no obvious action to address his problems.

At the same time, however, a number of his friends and supporters, both nobles and military colleagues, rallied to Essex's increasingly dangerous cause. Some zealous Protestants, perhaps attracted by his earlier plans for a grand European anti-Catholic and anti-Spanish alliance, were also among the growing group of supporters, and there was wild talk of taking some action to protect and promote his interests. The final drama of his life began on 7 February 1601, when a group of his supporters arranged for a public performance of Shakespeare's *Richard II* that included the banned deposition scene, in which Richard progressively discarded all that made him a king. There is a much-repeated tradition that later Elizabeth remarked to one visitor: 'I am Richard II, know ye not that?' What is known more certainly is that the next day Essex and some 300 supporters marched through London calling for supporters to join them. Their purposes were apparently confused for it seems that they all were, at best, lightly armed. Whatever the truth of that, it quickly became plain that, for Londoners, popular support for Essex did not imply rebellion against Elizabeth. It has been suggested that choosing a Sunday for the protest helped alienate the pious whom he had hoped to rally to him. That cannot adequately explain the wider failure to respond to Essex's desperate appeal.

The outcome was almost inevitable. By the end of the day Essex and many of his supporters had been arrested, including his particular companion in Ireland, Sir Thomas Lee. (Lee spent many years as a soldier in Ireland, and celebrated that with his 1594 portrait by Gheeraerts, showing him in Irish dress, surely the only Elizabethan to be painted with bare legs and feet!) Now Lee, loyal beyond the point of foolishness, tried to force his way into the queen's presence to save his lord; his only reward was a speedy trial and execution, on 25 February 1601. Essex and the Earl of Southampton were also tried for treason; Essex was executed in April and was reported to have died a good Christian death. Several reports of his pious behaviour before and at his execution were widely distributed following his death and revived during the next reign. Southampton, on the other hand, survived until the accession of James VI&I, in part because of Robert Cecil's argument that he was a weak man, led astray by Essex. Then he was set free, and it was such men as Francis Bacon, who led the attack at Essex's trial, that came under James's severe displeasure. The new king apparently did not find an attempted rebellion against his predecessor unacceptable.

Immediately after the death of Essex, there was some backlash against Elizabeth and her advisers for his execution. As a proclamation in April 1601 declared, some 'lewd and ungodly' persons had issued libels 'tending to the slander of our royal person' and seeking to stir up rebellion.[2] But such criticism soon either died away or was suppressed. Little is known of Elizabeth's own response to the death of Essex, the man whose erratic behaviour she had indulged more than any other, and from whom she had endured frequent defiance. There were some reports that after Essex's death the queen was distressed, weary and very tearful. Others suggested any such tears reflected her continuing grief at the death of Burghley who had died in 1598.

Her godson Sir John Harington, who had fought with and been knighted by Essex in Ireland, reported that she was so distracted by the outcome of the Essex affair that she had completely lost interest in her clothes and barely changed them for many days; he also left one account of the queen slashing the arras in fury. But, as was widely acknowledged, she could be easily moved to fury for a wide range of reasons, and Harington has long been regarded as a rather unreliable gossip. In those difficult months after the execution, any appearance of illness, of reluctance to take part in any activities, of a failure to dress to her usual standards of magnificence were all popularly attributed to her grief at Essex's death.

It was the case that the queen had made very few progresses and visits in 1600, and made even fewer in the early months of 1601. There were, however, many possible reasons for such interruptions to her usual patterns of movement, including her advancing years, her increasing health problems and the deaths of so many of her long-standing friends; as ever, there were also, always, pressing matters of state. Her health was certainly becoming more troubling. The Venetian ambassador to Spain received a report from England in February 1601, before Essex had gone to trial, describing Elizabeth as 'feeble and tottering' because of her illness, and referring to the rumours circulating that she could not live much longer. Elizabeth's response to Essex's death was, and perhaps still is, a matter of wide speculation, and since she never spoke of it in the many months remaining before her own death, conjecture it must remain. The whole episode is one example of how much gossip and guesswork there always was about the behaviour of England's queen, and on how little evidence much of it was based.

'Pacifying' Ireland and pursuing new colonies

After Essex abandoned his military campaign in Ireland, Elizabeth chose as his replacement Charles Blount, Baron Mountjoy, another scholar/courtier/soldier whose company the queen appreciated. As Essex's replacement Mountjoy soon began to make some progress, in part by following his instructions, as Essex had failed to do. Important Irish areas were restored to English control well before the Spanish made yet another attempt to support their Irish co-religionists. For the Spanish there was always still the double attraction of restoring Catholicism to all Ireland and establishing a strong launching pad for yet another planned attack on England.

Spanish leaders had chosen Kinsale in County Cork as their base, but under Mountjoy's command the ensuing three-month English siege of the Spanish garrison, until January 1602, proved an important turning point for the Irish wars. From that time, Irish leaders had to accept their declining fortunes and began to surrender. So did the Spanish who, rather to the irritation of Elizabeth, were allowed to return to Spain; she would have much preferred them dead instead of departed. Almost the last of the Irish to accept defeat was Tyrone himself; he surrendered on remarkably generous terms in 1603, without knowing that Elizabeth had died a week before.

Despite the English victory, what was to become only too clear in the next century was that Elizabeth's apparent recovery of authority in Ireland had done very little to address the problems of English Protestant rule in Catholic Ireland. The restoration of English control, moreover, had been achieved at a debilitating cost to the regime; even Elizabeth, most unusually, made her own contribution to the costs by selling some of her own jewellery. There was certainly an even heavier human cost of the unknowable number of lives lost on both sides, but there was no serious attempt to identify, let alone redress, the grievances of her Irish subjects. At whatever cost, however, Elizabeth was able to die in the belief that she had restored English 'supremacy' in Ireland.

Elizabeth did not view Ireland as necessarily the geographical limit of her dominions. On the contrary, in the later decades of her reign she had encouraged several drives for more settlements, even though the English settlements in Ireland had proved to be a major cause for the problems she was to face there. Essex had never been the only one to dream of establishing English colonies in new and little-known lands. His plans for England to take over Spanish possessions across the Atlantic had come to nothing, but another of Elizabeth's erstwhile favourites, Walter Raleigh, strongly influenced by his half-brother Humphrey Gilbert, had been pursuing the same objectives. After a notably brutal military career in Ireland, Gilbert had been granted a royal patent in 1578 to search out 'barbarous lands' not already in the possession of a Christian prince, where he might establish English settlements. Elizabeth granted Gilbert authority to rule in these lands and to grant tenures to those colonists who were licensed to leave England; but Gilbert found the settlements in the New World extremely difficult to establish, and achieved nothing permanent in his Newfoundland enterprise before he died in 1583.

Raleigh continued in Gilbert's footsteps, trying to establish colonies in the part of North America he had named Virginia in homage to his queen. Given the power of many 17th-century sources which once shaped much Elizabethan history, it is noteworthy that despite what was frequently claimed then, Raleigh was not responsible for the introduction to England either of the potato or of tobacco. Rather, tobacco was grown in England for at least a decade before Raleigh started his colonial exploration, and potatoes were known in Spain and had spread across Europe some time before that. But Raleigh did make an important if initially unsuccessful contribution to the establishment of English settlements to the New World. That Elizabeth endorsed the colonising impulse of both Gilbert and Raleigh is a significant indication that she too was turning from her earlier focus on recovering lost European strongholds (most notably Calais) to explore the potential riches of unclaimed parts of America, however tentatively she did so. It was, however, not until 1607 that a permanent settlement was successfully established in Virginia, and by then Raleigh had been a prisoner of James I for four years.

Despite the future wealth it was hoped such settlements might bring, Elizabeth was characteristically reluctant to commit many resources to new colonies. This time she had several sound reasons for that reluctance, since she was already facing the very high costs of the final years of her wars in Ireland, the uncertain costs of the ongoing struggles in the Netherlands and more general concern about Spain's intentions towards her realm. After the death of Philip II in 1598, his son Philip III had pursued very much the same foreign policy against both the heretic English queen and the remaining rebellious and heretic parts of the Netherlands. There, Elizabeth's costs had been reduced in a new 1598 Anglo-Dutch agreement by which the rebellious Dutch met many of the queen's costs, but she did still have troops there and still more in Ireland. On the other side of the struggles, the Spanish, having made peace with Henry IV of France, also in 1598, were then much freer to concentrate their efforts on reclaiming their lost territories in the Netherlands.

English military fortunes on the continent seemed to reach their lowest point in June 1601 when Spanish forces laid siege to Ostend, a port crucial to Anglo-Dutch interests. By mid-December, coincidentally about the time when in Ireland Mountjoy's siege of Kinsale was finally showing some signs of a good result, it was obvious that Ostend had become a major testing point for both sides, and that neither was prepared to give way. By the spring of 1603, some 7,000 Dutch troops and 18,000 Spanish had died there. One explanation offered for the continuing siege was that 'despite the terrible human cost involved, defending Ostend offered a means of tying up Spain's best troops and bleeding them into military anaemia.'[3] As a strategy for ultimate victory, it still had not achieved its final aim by the time that Elizabeth died.

Spanish commitments to both Ireland and the Netherlands at the beginning of 1602 were only part of the wider military campaigns being waged by Spain, and Spanish resources, which had once seemed infinite, were being ever more obviously strained. Even the relatively limited intervention in Ireland was proving too much of a military quagmire, but Philip III still dreamed of a successful invasion of England. There had been some negotiations for a peace from 1598, initially promoted by the dying Burghley, but Elizabeth had set her demands very high. Her terms included, for example, the renunciation of any Spanish claim to her throne, allowing English traders free access to the Spanish Indies, the end of any Spanish contact with English Catholics, and acceptance of English support for the English-backed, now independent parts of what had been the Spanish Netherlands.

There were further negotiations in 1600, during which Elizabeth instructed the English representatives to insist that the Spanish negotiators must agree that she had always been the innocent and wronged party; that proved to be, however, only one of several English barriers to positive negotiations. Modern historians suggest that the primary aim for the Spanish of those negotiations was always to secure a peace with the Dutch; for them peace with England was always a secondary concern. But it is also the case that the English terms for settlement indicate that Elizabeth was not seriously interested in peace. So mutual hostility dragged on until the accession of James I in 1603; in the following year, to the fury of a significant number of his more fiercely anti-Catholic Protestant English subjects but with the very strong support of Robert Cecil, the new king ended the Anglo-Spanish war, not least because he recognised the extent of the drain of warfare on the English economy and preferred, as he always did, diplomacy to war.

The last Elizabethan parliament

Elizabethan parliaments, like those called by her Tudor predecessors, met seldom and were not always highly regarded by the monarch. Indeed, Elizabeth redefined a number of issues, discussed by parliament in earlier reigns, as now being matters of royal prerogative and therefore no longer fit matters for parliamentary debate. Many financial issues were so redefined and, as indicated in earlier chapters, she worked hard to prevent parliament interfering with *her* church settlement. Nevertheless, there were occasions where she was obliged to give way; she sometimes demonstrated she could do so with apparent grace, provided the appropriate deferential niceties had been observed. So, for example, in 1571 one Walter Strickland, who was among those promoting further reforms in the church, was briefly barred from attending parliament. Parliamentarians appealed to their privileges, specifically their freedom to attend parliament, which they saw to be under threat. What looked like a serious impasse was resolved only when parliamentarians agreed not to stand on their traditional privileges, but humbly to sue the queen for his return. A request, rather than a stand on their right, and cast in suitably submissive terms, was much more agreeable to Elizabeth's understanding of the nature of her royal authority.

The queen's last parliament, called in 1601, gave rise to another potential impasse and led to Elizabeth delivering what became probably her most famous speech, and one that, unlike her so-called 'Tilbury speech', she undoubtedly did deliver. She may not have intended it as such, but it is now read as an apologia of her rule over almost half a century, in part because it came so late in the reign. The disputed issue which brought about this occasion was, as it had often been, that of monopolies, for in 1601 the new parliament refused to address even matters of money supply for the crown until their grievances, specifically about the continuing spread of monopolies, had been redressed. Monopolies were, it may be remembered, one means whereby the crown saved money and rewarded subjects by granting patents for monopolies in specific trade items, ranging from playing cards to wines to glass manufacturing and even salt. Earlier muted protests against some of those monopoly practices had been ignored by the Crown and suppressed by her councillors, but the 1601 parliamentarians were more committed to addressing at least some of the more abusive practices which had developed.

Faced with the insistent demands for redress of those grievances, Elizabeth issued a proclamation couched, as such proclamations often were, in terms of reiterating her enduring and utmost concern to guard all her subjects' interests, which did end some of the most offensive practices. Following that conciliatory move, she summoned a number of members of the House of Commons to her presence. To them she delivered what is now known as her 'Golden speech'. In it she declared her enduring thankfulness to her subjects, since 'nothing is more dear to us than the loving conservation of our subjects' hearts', and her own good fortune that she had always saved her subjects from 'foreign foes, from tyrants' rule and from your own ruin'.[4] It was an impressive, if not fully persuasive account of her rule since she had come to the throne; that exercise of royal graciousness by the queen sufficiently defused the issue of monopolies at the time. It did not mark any further moves against the practice of granting monopolies beyond those announced in the proclamation, but as already noted, the speech has enhanced her reputation ever since.

The anxious heir apparent

Elizabeth's anxiety about the possible claims of alternative heirs was always at least equalled by that of the Scottish king. James VI's search for support for his claimed right to the English throne had been wide-ranging; as earlier discussed, he had courted Catholics and Protestants, foreign powers and English subjects to ensure his accession. But after the final fall of the Earl of Essex his anxiety intensified, since Essex had been his most deeply committed supporter. James, with Essex's guidance, had concluded that first Burghley, and then his son Robert Cecil, favoured the Suffolk line, descendants of Henry VIII's younger sister, Mary. That line was then represented by the offspring of Edward Seymour and Katherine Grey. Elizabeth's move to debar their descendants from the succession had never prevented some from seeing them as next Tudor heirs. Given the lack of a direct heir, there was always a range of potential candidates, both within and beyond England, and James never felt he had extracted a sufficiently firm promise of her support, preferably public, from Elizabeth.

After Essex fell in 1601, James sent an unusually large embassy to Elizabeth, partly to request yet another declaration that the Scottish king was innocent of the old Valentine Thomas charges that he had sought Elizabeth's life (discussed in Chapter 8) and was also innocent of the new accusation that he had prior knowledge of the Essex uprising. Elizabeth preferred to reiterate that James had no cause for complaint against her, but did make a fresh offer to increase his pension, a gesture perhaps marred by her statement that James would need to earn it by good behaviour. But for James the most significant point was that the embassy made satisfactory contact with Robert Cecil, who flatly denied the recurrent rumours of discussions about any other preferred heir, let alone for a Spanish succession, and agreed to enter secret negotiations with James. Reassured by his new connections, from late 1601 James's relations with the ageing queen were less troubled. Feeling more secure in his inheritance, he wrote agreeably affectionate letters to Elizabeth and kept her informed of his foreign negotiations. His main remaining concern was that on Elizabeth's death, a foreign attempt might be made to establish a Catholic successor, but even that anxiety faded as Elizabeth's pre-eminent advisers made it repeatedly clear that they saw him as the legitimate future king.

So it was that by July 1602 James felt free to write to his godmother in particularly flattering terms: 'Your honorable integrity and princely disposition in true love towards me has shone so brightly ... that the honourable record thereof shall never wear out. .... And ... I shall ever account it the true pattern of a princely and heroic mind.' In his final letters he also took good care to make clear not only that he deeply distrusted the Spanish, but that he had advised the French king to do the same, detailing just how fully he had written to Henry IV, warning him against the 'boundless and insatiable ambition of Spain'.[5]

Elizabeth's last months

Although there had normally been a Venetian representative at earlier Tudor courts, there had been no Venetian ambassador at Elizabeth's court since the first years of her reign. The usual explanation was that the Venetian authorities were anxious not to alienate the Papacy by attending a heretic court. Be that as it may, the result has been that for most of her reign historians have been without those detailed Venetian reports of the court which abounded in the earlier Tudor reigns, offering political gossip, scandal, historical details, misleading insights and frequently astute comments on successive monarchs.

But one Venetian representative did come to her court in her final days and left a vivid image of the ageing queen. By his account, despite some signs of her many years, she still retained all her royal magnificence, her skill at sustaining the theatre of royalty and her verbal sharpness. Scaramelli, the Venetian representative, first visited the queen on Sunday, 16 February at Richmond. His report began with a detailed description of Elizabeth's dress of silver and white taffeta, setting off a spectacular abundance of pearls, rubies and other gems as well as gold ornaments set all about her person. Her hair, he commented, was 'of a light colour never made by nature', but by then she had worn a light red wig for many years. It is widely believed that she chose that colour to act as a reminder that she was indeed the daughter of Henry VIII.

After a mutually gracious exchange of courtesies, Scaramelli congratulated Elizabeth on being in such excellent health before addressing the substance of his message, a complaint about the many raids of English sailors on other ships in the Mediterranean. Elizabeth responded by commenting on the long absence of Venetian officials from her court, remarking that it could surely not be on account of her sex, since no other princes had refused to send ambassadors. But, she added, she understood that the reason for the absence was that Venice had not been able to 'receive permission from certain sovereigns to do so'. Scaramelli could only insist defensively that Venice was indeed a 'great Sovereign and free'. If Elizabeth still retained her flair for nuanced jibes, she showed another familiar characteristic when Scaramelli was required to reassure her that indeed she still spoke Italian well, despite having studied it only as a child.[6] Before he left the court, the Venetian did receive a promise that his complaints would be investigated, although subsequently little if anything was done to curtail the English pirates operating within and beyond Europe.

When Scaramelli reported back to Venice, he noted that indeed she did appear to be very well. As others reported, despite some problems with rheumatism in her final years, often she was still able to ride for up to ten miles and still took vigorous walks in the park, despite the advice of her medical advisers to avoid such exertions. But it was very soon after the Venetian visit that her health deteriorated quite sharply. It has been widely suggested then and since that her decline began after Katherine Howard, Countess of Nottingham, a member of Elizabeth's household since 1560, died on 24 February 1603. She was also a relative, being a daughter of Elizabeth's cousin Henry Carey, later Lord Hunsdon, and she had been a friend and close confidante of Elizabeth since at least 1560. It would have been surprising indeed if Elizabeth had not grieved at the loss of yet another of her closest friends.

Whatever the reason for her decline, once she retired from public view the queen put up an impressive resistance to what others already saw as the inevitable outcome. There are many varied and sometimes lurid accounts of her death, but one of the more plausible is that of Robert Carey, brother to Katherine Howard, who was present at court for several days before she died. As another of Elizabeth's second cousins, and the holder of several important positions, he had good access to the court and to the queen herself. He had arrived there in early March 1603, to find her seated on low cushions and 'ill-disposed'. When he wished the queen good health, she replied 'no Robin, I am not well,' and told him that for 10 or 12 days 'her heart had been sad and heavy.' What he did not add, but other accounts describe, was that she already had a very sore throat, which presumably compounded her depression, as well as explaining her refusal to take the remedies suggested by her doctors.

She tried but failed to attend chapel the day after Carey's arrival, but had the cushions on which she had been lying placed where she could hear the service. For another four days, back in her bedchamber, she remained on her cushions, refusing either to take any medication or to leave her cushions and go to her bed. It was the husband of the late Katherine Howard, the Earl of Nottingham, who finally persuaded her at least to move to her bed, but still she refused to take anything offered her. By 23 March, Carey reported, she had lost her power to speak, but she called her Council to her, and to their queries signalled that her intended heir was indeed James VI. Her final hours were spent with the Archbishop and her chaplains in lengthy prayer around her; she would not allow the clerics to cease praying with and for her. Finally Carey left her with her women about her and the prayers continuing. Very early the next morning, 24 March 1603, Carey found her women 'weeping bitterly' for their dead mistress, who, they said, had finally fallen asleep, and did not wake again.

It was probably with the tacit approval of Elizabeth that Robert Cecil had been in secret correspondence with James for some time. He had also chosen Carey who, as a relative of the queen, had previously taken messages to James on her behalf, as an appropriate messenger to carry the news of her death to the Scottish king. Carey rode to Edinburgh at an amazing speed, reaching there on the night of 26 March, having left Elizabeth's palace early on 24 March. He had completed the ride in some 40 hours. At Holyrood House he was taken to James's chamber, where, as he wrote, he saluted the Scottish king 'by his title of England, Scotland, France and Ireland'.[7] Elizabeth had still never publicly declared that James was her heir, but privately she had sent out many signals to that effect. It should not have been a surprise to James, but it must have been a considerable relief, not least because he was well aware that, because he was a foreigner, there was always some support for other English-born candidates.

'The queen is dead; long live the king'?

Days before the queen died, her councillors set arrangements in place to preserve the public peace, a move made the more necessary precisely because there was still no publicly acknowledged heir. Four days before her death, her Privy Councillors had already reported to the more remotely located nobility that they were then consulting with such noblemen as were closer to London about steps to maintain good order. As news of the queen's final illness spread, there were many rumours of both nobles and lesser men storing up weapons and food in the expectation of fighting to follow. Anxious subjects were made more anxious by reports of armed men gathering; the activities of prominent Catholics were closely watched, and some who were particularly feared were imprisoned. In the more distant north, where there was still a strong Catholic presence, there was even more consternation. Lady Margaret Hoby, a devout Protestant living at Hackness, a few miles inland from Scarborough, wrote that the news of the queen's illness 'wrought great sorrow and dread in all good subjects' hearts';[8] in York, inhabitants expected the imminent sacking of their city.

In London, as her councillors went to proclaim Elizabeth's successor publicly, their way was barred by the Lord Mayor and others until they were satisfied that the declared successor would indeed be James VI. The proclamation itself was a long document, of a length comparable to that declaring Lady Jane Grey was next monarch in 1553, and responding to a similar need to explain just who the next heir was. James's claim to the throne by lineal descent was set out in careful detail. The proclamation again reminded local officials of their responsibilities to prevent any disorder, let alone any attempt to deny the right to rule 'of our only undoubted and dear Lord and Sovereign that now is'. The proclamation may have been particularly cautious because so few Englishmen had visited him in Scotland and he had never visited England, so he was indeed an unusually unknown quantity. That the transition of monarchs was ultimately so peaceful may well owe rather less to that tacit acceptance of James by Elizabeth as her heir, and a great deal more to the apparent conspiracy of so many of her closest advisers to establish sound relations with their prospective next monarch.

The final rites for the old queen

As James set out from Edinburgh to claim his new throne in England, the dead and eviscerated Elizabeth lay in state in her palace. As for any monarch, embalming her body was a necessary prelude to the lengthy preparations for a funeral. Another traditional practice was that until her funeral, which marked the formal dissolution of her household, its normal functions were maintained as they had been throughout her reign. Since the queen had died at Richmond, inconveniently distant from London, her corpse was taken at night by barge to Whitehall Palace two days later. There, in addition to the familiar household activities, she was 'watched' each night by lords and ladies of the court, who rotated the responsibility of sitting with the dead queen. Although that practice was Catholic in origin, and had traditionally included prayers for the dead, it was a practice still observed by Protestants as a mark of respect for the departed.

The new king, setting out from Scotland, decreed that her funeral should be held on 28 April. Although in form the funeral echoed those of her brother Edward VI and her sister Mary I, in scale it far outdid both of them. That difference may have been in part because her two predecessors had each been succeeded by a monarch with different religious convictions. But the sheer scale of Elizabeth's funeral may also indicate the extent to which it had been organised by her councillors and household, rather than at the command of the still absent new monarch. Royal funeral processions, after all, were exceeded as great public spectacles only by coronations; those were the two great occasions for the full display of royal ceremony. Elizabeth's funeral conformed fully to those expectations. She had reigned so long that there were few of her subjects who could remember a time without her on the throne.

The magnificent and lavish funeral procession involved more than 1,500 attendants, and all reports agree than many thousands lined the streets of London. The procession itself began with some lesser officials whose function was to clear the roadway for what was to follow. After them came a few poor men and many more poor women, a reminder of the importance of charity on such occasions. There followed a vast array of her household servants, yeomen and others arranged in order up through the hierarchy of her households to gentlemen and finally the great officials. The centrepiece of the procession was Elizabeth's hearse, drawn by four horses draped in black velvet and with an effigy of the queen in full parliamentary regalia on top. Surrounding her effigy and bier were the banners and standards of Wales, Ireland and England, and over the queen's effigy was a canopy carried by six knights, in an echo of her coronation procession so many years ago. The procession included many other dignitaries, and banners representing Elizabeth's linear descent from Henry II. As formulaic and spectacular the procession was as an event honouring Elizabeth, the printed account of it dutifully concluded with acknowledgment of the new monarch: 'Vivat Jacobus, Angliæ, Scotiæ, et Hiberniæ Rex.'

After the spectacular funeral rites had ended with the placing of the queen's remains in the tomb of her grandfather Henry VII, one final matter remained: the form of the permanent commemoration of Elizabeth. But there a problem emerged as it became ever clearer that the attitude of James VI&I towards his English predecessor was at best ambivalent, if not actually hostile. He had not been pleased when he finally arrived in London to find the printing presses were still much occupied with producing expressions of grief for the dead Elizabeth instead of focusing their attention on the arrival of the new king. Moreover, she was praised in such terms as:

Spain's rod, Rome's ruin, Netherlands relief,
Heaven's Gem, Earth's Joy, world's wonder, Nature's chief.[9]

James's strong preference for peace rather than war may have been one reason he did not enjoy finding Elizabeth praised in such terms.

His reaction may also have been in part because of the many years during which he had to accept the strictures of the late queen and her advice about how to rule his kingdom. His own ambiguous commemorative verse for Elizabeth described her as having 'A King's state in a Queen' and 'A king's heart in a maid' but, curiously, concluded that 'Heaven hence by death did summon/ To show she was a woman'. He had often made clear he was not an admirer of female rulers, but never explicitly made such a comment to Elizabeth while she lived.

After her death, however, it could at least be hinted at. In June 1603, for example, James reportedly told a French ambassador that well before the death of Elizabeth he had effectively been directing her Council. After he came to London, and perhaps after he saw the prolonged celebrations for the late queen, he issued one entirely unexpected order. By it he decreed that there would be no mourning worn at his court for the late English queen. That this was a very recent decision is confirmed by the message he sent from London to his queen as she was about to leave Edinburgh to join him, that she need bring no mourning clothes with her. About this point he was most insistent; when the special envoy from Henry IV travelled to the new king's court he was informed that neither he nor any of his retinue, all fitted out with mourning as was conventional, would be admitted to James's court if they wore black. Officially, apparently, joy at his accession took precedence over any overt expression of grief for the woman he replaced.

That may be one reason why it was another 18 months before James was persuaded by Robert Cecil that he should approve a funeral monument for Elizabeth. A further complication was that James proved adamant that if Elizabeth was to have a royal monument, so must his mother, and in the same place. That royal command meant that in the following years the remains of Mary Queen of Scots were disinterred from her grave in Peterborough Cathedral and brought to the Lady Chapel. There James had commissioned a splendid tomb for her which was not completed until 1612. Close to Mary Stuart was built a second tomb, for Margaret Douglas, Countess of Lennox, who had died in 1578, and by it is a kneeling effigy of her son Henry Stuart Lord Darnley, James's father, killed in 1567. His family was now well represented within that part of Westminster Abbey which Henry VII had fashioned to commemorate the new Tudor dynasty

Elizabeth's body was moved from her grandfather's grave in 1606 to its current site, across the way from the Stuart tombs. Curiously, for reasons now unknown, her tomb covers not only her body but also that of her sister Mary I, whom she always resented.

Only Elizabeth, however, has on the tomb either an inscription or an effigy – the latter a superb one indeed and one which, their correspondence suggests, her erstwhile councillors had to work hard to have made. Given the conflicting religious views of the two sisters brought together by James VI&I, the message at the base of the tomb: – 'Partners in throne and grave, here we sleep, Elizabeth and Mary, sisters, in hope of the Resurrection' – is, it can only be said, noncommittal. Given the extent to which Mary I and Elizabeth I were separated by religion throughout their lives, the inscription added in 1977 might appeal more to modern sensibilities: 'Remember before God all those who divided at the Reformation by different convictions laid down their lives for Christ and Conscience sake.' It is a fitting end for the biography of a queen whose reign was so extensively shaped by religious difference within and beyond her kingdom, and whose family relationships had been made and marred by the same matter.

10 What can be known of Elizabeth I?

Promoting or knowing Elizabeth?

As has been suggested several times in this study, many of the surviving sources for the reign of Elizabeth are imperfect, although she is by no means the only monarch for whom 16th and 17th-century sources are often dubious. Indeed, royal biographies in the early modern era have more generally been described as belonging 'in the intersections of chronicle, politic history, panegyric, martyrology, hagiography, confessional polemic and ... ballads, poems, sermons, pageants, and plays'.[1] That was indeed true in the case for Elizabeth Tudor, and identifying the actual Elizabeth within the propaganda that shaped her multiple representations remains a significant problem. Indeed, those polemics began even before she took the throne, at a time when her both personality and her abilities were hardly known beyond immediate court circles. As the only plausible Protestant counter to the triumphant Marian resurgence of Catholicism and as the legal heir to Mary, it was inevitable that she was widely praised and promoted by Protestant hopefuls.

If the outpourings of praise and advice for Elizabeth were more plentiful than for other monarchs, one reason was that for so many of her subjects she remained a problematic monarch. Consequently her more supportive subjects competed to praise her ever more elaborately, not only to demonstrate their loyalty but also to persuade her to endorse their preferred judgements. Some of her doctrinal caution, a recurrent irritant to more zealous Protestants, was undoubtedly because, after Mary died in 1558, Elizabeth understood rather better than many of her advisers that she had inherited a predominantly Catholic realm.

Not only did she refuse to restore the more advanced Protestantism of the later Edwardian religious changes, but her own practices, which came to include a crucifix in her chapel and her retention of the church music which Mary had promoted, dismayed the more fervent reformers. They accordingly resorted to the conventional forms of counsel and exhortation in the guise of praise; that had long been a familiar strategy employed by preachers, poets, playwrights and pamphleteers to promote their own preferred practices. So it was that Elizabeth was soon surrounded by printed exemplars of the ideal Protestant queen, largely borrowed from Old Testament models. Those models had previously been applied to Mary to promote *her* religious views, but now the message was unambiguously Protestant.

The competing range of views on the nature of 'true' English Protestantism ensured that religious exhortations, well spiced with compliments, continued for much of her reign. As a further blow to the 'hotter' Protestants, Elizabeth was instrumental in preventing moves to coerce her Catholic subjects not only to be physically present at church but also to take the Anglican Communion. She was indeed unusual in the distinction she drew between political and religious obedience, and attendance at church was her own minimal requirement for her subjects.

As relations with Spain continued to deteriorate, however, her role as the bastion of Protestantism was reinforced. Although Elizabeth insisted that open war with Spain was never made formal, the undeclared war with Spain made the need to reinforce the queen's standing within and beyond England even stronger. It became inevitable that Elizabeth should be surrounded by ever more hagiography and flattery from those who wished to sustain her in the policies about which she was often ambivalent. Although there were numerous hostile Catholic accounts in response to the Protestant hagiography, there were very few dispassionate reports of Elizabeth's conduct or of her policies. Intermittent foreigners' reports about Elizabeth have survived, some of which have been quoted in previous chapters, but their outsiders' eyes could offer only very limited accounts of Elizabeth, her court and the politics of her regime.

Elizabethan polemics in the next generations

The polemics surrounding the late queen continued after James VI&I came to the English throne. His often cavalier attitude to his predecessor, and his own policy preferences, particularly his seeking peace with Spain, gave rise to ever more hagiographic accounts of Elizabeth for her resolutely Protestant stance and her continuous war against Spain. In her reign, hostility to Spain and to all things Spanish had become an integral part of the model Protestant Englishman, and after her death much was made of her role as a consistent defender of Protestant causes at a time when both military power and wealth weighted the contest heavily in favour of Catholic forces. James's pursuit of peace seemed to many a denial of the achievements of Elizabethan England in keeping Spain at bay.

Above all, fear of Catholicism remained a potent force under the several generations of Stuart monarchs. James's Catholic wife Anne of Denmark was less a problem for her English subjects than the attempt of their son Charles to marry a Catholic princess of Spain; that project failed, but he then married a Catholic French princess. When as Charles I he succeeded his father, his religious preferences were widely seen as moving to restore Catholic mores; one result was that ever more hagiographic accounts of Elizabeth and her Protestant ways continued to appear.

We have already seen in previous chapters that 17th-century authors substantially rewrote – or invented – official accounts of the queen's speeches and activities, which served to reinforce a fictive image of a deeply Protestant, widely beloved and loving queen. These accounts were designed to defend the Protestant cause, frequently in ways Elizabeth would not have endorsed. The revisions were more often intended to be politically prescriptive than historically accurate.

Elizabeth's chronic insecurity

Nevertheless, all the material produced to exhort and exemplify Elizabeth has not rendered her actual self completely invisible; there are many aspects of Elizabeth's character which *may* be deduced from her behaviour. Given the important achievements of her reign, above all the comparative religious and political stability during it, it might seem remarkable to suggest that indecisiveness and insecurity were two of Elizabeth's most marked characteristics; throughout her reign, her councillors had good reason to be repeatedly reminded of her indecisiveness, as many of them sought to involve her in further wars. More generally, her insecurity was causally connected to such indecision.

Elizabeth's insecurities can often be deduced from her actions and decisions. She never felt secure enough to marry (marriage being a normal expectation of any monarch) and she never felt secure enough publicly to name a successor, even after it was obvious that she was not going to provide an heir in the usual monarchical way. For some years she was not sufficiently secure on her throne to destroy the Scottish queen, although Mary Stuart so manifestly aspired to Elizabeth's throne and was prepared to take it from her with the aid of anyone who offered help. Similarly, later in her reign Elizabeth never felt secure enough to deal with the many times her commands were ignored by some of her officials and courtiers, most obviously and repeatedly Robert Devereaux, Earl of Essex.

The origins of the insecurity

It is surprising in these times, when most biographers pay close attention to the formative childhood years, that historians have not thought more about the first decades of Elizabeth's life. For her first three years, she was officially the only royal princess and acknowledged heir to the throne; she was surrounded with elaborately deferential protocols and served by a large household where foreign dignitaries paid homage to the elaborately dressed infant. Sometimes her mother, Queen Anne Boleyn, visited her and, less often, her father Henry VIII. But in 1536 that all came to an abrupt end, after the shameful trial and execution of her mother, followed by the declaration of Elizabeth's own illegitimacy.

The tradition that the royal infant asked why she was no longer treated as princess may well be apocryphal; that she was outgrowing her clothes without new ones appearing was probably of more concern to her governess, Lady Margaret Bryan, than to her. Lady Margaret remained the most constant presence in Elizabeth's life until October 1537, but she was then removed by King Henry to oversee the nursery household of the latest royal child, his son Edward.

At her age, just four when Lady Margaret left her, Elizabeth may have understood little of any of the changes. It is not known at what age she first learned of, let alone fully understood, the charges of multiple adultery against her mother, and the nature of her mother's death at the command of her father. It is, however, known that in the following years much more attention was paid at court to her previously scorned elder sister. In part this was because Elizabeth was still very young, but although her brother Edward was younger, he was always heir apparent and honoured as such. When she *was* at court she consistently received less attention and much less distinction.

The sequence of Henry's wives brought a succession of new stepmothers, more or less kind to the daughter of the now excoriated Anne Boleyn, but usually they found the king's other children more interesting – Mary because she was older and widely agreed to be an ornament to the court, Edward because although he was younger he was indisputably next heir. In many ways then, Elizabeth was frequently reminded of her lesser status around the court; one interesting consequence is that she alone of Henry's children had no explicit preparation for the throne.

Patrick Collinson, pre-eminent Elizabethan scholar, has suggested that the '"black dog" depression had always been Elizabeth's companion'.[2] Given her uncertain early decades, this seems very likely. Depression, like her sense of insecurity, could only have been compounded by the publicity, within and beyond England, which surrounded her adolescent affair with Thomas Seymour in 1547, at the home of his wife and her guardian, Katherine Parr; Elizabeth's need to request the Edwardian Council for an official denial of the rumours within and beyond England that she was pregnant (a request they refused) could only have distressed her further. By then she would also have understood the force of contemporary beliefs that an immoral mother could easily pass on that corruption to her child.

The later years of Edward's reign (1547–53) did see some moves to defend the reputation of Anne Boleyn, but the young king himself was not interested (perhaps because defence of her could lead to aspersions about her successor, his mother). Elizabeth was not often at court. Officially she was still at her studies in those years, although now her scholarly achievements are thought to be less impressive than her contemporary admirers and polemicists claimed. One example of such exaggeration was the praise Roger Ascham offered for Elizabeth's command of other languages, asserting that 'they be few in number in both the universities or elsewhere in England, that [have linguistic skills] comparable to her Majesty.' Modern scholars take a rather less enthusiastic view of her linguistic skills, not least because, in Latin as in other languages, she, like many beginners, consistently used the English word order.[3] Undue praise for skills beyond her capacities may not have done anything for Elizabeth's self-esteem.

More generally, during Edward's reign Elizabeth was held of little account, despite some later romantic tales about the close friendship between brother and sister. They were, in fact, seldom together, and when he was dying Edward rejected both his sisters as possible next heir, not least for their illegitimacy but also for what he saw as the possible threat to his established Protestantism from either of them; he preferred the less royal but firmly evangelical Lady Jane Grey, who had the added benefit of being safely married to another Protestant. When Catholic Mary took up arms to defend her right to the throne in accordance with the final statute of succession of Henry VIII and against the usurping Lady Jane Grey, Elizabeth stayed well away from supporting either, taking to her bed until the victor emerged.

It quickly transpired that Mary had been in no need of her support. But during Mary's reign, Elizabeth's own early knowledge of and silence about the Wyatt conspiracy against Mary's proposed marriage, and her foreknowledge of other plots (which always had some French support) throws light on her later resistance to ever publicly naming an heir. After her own conduct she apparently could not imagine that any heir would be trustworthy. If she had a low public profile in the reign of Edward, in the reign of Mary much of the publicity she did incur was because of suspicions about her complicity in conspiracies against her sister. All in all, the rather chequered early decades of Henry's third successor go some way to explain why she may well have been chronically insecure as a person and on her throne.

That insecurity may also be the reason for one of Elizabeth's more enduring but in some ways unlikely friendships. Kat Astley had joined her household in 1536, but little is known of the early relationship between the two. By 1545, however, Kat was sufficiently securely established in the household to be appointed Elizabeth's governess, and she may well have given the young princess a degree of emotional support she did not receive from other sources. Nevertheless she was manifestly not the ideal model of sound judgement. Kat was, for example, three times imprisoned in the Tower for her indiscreet promotion of marriage proposals for her mistress. The first and most severely punished incident was her support of the lecherous and dangerously ambitious Thomas Seymour, the last her advocacy of the always improbable, but not yet mad, Erik XIV of Sweden. Despite all that, Elizabeth retained Kat in her household until her death in 1565 as a particularly favoured companion. A strong emotional bond between the two seems the most likely explanation for her continuing close association with Elizabeth, despite her noteworthy indiscretions. But, in the absence of more evidence, that bond remains at best a probability, no more than that.

Another aspect of Elizabeth's insecurity was implied in reports of ambassadors attending her court, suggesting that she often interrogated them in ways which reflected her need for reassurance. In 1564 the Scottish Melville reported the questions that Elizabeth asked about Mary Stuart's height, her musical skills and her facility at dancing – and her responses (discussed in Chapter 4) reflect some anxiety about her own abilities and attributes. Such anxiety recurred throughout her reign; apparently even in her dying days she was seeking reassurance from the Venetian ambassador that despite her many years without speaking it, her Italian was good. Such self-doubt, after all is a not uncommon human trait.

There was also the matter of her public demeanour, consistently an exercise in visible majesty. Within her most intimate circle she could and did relax. One intriguing episode which illustrates this is the occasion in 1560 when Elizabeth disguised herself as maid to her cousin Katherine Carey, to watch Robert Dudley take part in a competition at Windsor in 1561. But there are few such anecdotes. She reportedly ate sparingly, but for her meals she was always given a wide choice of a complete range of dishes, even the more frugal of which cost much more than a common labourer could earn in a year. This practice was retained in her later years when, perhaps because of her bad teeth, she chose to eat more privately. In all these ways her self-presentation was frequently very different to that of Europe's most powerful monarch, Philip II, who habitually dressed in black, on occasion publicly ate the local foods his subjects ate, and sometimes walked their streets without royal grandeur. On her public outings, Elizabeth, richly attired, took care to show herself to the crowds that gathered for the royal spectacle, but was always somewhat distant, on horseback or in a carriage, and surrounded by her considerable entourage.

'The Queen is a woman'

There are two aspects of the second Tudor queen regnant which are indisputable but often seen as problematic: that Elizabeth was indeed a woman, and that she never married. Despite a long tradition to the contrary, the first was of less consequence, for in her own time she was not particularly unusual as an authoritative female. *Because* she was a woman, it might well be argued that she has often been assessed by criteria different from those applied to male rulers. Subtexts of emotional and irrational responses recur much more frequently in histories of her reign than they do, for example, in the reign of her father. That, however, does not alter the point that the uniqueness of her female rule is easily overstated.

She was, after all, the second queen regnant of early modern England, immediately after the five-year rule of her half-sister Mary. As long as 16th century English history was treated essentially as the time when England finally broke away from the Catholic Church, Mary's rule was treated simply as a deviation and as a warning of how not to reign. More recent research has offered a quite different portrait of that queen. She is now often seen as a much more positive exemplar of female rule than has been traditionally understood. Elizabeth was often well placed to observe and learn from Mary's examples – in both positive and negative ways.[4]

Although ultimate authority in the 16th century was normally viewed as a male prerogative, Elizabeth had many exemplars of female authority as well as the precedents set by Mary I. Before the reign of her elder sister, there was, for example, the sister of Charles V, Mary of Hungary, briefly regent of Hungary following her husband's death, and later regent of the Netherlands on her brother's behalf from 1531–55. Christina of Denmark, Duchess-consort of Lorraine, was regent for her son from 1545–52. Mary Queen of Scots, nominal queen of Scotland within a week of her birth, may have returned reluctantly to her own realm as its ruler in 1561, but it was a realm she ruled with some success until her disastrous marriage choices. The France Mary left had entered a period of underage kings, and was dominated by the queen mother, Catherine de Medici, who was powerful during the reign of her young son Francis II (died 1560) and for a time regent for Charles IX (died 1574). Her influence continued in the reign of her third son, Henry III, until her death in January 1589. And that is only to name significant women in the countries close to England.

In that hierarchic world, both social status and inherited office could outrank gender difference. More generally, even the most sweeping generalisations about female inferiority were always subject to exceptions; not even the most misogynistic male argued that all women were inferior in all ways to all men.[5] In brief, the peculiarity of Elizabeth's position as queen can be easily overstated, not least because she had first been confirmed as the successor to Mary by parliamentary statute in 1543. Indeed the two Tudor queens between them notched up six decades on the throne, which suggests *prima facie* that female monarchy was not necessarily a particular problem for the majority of their subjects. For the two English Tudor queens regnant, their religious allegiances were to prove more problematic for many subjects than their gender.

There was one aspect of Elizabeth's female rule which was unusual in a 16th century monarch. In this study it has been argued that one reason for Elizabeth's reluctance to wage war may have been that she did not share the traditional masculine impulses to seek chivalric glory. A corollary to that, however, may be her reluctance to allow defeated enemy troops to retreat with honour. Two episodes, both discussed in previous chapters, point to that reluctance to follow the chivalric code. Whoever devised it, she certainly concurred with the delay in granting safe-passage to English ports for some 600 Spaniards from the Armada in 1588. That delay was intended to win time to advise Philip's Dutch rebels that the unarmed sailors were about to be returned to the Netherlands; as they approached that coast, some 300 of them were slaughtered or drowned by Elizabeth's allies as they tried to evade the Dutch attack. Another occasion arose as the siege of Kinsale ended in an English victory. As was conventional the Spanish, having accepted defeat, were granted safe passage from Ireland back to Spain; Elizabeth, too late, made it very clear she would have much preferred that they had been killed.

The unmarried queen

If her lack of interest in the code of chivalry was unusual, much more remarkable was her failure to marry; the reasons for this may well include her constant insecurity. Certainly there is a strong argument that her Council could never agree on a suitable candidate, and she was reluctant to proceed without more support. But it is noteworthy that neither her father nor her elder sister had made their marriage choices conditional on conciliar support. Her failure to wed was indeed a remarkable omission, not least since no adult English monarch, for at least the previous 500 years, had remained unmarried.

In the past, a popular explanation for that omission was that she believed the marriage of Mary I and Philip II of Spain to have been a political disaster. That was the point made by some Protestant polemics, but chiefly to make a point about Catholic monarchs, not to endorse the reign of an unmarried one. It is a point which might have seemed more persuasive if not for the fact that the marriage treaties for Philip and Mary made it clear that regal authority rested solely in Mary. Indeed, those treaties were repeatedly cited by Elizabeth's councillors as an appropriate basis for negotiations for her marriage as well. Since Elizabeth approved that model and knew more of the marriage of Mary and Philip than most, it would appear that was not the reason for her remaining unmarried.

She also understood that, as Mary's husband, Philip II had been an important means of reconciling several important families previously committed to Lady Jane Grey in her brief reign. He won over some of his wife's opponents by including them in the very masculine activity of jousting, and when the nobility's traditional function of leadership in war in Europe was on offer some of his more vehement former opponents, even members of the Dudley family whose brother had married Jane Grey, joined Mary's husband in his campaign against France. Warfare was so important to male members at the higher levels of society that, as the then Earl of

Westmoreland put it in 1557, 'as long as God shall preserve my master and mistress together, I am and shall be a Spaniard.'[6]

Elizabeth's unmarried status also helped to complicate relations between her and some of her male courtiers, reducing several of them to behaving at times like petulant schoolboys as they competed for her favour. In February 1566, the Venetian ambassador in France reported that Dudley was sufficiently driven by jealousy of a new favourite (probably Sir Christopher Hatton) that he retired to his own rooms at court and stayed there for four days. But the stakes in reputation, advancement and fortune were far greater than anything to which a schoolboy might aspire, and the Venetian report ended with a new rumour that Dudley was about to be made a duke, and married, by the queen. That was indeed part of a plan, but the intended bride was Mary Stuart.

The history of the Earl of Essex is one more indicator that her unmarried status put her at a disadvantage; the authority of a king consort for Elizabeth might well have been exercised, as Philip's was, to reduce dissatisfaction among courtiers. It is surely, for example, inconceivable that Essex would have dared to pursue his overweening military ambitions in the manner that he did if there had been an authoritative military figure at Elizabeth's side. It is worth remembering that there were also a number of other discontented members of the Elizabethan elite only too willing to endorse Essex's discontent.

Even more important in the eyes of her subjects was that Elizabeth, by failing to marry, foreshadowed the end of a dynastic line of which she was the last survivor. Her father's marital history may well have been atypical, but it did serve to underline the importance of securing the dynastic succession; male heirs were preferable, but female heirs were better than no direct heirs at all. There have been many who have lauded the queen for her single life; her courtiers and poets had little choice but to do so, at least in public. A number of later biographers have also ignored the many dangers that the lack of a clearly identified heir brought to Elizabeth's England, although her councillors were always conscious of the danger. That had first been made clear by French insistence at Elizabeth's accession that Mary Stuart was the true heir. Indeed, as long as she appeared a strong contender for the succession, the consequences of the poisonous presence of Mary Stuart in England included the many plots to replace Elizabeth. The absence of an obvious English heir also fed the plans of Philip II of Spain to install his daughter Isabella on Elizabeth's throne. Isabella did have a claim at least as plausible as some other potential aspirants. The confusion, debate and anxiety about which criteria determined the succession prevailed to the final days of Elizabeth's rule. In the end, it was less the tacit actions of Elizabeth than the covert agreements of those around her that ensured the succession of James VI&I despite widespread doubts as to whether a foreign-born 'alien' could succeed to the English throne.

Elizabeth's religion

One reason for the veneration that later generations showed for Elizabeth was the extent to which she was seen as having provided a secure and enduring foundation for the Church of England, in part by developing what Francis Bacon described as a reluctance to make windows into her subjects' souls. Her own religious beliefs, however, are difficult to identify. Even more confusing is what she might have believed about the existence of a coherent true faith. When she argued so consistently that the monarch of each realm had a God-given right to define the official, public religion of his or her subjects, she was surely inviting a diversity of religious belief according to the inclination of each monarch. As Archbishop Grindal's fate demonstrated when he suggested she might consult with her clergy before taking theological positions, her belief in her own right to decide such matters was not negotiable (see Chapter 8). But that she apparently accepted that other monarchs had the same right might be thought to set out a fresh interpretation to Jesus' observation that 'In my Father's house are many mansions' (John, 14, 2).

The various prayers published in the queen's name are an unreliable source for her religious beliefs, since there are few guidelines as to which were actually written by her. A careful study of her correspondence, and those prayers she wrote (as distinct from those which were published under her name), establishes that she did believe in the Real Presence, but little more can be said either about the precise nature of that belief or about other aspects of her own theology.[7] There is widespread agreement only that the queen's

Protestantism was rather less rigorous than that of many of her clergy, particularly among those who were influenced by the Calvinist reformers.

She particularly mistrusted popular preaching. Although she heard many sermons herself (and did not flinch from showing her disapproval of the subject matter, if she felt so inclined), she seems to have believed that her subjects would more reliably benefit from observing the rites prescribed in the Book of Common Prayer than from too much preaching. For her, a primary concern may well have been that her subjects should conform to their legal requirements for church attendance at the specified time. There the congregations were able to hear homilies read to them about their duties, to read the Ten Commandments on the church walls, and to view Elizabeth's Coat of Arms, placed as a reminder that the English monarch was indeed head of the English Church.

The visible queen

One important feature of Elizabeth's life and reign was that hers was never a wealthy regime. The constraints on her financial resources were as much a factor in her reluctance to enter into military adventures as were her anxieties about the perils of such military commitments. Her financial resources also limited her own expenditure, despite the lavish displays of food her meals involved. Portraits of Elizabeth usually pay close attention to the complex details of her dress and the rich jewels adorning both her body and her head. Those familiar images express accurately the contemporary beliefs about the necessity for monarchs to embody the magnificence of their realm, but in the case of Elizabeth it might be thought to be something of an illusion. Careful examination of her portraits has revealed how many aspects of her attire and jewellery recur in portraits across her reign; careful work on her wardrobe accounts illustrates how frequently her existing garments were refurbished, remodelled and, as she grew older, refashioned to accommodate her thickening body – a feature which does not appear in the later portraits. That reflects just one aspect of what Roy Strong described as a policy of recurrent royal rejuvenation in her portraits.

Royal jewels and the contents of the royal wardrobe were

regularly passed on from generation to generation. Those resources Elizabeth augmented by encouraging gifts of fabric and, above all, of jewels from her courtiers and subjects, particularly during the main gift-exchange period of New Year. Despite her rich attire, her wardrobe costs were relatively modest when compared with the annual expenses of her mother, her half-sister Mary I, and even Mary Queen of Scots. In this, as in other ways, Elizabeth protected her own resources, and encouraged her subjects – and fellow rulers – to present her with a significant proportion of the means she needed to maintain her royal magnificence.

Very little is known with certainty about the physical appearance of Elizabeth at any stage of her life. The earliest known portrait of Elizabeth, c. 1546 (Plate 2), shows a carefully demure young woman. That she may well have been, reflecting the years she had spent as the king's other illegitimate daughter. We have much less idea of what Elizabeth looked like at any stage of her later life. It is very likely that, at most, two images of her were based on direct observation: the Zuccaro drawing (Plate 5) and, perhaps, the Hilliard miniature (Plate 4). That may seem the more surprising since there developed an expectation that loyal subjects would display a portrait of the queen, in the genre suitable to their social status. Her officially approved portraits were based on patterns which standardised her features; variations in most portraits are more to be found in dress, jewellery and specific symbols. (Much less attention was paid to the cruder woodcuts favoured by the lower orders in the later decades of her reign.)

On several occasions, the portraits referred to the commissioner of the portrait as much as to the queen's physical presence. One example is the famous Ditchley portrait, which has Elizabeth standing on southern England, clearly reflecting Saxton's mapwork. It might suggest her dominance over her realm, but it also reflects some glory on the man who commissioned the portrait, Sir Henry Lee, whose home was Ditchley. Painted about 1592, it commemorated her visit to his estate, to which her toe points. Such dual-purpose portraits became more widespread in the last years of her reign, perhaps as she became less concerned by such use of her image.

Direct observers of the queen who have left descriptions of her differed about almost all aspects of her physical appearance. In 1557, a Venetian ambassador called her 'tall and well formed', and admired her eyes, although he thought her skin 'swarthy', a feature not suggested in the earlier portrait. By 1596 descriptions had varied remarkably; she was then, by one account, 'short and ruddy in complexion'. That was apparently not the effect of age, however, since the next year another observer saw her figure as 'tall and fair and graceful in whatever she does'! The next year Hentzner thought her face was 'oblong, fair but wrinkled, her nose a little hooked'.[8]

As these reports indicate, her face was never a crucial aspect of her image. The art of physiognomy, of reading character from facial features, was still in its very early development by the early 17th century, and features therefore were of less general interest than was dress. The sumptuary laws defined in careful detail precisely the fabrics and precious metals with which the higher orders of the nobility might adorn themselves, all carefully graduated to define the precise status of each individual.

It followed that the very apex of the social hierarchy, the monarch, was the one person whose dress was not constrained by rank. Rather, it was a political imperative that she should outshine all others. And, by all accounts, Elizabeth usually did. Although less attention was paid by observers to Elizabeth's facial appearance, sometimes her opponents attacked her image, since there was a widespread magical belief that defacing or destroying a portrait could harm the sitter. There were of course, also many obscene and scandalous caricatures of Elizabeth created on the continent and smuggled into her realms, particularly Ireland, aimed at subverting her royal mystique. But that was a long way from the official representations of the queen.

Promoting royal authority

There were good political reasons that so much surviving English literature, including that written before her accession, presented an idyllic picture of Elizabeth. Little was known of her in the international community before her accession, although that had not prevented many scurrilous tales about her as well as about her mother. As it became clearer that she was likely to be the next English monarch, inevitably she became the subject of more personal, diplomatic and political interest. One aspect which impressed – and confused – those who came into contact with her, and the early ambassadors at her court, was her mastery of the ambiguous and convoluted utterance. Her skill in charming ambassadors with her conversation while deftly evading any commitment to their proposals was a common topic of their reports back to their masters.

Very early in her reign Elizabeth insisted that in the days when she was Queen Mary's prisoner in the Tower, far from having been protected by Philip of Spain, as his representative had claimed, she was actually saved by the love of the people. However implausible that claim may have been, the 'love' of her people became a central feature of Elizabeth's image, the primary explanation for whatever interest her subjects of lesser degree showed in the queen. Her use of the language of love as marking an ideal relationship was not novel, though her extending it to her more lowly subjects probably was. Politically, the use of 'love' was already understood to invoke the ideal of a mutually beneficial political relationship, gradually replacing the older feudal relationships of obligatory submission. It was a language which had been used by successive Tudor monarchs to signify that ideally less coercive, more willing compliance with and obedience to the ruler. (For a fuller discussion of this, see Chapter 5.)

But, as Elizabeth was to demonstrate in 1569, that language did not constrain her when dealing with subjects she deemed had been disobedient. Historians have debated how many of the lesser sort were killed out of hand in the aftermath of the Northern Uprising, but it was certainly several hundred (see Chapter 4). It is instructive to compare those many humble deaths with the response of Mary Tudor to several hundred lowly followers of the failed Wyatt rebellion early in her reign. Her prisoners were marched through the streets of London with ropes around their necks to a royal courtyard where Mary, having reminded them of their likely fate, pardoned and dismissed them all to their homes. To return to an earlier theme: Elizabeth was a more insecure monarch and therefore, arguably, more ruthless than her immediate predecessor.

Throughout her reign, a good deal of literature – religious meditations, prayers and poems – was issued in Elizabeth's name, all reinforcing her image as a pious and Protestant queen, perhaps in part to counter moves by more radical Protestants for further religious changes. Over the years, many scholars have constructed and reconstructed images of Elizabeth from writings issued in her name. One problem with those readings is that it is almost impossible to know which of those writings were actually her work and which simply carried her name as an imprimatur. Some of the prayers issued in her name, for example, were demonstrably reprints of previously collected works. The queen's promotion of her preferred image was undoubtedly tinged with the skilled dissimulation which was undoubtedly one of Elizabeth's talents.

Achievements of England's second queen regnant

However difficult it may be to judge the personality of the queen, the consequences of her rule can be much more easily assessed from this distance. Some have said that the most important achievement of Elizabeth's reign is that, despite the intermittent splutters of rebellion, there was no sustained civil war during her reign. Given the range and intensity of religious divisions across Europe, and the resulting religious and civil wars, the relative peace within her realm was indeed a remarkable achievement. To the extent that it was true in England itself, it was particularly impressive given the numerical dominance of Catholics at her accession and the gradual emergence of a Protestant majority. Moreover, this relative tranquillity owed a great deal to Elizabeth herself.

The claim that there were no divisive wars in her realms, however, never held true in Ireland. For that realm she showed little interest, beyond seeing it as a source of confiscated lands which she could dispense to favoured courtiers such as Raleigh. That way she rewarded them at little cost to herself – at least in the short term. In the longer term however, the policy of relative neglect, leaving control of that realm to frequently venal lesser English officials, forced her in the last decade of her reign into the most expensive war of all, in terms of both money and lives.

Ireland apart, however, during her long reign one important feature was the progress of centralisation made across the disparate regions the Tudors ruled. The southwest, most significantly Devon and Cornwall, which had proved a serious problem for the Edwardian regime (1547–53) for both linguistic and religious reasons, was more completely incorporated into the realm by the end of her reign. It was also by then a region which produced courtiers and several of the more remarkable sailors of the 16th century. By the last years of her reign, the north was also under more centralised control, in part because of the progressive destruction of leading Catholic families and their replacement by Protestants, whose rise owed much to the confiscation and redistribution of church lands in the reign of Henry VIII.

Catholicism was still widespread in the 'dark corners' of the north even at the end of her reign, but the loss of significant leadership made those 'false believers' much less threatening. In the aftermath of the Northern Uprising, the parliamentarian and polemicist Thomas Norton spelled out in detail the hierarchy of obedience which northern subjects should observe. He acknowledged their customary local bonds as tenants and servants with obligations to their local lords, but insisted that they also had a higher obligation: 'Is Percy and Neville more ancient, more beloved and dear to you than your natural Sovereign Lady, the Queen of England?' (If the truth be told, their honest answer was then probably 'Yes'.) Such local loyalties, he added, were important but always secondary to their 'allegiance to your Sovereign queen'.[9] There followed further reinforcement of the idea that their primary obligation was to the (always remote) queen. Once the killings had stopped, even the poor and landless were required to take an oath condemning the recent rebellion and promising unqualified loyalty to Elizabeth before they were allowed to return to their homes. There was indeed a far-reaching drive to incorporate all Elizabeth's subjects more actively into her regime.

As a footnote to the extension of royal authority within her realms, it is worth remembering that Elizabeth herself came to encourage the historically significant shift from the traditional focus on recovering lost English footholds in Europe to encouraging the search for sites for English colonies in new lands, a development which proved central to the growth of English – and then British – prominence for centuries.

The benefits (and problems) of print

During Elizabeth's reign, the reach of royal authority was made much more effective as the print medium expanded and grew more diverse. The great increase in the number of proclamations issued across her reign is only one instance of the improved government capacity to communicate with all subjects through print; the still relatively low levels of literacy were not a barrier since many royal proclamations were read out in church. The regime's control of print, however, was never complete, in part because of the relative ease of importing subversive material from the continent. Books, already subject to censorship, became important across a much wider spectrum of society. The more educated audience for Elizabethan prose and poetic works is familiar enough, and Foxe's *Book of Martyrs* is the most obvious example of a work widely popular for its polemical attacks on Catholicism, its promotion of Protestantism and for its graphic images. (Drake is said to have whiled away some time circumnavigating the world by colouring in its pictures. Surviving copies certainly make it clear that some readers did so.)

Cheaper print and the use of woodcuts also became much more common and helped spread Elizabethan messages and propaganda. Although the population was only partly literate, all communities could produce some person who could read, and the texts often included illustrations emphasising the more important points of a pamphlet. One popular issue which lent itself to eye-catching images was caricatures of the Papacy and its 'pretended' powers. Ballads could also be used to reinforce the status and significance of the monarch in places and across social levels where there had previously been few reminders of a distant ruler. It is likely that there were many cheap woodcut images of Elizabeth, since they were readily produced in considerable numbers, though of a quality which meant few have survived. At a time when it was desirable to show loyalty to both queen and Protestantism, one way of doing so was by having a portrait of the queen on show. Taverns and inns, at least in London, often did that, and some poorer homes made the same gesture in that humble medium, as did the many great households which had portraits of the queen. At all social levels, the rapid spread of printed material gave unprecedented coverage to the English queen.

Who ruled in Elizabeth's reign?

It was part of her good fortune that Elizabeth's reign had been preceded by ferocious attacks by her father on the older feudal families. Their decline, intensified in the aftermath of the Northern Uprising, was supplemented by redefinitions of what constituted subject loyalty directly to the monarch. The growth of royal authority over all parts of England was significant, and an important achievement of the decades that Elizabeth ruled. But it was also important that the queen knew how to make good use of the opportunities those changes offered.

A surprising number of historians still write as if the politics of Elizabeth's reign were consistently determined by her Council and individual councillors, rather than by the queen herself. It was, however, her early good judgement that led to the pre-eminence of Cecil, later Burghley, for so many years. And Burghley had no doubt where ultimate authority lay. As he explained to his son Robert, Elizabeth was indeed a divinely sanctioned monarch, who should be counselled, and must be obeyed. She often dismayed her Council by rejecting their policy recommendations, and there is a great deal of evidence of complex strategies to win her agreement. But she remained in principle, and usually in practice, the final arbiter of policy decisions. The occasions to which historians pay much attention include those when she vetoed open warfare, but her opposition was based on her eminently sensible view that wars were precarious and infinitely wasteful of scarce resources. And she had better reason than most to know just how limited were her realm's financial resources.

There were, however, two notable cases in which it seemed her authority was challenged. One was the recurrent disregard of her orders by Essex, whose career was certainly atypical in the frequency with which he flouted her commands and survived. Satisfactory explanations for that toleration are certainly hard to find. Apart from that, the best-known case of apparent disobedience was the forwarding of the paper she had signed – and passed on – for the execution of Mary Stuart. But Elizabeth knew very well the formal consequences of that action. It is worth considering further the extent to which her passionate responses to the actual execution were due to her dread of what consequences might follow. In signing that death warrant she had, after all, denied her own most deeply held beliefs about the sanctity of monarchy. She had also probably alienated her two more important neighbours, who might even be drawn back to the traditional 'Auld Alliance' between France and Scotland, a combination which inevitably threatened England. She had also provided strong grounds to Philip of Spain for an attack on England with papal support, and had cleared away his most obvious barrier to placing a Spanish candidate on the English throne. The period immediately following Mary's execution was Elizabeth's most dangerous time, and her assaults on the councillors who had connived at Mary's execution were very probably more about her terror of possible consequences than astonishment that they had enacted the death sentence she had signed and sent on. It was a very dramatic time, and she made very dramatic responses. But the likelihood is that behind that emotional display was the knowledge that she and she alone had taken the final step in the process. Even in that, then, she was ultimately in control.

In conclusion

Elizabeth has been described in many ways, by her contemporaries and ever after. Hostile accounts of her across the centuries are more than countered by implausibly romantic fantasies which often disregard the harsh imperatives of being – and remaining – a monarch in early modern Europe. What can be said of her is that, despite her unpromising beginnings and dubious reputation, Elizabeth was an interesting and impressive monarch, capable of considerable charm when she was so inclined. She was not always a likeable one, but likeability is not necessary for successful rule, even for a female monarch. Her most striking deviation from regular royal practice, and one for which she has often, and in the eyes of this author perversely, been admired was her failure to marry and secure the succession, despite the demands of her councillors and parliament that she should either do so or name an heir.

Elizabeth certainly enjoyed good fortune at crucial times, most notably with the weather on the several occasions when Philip sought to despatch an armada to invade England, She was, on those occasions fortunate. But it was substantially by her own actions and qualified acceptance of council advice that Elizabeth brought her reign to a satisfactory conclusion and a peaceful transition. Despite the many criticisms which might be made of her reign, the ultimately peaceful and easy transition of her realm to the next ruler remains, with all the benefits of hindsight, one important mark of a sufficiently successful monarch. But that she survived to secure that succession might also be counted as another mark of her own remarkably good fortune in often difficult times.

Notes

1 Elizabeth, briefly Princess of England

1 All scriptural references are to the King James translation of the Bible.
2 Reproduced in *Tudor Tracts 1532–1588,* ed. A.F. Pollard, first published 1903, pp.10–27, p.17.
3 *Letters and Papers of Henry VIII* viii, No. 501.
4 *Letters and Papers of Henry VIII* x, No. 141.
5 This case is most recently made by Eric Ives, *The Life and Death of Anne Boleyn 'The Most Happy'* (Oxford, 2004).
6 *Letters and Papers of Henry VIII* ix, No. 205.
7 *Letters and Papers of Henry VIII* xi, No. 312.
8 *Letters and Papers of Henry VIII* xi, No. 1219.
9 *L&P xviii pt 1* No. 364.
10 *Letters of Royal and Illustrious Ladies of Great Britain,* ed. M.A.E. Green, 3 vols (London, 1846), i., pp.193–4.
11 Sheila Cavanagh, *'The Bad Seed.* Princess Elizabeth and the Seymour Incident', in *Dissing Elizabeth: Negative Representations of Gloriana,* ed. Julia M. Walker (Durham, North Carolina, 1998), p.16.
12 For details of that ongoing conflict, see my *Mary Tudor* (Routledge, 2008) Chapters 5 and 6.
13 The details of their properties and the political significance of that landowning is extensively discussed in Chapter 4 of J.L. McIntosh, *From Heads of Household to Heads of State: The Preaccession Households of Mary and Elizabeth Tudor* (Columbia University Press, 2008).

2 From suspect 'second person' to Queen of England

1 The original title was *Actes and Monuments of these latter and perilllous dayes, touching matters of the Church...* Foxe himself produced four editions, each with fresh material and his work was subsequently republished, added to and modified by many Protestant traditions. It remained a standard text for Protestants into the 20th century, and its many woodcuts illustrating the

suffering of godly martyrs made it unusually attractive to children. The
original texts – and woodcuts – can be found at http://www.hrionline.ac.uk/
johnfoxe/.
2   CSPVen, v. 5, No. 539, 18 Aug 1554.
3   *State Papers of Mary I,* ed. C.S. Knighton (PRO, 1998), No. 25 (SP 11/2, No.
    2).
4   *The Diary of Henry Machyn ... from 155 to 1563,* ed. J.G. Nichols (London,
    1848), p.57.
5   For the complete letter, see *Elizabeth 1 Collected Works,* ed. Leah S. Marcus,
    Janel Mueller and Mary Beth Rose (Chicago, 2000), pp.41–2.
6   *The Chronicle of Queen Jane and of Two Years of Queen Mary,* ed. J.G. Nichols
    (London, 1850), pp.70–1.
7   David Starkey, *Elizabeth: Apprenticeship* (London, 2000), p.142.
8   Foxe (1563), p.1711.
9   'Deposition of Henry Peckham', SP 11/8, No. 51; *Calendar of State Papers ...
    Mary I 1553–58,* ed. C.S. Knighton (London, 1998), No. 423.
10 Report of Sir Thomas Pope of Princess Elizabeth's answer, SP 11/12, No. 70;
    Calendar of State Papers ... Mary I 1553–58, ed. C.S. Knighton (London,
    1998), No. 753.
11 'The Count of Feria's dispatch to Philip II of 14 November 1558', ed. M.J.
    Rodriguez-Salgado and Simon Adams, *Camden Miscellany,* 28 (London, 1990),
    p.331.
12 Wallace MacCaffrey, *Elizabeth I* (London, 1993), p.28.
13 *The Diary of Henry Machyn ... 1550 to 1563,* ed. J.G. Nichols (London, 1848),
    pp.179–80.
14 Christopher Haigh, *English Reformations Religion, Politics and Society under the
    Tudors* (Oxford, 1993), p.238.
15 For a fuller discussion of that issue see my 'Love and a Female Monarch: The
    Case of Elizabeth Tudor', *Journal of British Studies,* 1999, Vol. 38, No. 2, pp.
    133–60.
16 *Calendar of State Papers, Venetian* (1558–1580), Vol. 7, No. 10 (23 January
    1559).

3 Establishing the new reign

1   J.E. Neale, 'Sir Nicholas Throckmorton's advice to Queen Elizabeth', *English
    Historical Review,* 65 (1950), pp.91–8, 98.
2   Kevin M. Sharpe, *Selling the Tudor Monarchy: Authority and Image in Sixteenth-
    century England* (New Haven, Conn., 2009), p.331.
3   *Calendar of State Papers (Venetian),* Vol. 7, No. 2, 31 December 1588.
4   Steven G. Ellis, *Ireland in the Age of the Tudors 1447–1603* (London, 1998),
    p.226.
5   Wallace Macaffrey, *Elizabeth I* (London, 1993), p.66.
6   Calendar of State Papers, Spanish (Simancas), No. 24, 11 April 1559.
7   CSP Sp (Simancas), No. 27, 18 April 1559.
8   See Simon Adams' entry 'Robert Dudley' at *http://www.oxforddnb.com.*

4 Mary Queen of Scots, the English succession and other problems, 1563–7

1 *The Memoirs of Sir James Melville of Halhill,* ed. Gordon Donaldson (London, 1969), pp.33–40.
2 For a fuller discussion of this matter, see Thomas S. Freeman, '"As True a Subject being Prysoner": John Foxe's Notes of the Imprisonment of Princess Elizabeth, 1554–5', *English Historical Review,* Vol. cxvii, No. 470 (February 2002), pp.104–16.
3 For details of that particularly confusing episode and its immediate implications, see MacCaffrey, *Elizabeth I*, pp.158–63
4 The text, in both the original Latin and English can be found in *The Tudor Constitution,* ed. G.R. Elton (Cambridge, 1982). It is also reprinted in English in Stump and Felch, *Elizabeth I*, pp.155–7.
5 *Calendar of State Papers, Domestic, Addenda 1566–79,* Thomas Hargrave to Cecil, February 1570, p.221.

5 The queen and her realm mid-reign

1 Latymer's account of Anne Boleyn's religious practice was edited by Maria Dowling in *Camden Miscellany,* Vol. 30 (London, 1990), pp.23–65.
2 There are several examples of the dress – and diet – regulations that helped sustain the social hierarchy in the three volumes of *Tudor Royal Proclamations,* ed. Hughes and Larkin.
3 There are several detailed accounts of gifts given and received in *Progresses and Public Processions of ... Elizabeth,* ed. Nichols.
4 For further discussion this see Janet Arnold, *Queen Elizabeth's Wardrobe Unlock'd* (Leeds, 1988).
5 The details of this rather strange occasion are discussed in the opening pages of Helen Hackett, *Virgin Mother, Maiden Queen* (Basingstoke, 1995).
6 For a fuller account of the evolution of 'love' as a term of political relationship, see my 'Love and a Female Monarch: The Case of Elizabeth Tudor', *Journal of British Studies,* Vol. 38, No. 2 (April 1999), pp.133–60.
7 For one helpful discussion, see the essay by S. Doran, 'Elizabeth I's Religion: The Evidence of her Letters', *Journal of Ecclesiastical History,* Vol. 51, No. 4 (October 2000), pp.699–720.
8 I am grateful to A.R. Disney for drawing this episode to my attention. It is mentioned in his *A History of Portugal and the Portuguese empire* (Cambridge, 2 vols. 2009), Vol. I, p.173.

6 Old problems and new in the queen's middle years

1 *Tudor Royal Proclamations,* ed. P.L. Hughes and J.F. Larkin, 3 vols (New Haven, 1964–9), Vol. 2, pp.445–9.
2 Helen Hackett, *Virgin Mother, Maiden Queen* (Basingstoke, 1995), p.83.

3   Quoted more extensively in *Elizabeth I and her Age*, ed. D. Stump and S. Felch (New York, 2009), pp.304–6.
4   For a more complete account see Jean Wilson, *Entertainments for Elizabeth* (Woodbridge, 1980), pp.43–7.
5   The final text of the Act is to be found in *The Tudor Constitution*, ed. G. R. Elton.

7 Killing a queen and facing invasion 1585–9

1   *The Letters of Queen Elizabeth I,* ed. G.B. Harrison (London, 1968), p.180.
2   *Ibid.* Her reply is found at pp.185–7.
3   Peter E McCullough, '"*Out of Egypt*": Richard Fletcher's Sermon before Elizabeth I after the Execution of Mary Queen of Scots', in *Dissing Elizabeth: Negative Representations of Gloriana*, ed. Julia M. Walker (Durham, 1998), p.139.
4   *Letters of Queen Elizabeth and King James VI…*, ed. John Bruce, Camden Society, 46, 1849, pp. 45–6.
5   Martin and Parker, *The Spanish Armada*, p.257.
6   Susan Frye, 'The Myth of Elizabeth at Tilbury', *Sixteenth Century Journal*, Vol. 23, No. 1 (Spring, 1992), pp.95–114.
7   For further discussion of this point see my 'The English Accession of James VI: "National" Identity, Gender and the Personal Monarchy of England', *English Historical Review,* Vol. 117, No. 472 (2002), pp.513–35.

8 An ageing queen and the difficult later years of her reign

1   For a comprehensive discussion of the problems, see Jim Sharpe, 'Social strain and social dislocation, 1585–1603', in *The Reign of Elizabeth I: Court and Culture in the Last Decade*, ed. John Guy (Cambridge, 1995), pp.192–211.
2   For more details on prophesyings, see Patrick Collinson, *The Religion of Protestants* (Oxford, 1982), pp. 129–31.
3   Thomas Wilson, 'The State of England A D 1600', Camden Miscellany, Vol. 16 (London, 1936), p.5.
4   For further details of this and other aspects of court splendour as seen through foreign eyes, see 'Extracts from Paul Henzner's Travels in England, 1598', in *England as Seen by Foreigners,* ed. William Brenchley Rye (New York, 1967).

9 Elizabeth's final years

1   *The Memoirs of Robert Carey*, ed. F. Mares (Oxford, 1972), pp.30–1.
2   *Tudor Royal Proclamations*, ed. Paul L. Hughes and James F. Larkin, Vol. 3 (New Haven, 1969), No. 810.
3   Paul Hammer, *Elizabeth's Wars* (Basingstoke, 2003), p.230.

4   The full text is reproduced in *Elizabeth I and her Age*, ed. D. Stump and S. Felch (New York, 2009), pp.506–7.
5   *Letters of Queen Elizabeth and King James VI of Scotland,* ed. John Bruce (Camden Society, Vol. 46, London, 1849), pp.146–7, 149. Spelling modernized.
6   CSP Ven v. 9, Scaramelli to Doge and Senate, 19 Feb 1603.
7   *Memoirs of Robert Carey*, p.63.
8   *The Private Life of an Elizabethan Lady: The Diary of Lady Margaret Hoby 1599–1605*, ed. Joanna Moody (1998, Stroud), p.186.
9   Anon BL:Eg 2877 (f.13v).

10 What can be known of Elizabeth I?

1   Paulina Kewes, 'Two Queens, One Inventory: The Lives of Mary and Elizabeth Tudor', in *Writing Lives: Biography and Textuality, Identity and Representation in Early Modern England*, ed. Kevin Sharpe and Steven N. Zwicker (Oxford, 2008), p.187.
2   See Patrick Collinson's biography of Elizabeth at *http://www.oxforddnb.com*.
3   Susan Doran, 'The Queen', in *The Elizabethan World*, ed. Susan Doran and Norman Jones (London, 2011), p.58. (Spelling modernized.)
4   See, for example, my 'Examples and Admonitions: What Mary I Demonstrated for Elizabeth I', in *Tudor Queenship: The Reigns of Mary and Elizabeth*, ed. Alice Hunt and Anna Whitelock (Basingstoke, 2010).
5   Margaret Sommerville, *Sex and Subjection: Attitudes to Women in Early-Modern Society* (London, 1995).
6   C.S.L. Davies, 'England and the French Wars 1557–9', in *The Mid-Tudor Polity c.1540–1560*, ed. Jennifer Loach and Robert Tittler (London, 1980), p.162.
7   Susan Doran, 'Elizabeth I's Religion: The Evidence of her Letters', in *Journal of Ecclesiastical History*, Vol. 51, No. 4 (2000), pp.699–719.
8   For a further discussion of this, see Roy Strong, *Gloriana: Portraits of Elizabeth I* (London, 1987), pp.17–9.
9   Thomas Norton, *To the Queenes Maiesties Poore Dececeived Subie*ctes… (London, 1569).

Index